THE 50 GREATEST PLAYS
in NEW YORK GIANTS
Football History

JOHN MAXYMUK

TRIUMPH
BOOKS

Library of Congress Cataloging-in-Publication Data

Maxymuk, John.
  The 50 greatest plays in New York Giants football history / John Maxymuk.
    p. cm.
  Includes bibliographical references.
  ISBN-13: 978-1-60078-109-4
  ISBN-10: 1-60078-109-8
  1. New York Giants (Football team)—History. 2. Football—New York (State)—New York—History.
I. Title. II. Title: Fifty greatest plays in New York Giants football history.
  GV956.N4M37 2008
  796.332'64097471—dc22

                                      2008003685

This book is available in quantity at special discounts for your group or organization. For further information, contact:

Triumph Books
542 South Dearborn Street
Suite 750
Chicago, Illinois 60605
(312) 939-3330
Fax (312) 663-3557

Printed in U.S.A.
ISBN: 978-1-60078-109-4
Design by Sue Knopf
Page production by Patricia Frey
Photos courtesy of Getty Images unless otherwise indicated.

There are Giants in my home and heart;
their names are Suzanne, Katie, and Juliane.

CONTENTS

FOREWORD

When I came to the New York Giants in 1958, it represented a turning point in my career. I had spent five of my first six seasons with the Chicago Cardinals, a team that had little spirit, little direction, and little success. I can't say we expected to lose, but it certainly came as no surprise when we usually did. With the Giants, though, we not only expected to win, but did. In three of my four seasons as a Giant, we played in the NFL Championship Game.

The Giants were clearly more talented than the Cardinals, but they had a more positive attitude as well, and I noticed that from the first day I reported to their training camp. I could see immediately that my new Giant teammates were smart, classy, and charismatic. Kyle Rote was so revered by his fellow players that eight of his teammates named a son after him; I would be one of them. Frank Gifford, our multi-talented leader on the field, was also leader in the locker room. My roommate was our 37-year-old quarterback, Charlie Conerly, a taciturn ex-Marine who the team loved and respected most of all. He had maintained his dignity and composure through good times and bad. Any of us would do anything for Charlie.

Perhaps the most remarkable thing about that team, though, was its two assistant coaches: Vince Lombardi on offense and Tom Landry on defense. Since I was a backup tight end and backup defensive end, I got to watch both men closely. I remember coming to my first meeting on the Giants, sitting down next to reserve quarterback Don Heinrich, and getting the feeling that I was joining a raucous party. Then a short, barrel-chested guy with thick black hair and thick black glasses walked in and the room was instantly silent. Lombardi. Vince commanded respect as any great teacher does, especially one as vocal, dynamic, and detail-oriented as he was.

Landry, who was not only the defensive coach but my kicking coach as well, was Lombardi's polar opposite. Tom was just as detail-oriented, but was cool and distant. He told his defense exactly what he wanted them to do, and there was no discussion. His expectations were high, but he offered little praise for his great defense. Tom studied my kicking and recommended I swing my leg like one would a golf swing. With his tips, I had my greatest place-kicking success as a Giant.

Without the support of Landry and my teammates, I doubt I would have made the 49-yard field goal through the snow that forced a playoff for the Eastern Division crown at the end of my first season in New York. Going into the season finale against the Browns at Yankee Stadium, we trailed Cleveland by one game. On a cold and snowy day, the two teams were tied at 10–10 in the last quarter when I shanked a 31-yard field-goal try. Coming off the field I was lower than low, knowing I had probably just cost my teammates a chance at the title. Then linebacker Cliff Livingston patted me on the shoulder and said not to worry because, "we're going to get you another chance." Did I mention I had great teammates?

And smart ones, too. We did get the ball back and drove to the Browns' 42 before three straight incompletions left us facing fourth-and-10. If I was surprised when head coach Jim Lee Howell sent me in to try a field goal from midfield, you can imagine how shocked my teammates were. Charlie Conerly, my roommate and holder, asked what the heck I was doing on the field. However, he and I chipped out a little clearing in the snow, center Ray Wietecha gave me an accurate snap, Charlie gave me a perfect hold, and I booted the ball through the falling flakes. As I came off the field mobbed by my teammates, Lombardi pushed his way through and shouted at me, "You son of a bitch, you know you can't kick it that far."

We won that game and the following week's playoff against the Browns to put us into the sudden-death championship game that changed the image of football forever. Without Johnny Unitas's late-game heroics, the Giants would have been champs and yours truly would have provided the margin of victory just as I had when we beat the Colts 24–21 earlier in the season. After three more wonderful seasons in New York, I began what would prove to be a 40-year second career as a broadcaster and got to witness many more exciting NFL games, several involving the Giants.

It's fun to relive those games and the key plays that decided them in this book. In the following pages, the whole of New York Giants history is described—from a fake punt that keyed the first Giants title in 1927 to the David Tyree catch that keyed another New York championship 80 seasons later. This book brings to life the greatest plays by some of the greatest players in Giants history, including Mel Hein, Lawrence Taylor, Phil Simms, and Tiki Barber. It's a delight to remember several of the colorful players and coaches that have given the New York Giants such a rich tradition of which I was proud to be a part.

—Pat Summerall

PREFACE

So what constitutes a great play, and how do you choose the 50 greatest of them from more than 80 seasons of games? For this book, great plays are the ones that are the most memorable and most historically significant. The most obvious choices are game-winning or turning-point plays in the biggest games: playoff games, championship games, and Super Bowls. That is clearest when the Giants win the ultimate prize (see Play 1, Play 2, or Play 4). Even title losses, though, produce plays of expediency and cleverness that deserve to be recalled (see Play 24 or Play 32).

Great plays can come in more mundane settings, as well. After all, a last-minute, game-winning 85-yard screen pass is a great play (see Play 29) under any circumstances, as is an 89-yard fly pattern that was celebrated with the first end zone spike (see Play 36). Record-setting performances are also represented (see Play 22), and it would be unconscionable to forget offensive-line brilliance (see Play 37). Perhaps the most fun to recreate in print are the spectacular trick plays of imaginative design (see Play 28 or Play 17).

Defense has been a big part of the Giants' success over the years, from the beginning of modern defensive alignments (see Play 19) to a key interception on Thanksgiving Day (see Play 25) to a monster hit on a fearless foe (see Play 9) or a thunderous goal-line stand (see Play 48). Even a simple field goal can be unforgettable if it's a 49-yarder in the snow with playoff implications (see Play 3).

And then there are the disasters that Giants fans would like to forget. They may not have been "great" for the Giants, but they hold great importance to the team's past. An opposing linebacker laying out the biggest Giants star (see Play 27) is celebrated in one of the most familiar photographs in NFL history, as is another famous shot of an aging New York quarterback on his knees (see Play 45). Painful or not, the most replayed fumble in team history can't be ignored (see Play 5).

The Giants have had a long, proud, and exciting history as a cornerstone franchise in the NFL. Returning to their greatest plays is a terrific way to relive that legacy. Little did I realize when I began this project that the greatest of all Giants moments would unfold at the end of the 2007 season; history never stops renewing itself. I hope readers will find this retelling of a glorious past a worthwhile experience that heightens interest in witnessing the next 50 to come.

ACKNOWLEDGMENTS

I would like to thank a number of individuals who helped me with this book. Marcia Schiff and Matthew Lutts at AP Images, and Christiana Newton and Tamyka Muse at Getty Images provided able assistance in researching photographs for the book. Mary Anne Nesbit at Rutgers University has always been helpful in borrowing obscure materials from other libraries. John Gibson, also at Rutgers, has helped me unfailingly with technology questions for many years now. A couple of Giants fans, Alan Ludwig and Dr. Ken Leistner, offered advice during the project. Finally, all the pros at Triumph Books made this book a delightful experience.

January 5, 2003

SEASON ENDS IN A SNAP

Giants Lose to 49ers on a Botched Field-Goal Attempt

On a sunny afternoon of big plays, big leads, big comebacks, and bigger mental and physical lapses from both sides of the field, this NFC Wild-Card Game came down to the simplest of plays with six seconds remaining: a medium-length field goal. Unfortunately, the Giants botched it for the second time in three minutes. However, as several players noted after the game, it never should have gotten to that point. The 49ers beat New York 39–38 by erasing a 24-point second-half deficit; in the history of the NFL postseason, only the 1991 Bills' 32-point comeback against the Oilers outranks this Giant collapse.

The 49ers struck first in this wild contest, with a 76-yard touchdown pass to Terrell Owens on their first play, five minutes into the first quarter. The Giants answered with a 12-yard touchdown pass to Amani Toomer, one of three scores Toomer would grab during the afternoon. Quarterback Kerry Collins hit Jeremy Shockey for a two-yard score just three minutes later, but the 49ers responded with a Kevan Barlow touchdown run to tie the score at 14–14.

The Giants took control of the game before halftime with two more Collins-to-Toomer touchdowns, of eight and 24 yards, in the last three minutes of the half; they went to the locker room with a 28–14 lead. New York continued its dominance in the third quarter with a Tiki Barber touchdown run and a Matt Bryant 21-yard field goal to stretch the lead to 38–14 with less than 20 minutes to play.

But the first signs of the Giants' unraveling had begun to appear. The Giants had to kick that field goal because Shockey dropped a pass in the end zone that would have made the score 42–14. A less obvious sign was the departure of defensive end Kenny Holmes after separating his shoulder earlier in the third quarter, diluting the quality of a defensive line that was already thin. Up to that point, the Giants' pass rush had allowed the mobile Jeff Garcia to roam from the pocket only three times.

Down 24 points, the 49ers went to a no-huddle offense that put additional pressure on the tiring Giants defensive line, which was unable to substitute players because of the faster pace. With two minutes left in the quarter, Garcia hit Owens for a 24-yard touchdown, and followed that with a two-point conversion on which Garcia scrambled

A botched snap and a pass interference call that never came left Rich Seubert (69) and the Giants dazed and confused in a wild 39–38 playoff loss to the 49ers in 2003. *(Photo courtesy of AP Images)*

TREY JUNKIN

Trey Junkin was a proud man who spent 19 years in the NFL, from 1983 to 2001, playing for the Bills, the Redskins, the Raiders, the Seahawks, and the Cardinals, where Jim Fassel came to know him. Junkin started as a backup linebacker as well as a long snapper, but he also played some tight end. He was so proud of his snapping that he once grabbed the ball from the official after completing 1,000 consecutive successful punt snaps. He was proud that of his 17 NFL receptions, seven were touchdowns and the other 10 were all for first downs. And he was proud of having played in 281 games, placing him among the all-time leaders among non-kickers.

The Giants had been having a problem with special-teams snaps all season and had already used three snappers and three holders during the 2002 season. When Dan O'Leary was lost due to injury, regular center Chris Bober took over the duties. For the playoffs, Fassel decided to bring in the recently retired Junkin, whom he remembered from his time in Arizona. After a few days of practice, Fassel decided to go with the experienced and reliable Junkin. After his disastrous final NFL game, though, Junkin stood at his locker, choking back tears: "I cost 58 guys a chance to go to the Super Bowl. Quite honestly, I screwed up. And there it is. That's it. I'm retired."

to buy time for Owens to get open. Still leading 38–22, New York's offense went three-and-out, and the Giants were forced to punt from their own 12-yard line. Matt Allen delivered a lame 30-yard punt that Vinny Sutherland of the 49ers caught at the New York 42, as Dhani Jones plowed into him on a boneheaded play for which the Giants were penalized 15 yards.

Starting at the New York 27, San Francisco scored quickly on a 14-yard scramble on the first play of the fourth quarter. Another scramble on the two-point conversion allowed Garcia to find Owens again to make the score 38–30 with just under 15 minutes to play. Once again, the Giants offense was forced to punt after just three unsuccessful plays, and the 49ers drove down the field and kicked a field goal halfway through the quarter to make the score 38–33.

Finally, the Giants offense woke up and marched from their 36 to the 49ers' 24. On fourth-and-one, coach Jim Fassel elected to go for the easy 42-yard field goal that would restore their eight-point lead with 3:06 to go. In an ominous bit of foreshadowing, newly signed veteran long-snapper Trey Junkin fired a bad snap that holder Matt Allen was barely able to get down, and a confused Matt Bryant missed the kick to the left. From their 32, the 49ers moved down the field again on the legs and arm of Jeff Garcia, who hit Tai Streets for a 13-yard touchdown to take a 39–38 lead with 1:05 to play. Will Allen intercepted the two-point conversion intended again for Terrell Owens, and Owens flung Allen out of bounds, drawing a flag for unnecessary roughness. However, Giants safety Shaun Williams retaliated against Owens and drew his own offsetting penalty, so the Giants would get no advantage on the ensuing kickoff.

Despite this mental error, the Giants got a big return from Delvin Joyce and started at their own 48 with one minute left. Kerry Collins went to work and hit Ron Dixon twice before missing Toomer. With six seconds left, Collins hit Toomer on a five-yard out at the 23 to set up the potential 41-yard winning field goal.

The field-goal unit came onto the field. Allen told Bryant to trust him and expect the ball to be down despite the bad snap of three minutes before. Allen then told Junkin, the snapper, "You've been in this league for 19 years; you've got to come through for us." Once the team was set, Allen called for the ball, and Junkin

GAME DETAILS

New York Giants 38 • San Francisco 49ers 39

Date: January 5, 2003

Location: 3Com Park, San Francisco

Attendance: 66,318

Significance: NFC Wild-Card Game

Box Score:

Giants	7	21	10	0	**38**
49ers	7	7	8	17	**39**

Scoring:

SF	Owens 76-yard pass from Garcia (Chandler PAT)
NYG	Toomer 12-yard pass from Collins (Bryant PAT)
NYG	Shockey 2-yard pass from Collins (Bryant PAT)
SF	Barlow 1-yard run (Chandler PAT)
NYG	Toomer 8-yard pass from Collins (Bryant PAT)
NYG	Toomer 24-yard pass from Collins (Bryant PAT)
NYG	Barber 6-yard run (Bryant PAT)
NYG	Bryant 21-yard FG
SF	Owens 26-yard pass from Garcia (Owens pass from Garcia)
SF	Garcia 14-yard run (Owens pass from Garcia)
SF	Chandler 25-yard FG
SF	Streets 13-yard pass from Garcia (pass failed)

Team	FD	YDS	RUSH	PASS	RTN	A-C-I	Sacked	PUNT	FUM	PEN
Giants	26	446	29-119	327	181	44-29-1	2-15	4-39	1-0	5-50
49ers	23	446	20-90	356	131	45-28-1	0-0	3-47	1-1	2-20

Giants: Barber 115R, Collins 342P, Toomer 136C
49ers: Garcia 331P, Owens 177C

squirted the ball low and so far to the right that Allen grabbed it, rose up, and yelled "Fire" to his teammates to signal a broken play.

Allen rolled out with 49ers in pursuit as guard Rich Seubert, an eligible receiver on this play, went out for a pass. Allen unloaded the ball in the direction of Seubert, who was open at the 2-yard line, but Chidi Okeafor of the 49ers tackled Seubert as penalty flags flew and the pass fell incomplete. To the amazement of everyone, the Giants were called for having an ineligible receiver downfield because guard Tam Hopkins was also inexplicably at the goal line, but interference was not called on Okeafor so there were no offsetting penalties, and the game was over.

Fassel pointed out after the game that Allen was supposed to simply call timeout in that situation, and others speculated he could have quickly thrown the ball out of bounds to stop the clock. However, as Michael Strahan complained afterward, "Screw the botched snap, screw the calls after that. It should never have come to that. This game was like our season—look about as good as you can look on a football field and look about as bad as you can look."

Two months earlier in Arizona, Junkin had been interviewed for a piece in *Sports Illustrated* in which he described the anonymous nature of his long, strange career: "Ideally, my name should never come up. If it does, I've made a mistake," he said. Unfortunately, Junkin did just that on the immense stage of the NFL playoffs.

One day later, the NFL admitted its officiating error and said that interference should have been called and that the offsetting penalties should have resulted in a rekick for New York. San Francisco head coach Steve Mariucci responded sarcastically to the news with the comment, "Bummer," but his fortunate 49ers lost the following week in Tampa to the eventual champion Bucs.

The NFL also altered its procedures to allow for more consultation among officials in the future, but nothing could change the result of the game. One direct carryover for the Giants came in Week 2 of 2003, when Fassel had his field-goal unit kick a lead-changing field goal against Dallas with too many seconds left on the clock, allowing the Cowboys enough time to kick a 52-yard game-tying field goal on the final play of regulation. Dallas won in overtime. New York finished 4–12 and Fassel was fired.

Quarterback Kerry Collins stares in disbelief after the Giants fell to the 49ers 39–38.
(Photo courtesy of AP Images)

November 17, 1929

 # BENNY BOMBS THE BEARS

A Record Four Touchdown Passes

On an overcast November day at the Polo Grounds, Benny Friedman and Hap Moran rained down passes on the Bears for more than 250 yards and five touchdowns, leading a 34–0 trouncing by the undefeated Giants. Friedman, the greatest passer of his time, tied the NFL record with four scoring tosses on his way to a record 20-touchdown pass season in 1929. This match with the Bears served as a tune-up for the anticipated contest with the undefeated Packers one week later.

Against the Bears, Friedman opened the scoring in the second quarter by connecting with Glenn Campbell for a 30-yard touchdown. Friedman's pass was to the 15-yard line, and Campbell followed his teammates' blocking into the end zone untouched. In the third quarter, Friedman was unstoppable. A 35-yard pass to Len Sedbrook set up a six-yard score to Hap Moran. Another 35-yard pass to Sedbrook culminated in a 15-yard score, again to Moran. Finally, a 40-yard pass to Tiny Feather led to a 20-yard touchdown to Jerry Snyder. In the final quarter, Moran finished the aerial onslaught with a 35-yard touchdown pass to Feather.

The four touchdown passes by Friedman equaled that of three previous great performances by 1920s passers Elmer Oliphant, Red Dunn, and Ernie Nevers. For Benny, though, this was no freak occurrence. Friedman would set a new mark of five touchdown passes the following year in a 53–0 rout of Frankford. That would not be topped until Sammy Baugh threw six in a game in 1943. Friedman's seasonal standard of 20 touchdown passes would not be equaled until Cecil Isbell threw 24 in 1942.

> The things that a perfect football player must do are kick, pass, run the ends, plunge the line, block, tackle, weave his way through broken fields, drop- and place-kick, interfere, diagnose plays, spot enemy weaknesses, direct an offense, and not get hurt. I have just been describing Benny Friedman's repertoire to you.
>
> —SPORTSWRITER PAUL GALLICO

Giants captain Benny Friedman (right) threw four touchdown passes to beat Red Grange (left) and the Bears in 1929. To appreciate the lowly status of pro football in those days, note the tattered jerseys that both stars are sporting.

TIMOTHY MARA

Benny Friedman was brought to New York because the owner of the Giants, Tim Mara, needed a drawing card and a winner. Much is made of the fact that the Giants' first season was saved financially with a late-season appearance by the legendary Red Grange, barnstorming with the Bears. What is forgotten is that in 1926, Mara lost $60,000 competing against Red Grange's American Football League Yankees. The Giants won the title in 1927, but were back in the red in 1928, losing $40,000. Mara's solution was to buy Friedman's contract from Detroit, but owner/coach Leroy Andrews was not interested in selling just Friedman. So Mara bought the entire team and installed Andrews as the Giants' coach. This was a great deal for the Giants because not only did they get Friedman, but they also added eight of the other 18 players on the third-place Wolverines to the sixth-place Giants roster, resulting in 13-win second-place finishes in 1929 and 1930.

Timothy Mara had dropped out of high school to help support his family and worked his way up from nothing to become a great success as a legal bookmaker. When he bought the Giants franchise for $500 in 1925, he knew nothing about the game, but was determined to go first-class. In so doing he created a great and lasting legacy for his sons: Jack, who took over the business side of things, and Wellington, who took over the personnel side. The success of Mara's New York franchise was a major reason for the growth and success of pro football and the NFL.

Mara would face an even more costly challenge to his franchise and to the NFL with the All-America Football Conference, which put franchises in Yankee Stadium and Brooklyn's Ebbets Field in the late 1940s to compete directly with the Giants. Secretly, Mara took out loans from a local bank that were not fully paid off until the 1960s, according to sportswriter Jerry Izenberg. Tim Mara died in 1959, the same year as Commissioner Bert Bell, and both were fully qualified members of the Pro Football Hall of Fame's inaugural class of 1963.

Giants owner Tim Mara purchased the franchise for $500 in 1925. *(Photo courtesy of WireImages)*

GAME DETAILS

New York Giants 34 • Chicago Bears 0

Date: November 17, 1929

Location: Polo Grounds, New York

Attendance: 15,000

Significance: Record-setting day in a record-setting season for the game's first great passer

Box Score:

Bears	0	0	0	0	**0**
Giants	0	7	20	7	**34**

Scoring:
NYG Campbell 30-yard pass from Friedman (Friedman PAT)
NYG Moran 6-yard pass from Friedman (Friedman PAT)
NYG Moran 15-yard pass from Friedman (Friedman PAT)
NYG Snyder 20-yard pass from Friedman (PAT failed)
NYG Feather 35-yard pass from Moran (Plansky PAT)

BENNY FRIEDMAN

It took over 40 years for Benny Friedman to be elected to the Pro Football Hall of Fame, despite the fact that he was far and away the greatest passer of his time and a revolutionary figure in the history of the game. For one reason, the statistics from the time are incomplete and unofficial. For a second, the numbers we do have for Friedman cannot be compared to the numbers of modern players playing the modern passing game that Friedman pioneered. For a third, Friedman was an opinionated man who was sometimes too clever for his own good. As an example of his supreme self-confidence, he wrote an article for *Sport* magazine in 1953 entitled "I Could Play Pro Football—And I'm 48."

Friedman was an All-American at Michigan under Fielding Yost before turning pro in 1927 with Cleveland, where he led the NFL in touchdown passes. The following year in Detroit, he led the league in touchdown passes again. Tim Mara brought Benny to New York in 1929, and Friedman led the league in touchdowns and led the team to 13 wins; then he repeated the trick in 1930. Both the team and Friedman suffered a bit in 1931, and it was time to move on again. When Friedman was unable to buy into the ownership of the Giants, he left for the Brooklyn Dodgers and finished his career there.

Benny was the first passer who made a habit of passing on any down. He reasoned, "Why wait until third down when the defense is looking for it?" Defenses were forced to adjust to a more wide-open game when playing against Friedman by having the center on the defensive line drop into a linebacking position to deal with the pass. Friedman even authored one of the first football primers, *The Passing Game*, in 1931.

December 10, 1989

FROZEN OUT

Giants' Big Stop in the Snow Beats Broncos

After starting the 1989 season 8–1, the Giants hit a rough patch and dropped three of the next four games. Headed for a road game in Denver with Lawrence Taylor unlikely to play, New York's run for the playoffs was beginning to disintegrate. Moreover, at game time the temperature was 23 degrees with a 15-mph wind and heavy snow falling. It was a day for defense, and led by inside linebacker Gary Reasons's 14 tackles, the Giants delivered.

New York got the ball for the first time on its own 15-yard line. A slow, steady 15-play mix of runs and passes culminated eight minutes and 53 seconds later with an Ottis Anderson three-yard touchdown run at the outset of the second quarter. Five minutes later, the Giants got the ball again in great field position after Dave Meggett's 26-yard punt return put the ball on the Denver 36. However, a penalty and a sack left the Giants with a seemingly impossible third-and-31 from their own 43. Phil Simms dropped back and flipped a little screen pass out to Meggett, who juggled the ball before securing it and took off with blockers in front of him. Meggett juked by a couple of Broncos and then cut back across the field and outran the Denver defenders

to the end zone for a spectacularly unlikely 57-yard score that put New York up 14–0 in the first half.

From there, the Giants' defense took over. In one remarkable sequence in the third quarter, Leonard Marshall, who provided pressure on quarterback John Elway all day, drew two holding calls against Broncos tackle Gerald Perry that wiped out Denver gains of 50 and 22 yards—in addition to the 20 yards in penalties.

Later in the third period, Elway drove the Broncos to the Giants' 1. On third-and-goal from the 1, Bobby Humphrey ran left out of the I-formation and was stopped by linebacker Steve DeOssie just half a yard from the end zone. On fourth down, Humphrey went right from the I-formation, but Gary Reasons read the play perfectly and leapt into the hole where Humphrey was headed, meeting him with a thunderous hit that knocked Humphrey backward while Reasons wrapped him up and sent the Broncos' offense off the field. The two banged helmets so hard that Humphrey's earflap went flying out of his headgear. Parcells said, "It was a big-time hit. It will probably be in the highlight reel." It was the key play of the game.

Gary Reasons leads the triumphant Giants defense off the field after a thrilling goal-line stand in which Reasons stoned Broncos runner Bobby Humphrey at the 1-yard line on fourth down. *(Photo courtesy of WireImages)*

BILL BELICHICK

That the Giants could come into Denver and shut down the AFC's best team in the snow—after having dropped three of their last four games—was one more example of the brilliance of Bill Belichick as a defensive coach. Belichick never played professionally, but he learned the game from his father, Steve, a longtime coach and scout at the Naval Academy. Belichick worked his way up from a gofer on Ted Marchibroda's Colts staff in the 1970s to special-teams coach on the Giants. When Bill Parcells was named head coach in 1983, Belichick moved up to defensive coordinator. The two would work together in New York for the next eight years,

sharing an acute attention to detail, a demanding and competitive intensity, and an affinity for tough defense.

In his time in New York, Belichick was called "Doom" by the players for his relentless, abrasive personality, while the writers referred to him as "Captain Sominex" for his deliberately dull and monotonous responses. It was clear that his first love was the Xs and Os of designing different and creative defenses each week, exploiting his opponents' weaknesses through the best usage of his defenders' talents. His own weakness was his personality; he did not yet have Parcells's personal touch with the players.

After a failed five-year tour as head coach in Cleveland, Belichick returned to Parcells's staff in New England and then followed him to the Jets, even briefly becoming the Jets' coach while a deal for compensation for Parcells leaving New England was worked out. When Parcells stepped down as Jets coach to become head of football operations, Belichick was named his successor, but resigned the following day with a brief, bizarre note.

Rather than continue as Parcells's acolyte, Belichick returned to New England, where he has enjoyed control over personnel and found his own voice and remarkable success. Over the years, the Giants have had seven coordinator-level assistant coaches who became head coaches and who led a team to the NFL's championship game. Allie Sherman, Jim Fassel, and John Fox won no titles; Tom Landry and Bill Parcells each won two; Vince Lombardi won five; and now Belichick's Patriots have won three. Ultimately, he may prove to be the greatest in a long line of great Giants assistant coaches.

Bill Belichick was one of the architects behind the ferocious Giants defense of the 1980s.
(Photo courtesy of AP Images)

GAME DETAILS

New York Giants 14 • Denver Broncos 7

Date: December 10, 1989

Location: Mile High Stadium, Denver

Attendance: 63,283 (12,771 no-shows)

Significance: Having lost three of four games, the Giants were in danger of falling out of the playoff race as they faced the team with the best record in the AFC

Box Score:

Giants	0	14	0	0	**14**
Broncos	0	0	0	7	**7**

Scoring:

NYG Anderson 3-yard run (Nittmo PAT)

NYG Meggett 57-yard pass from Simms (Nittmo PAT)

DEN Young 32-yard pass from Elway (Treadwell PAT)

Team	FD	YDS	RUSH	PASS	RTN	A-C-I	Sacked	PUNT	FUM	PEN
Giants	16	261	37–113	148	56	22–13–0	3–23	7–41	1–0	2–21
Broncos	18	367	24–83	284	79	47–23–0	1–8	5–37	0–0	8–62

Giants: Simms 171P
Broncos: Elway 292P

The Broncos kept up the pressure, with a scrambling Elway passing for 100 of his 292 yards in the final quarter. However, they could only reach pay dirt once—on a 32-yard pass early in the period—and the Giants defense, led by Reasons and Marshall, had ensured a critical victory.

New York then won its last two games to win the Eastern Division crown, but they would lose a heartbreaker to the Rams in the playoffs. Nonetheless, their ferocious, unyielding defense made an unforgettable stand that December day in eight inches of Colorado snow.

December 5, 1999

TOOMER TOASTS THE TUNA WITH THREE TOUCHDOWNS

Giants Beat Jets 41–28

In many ways, this 1999 win over the Jets signaled a new beginning for the Giants under Jim Fassel. It was just the second start as a Giant for free-agent quarterback Kerry Collins, and on this day he would become the first Giants quarterback to exceed 300 yards passing since Phil Simms six years earlier. With Fassel mourning the death of his mother and the team mired at 5–6, it was the first chance for quarterbacks coach Sean Payton to call the plays and open up the offense.

On the other sideline, it would be the first time that former coach Bill Parcells returned to Giants Stadium as a visitor and lost. It would be the first and only time that injury-prone Giants runner Joe

Montgomery gained more than 100 yards, and it would be the first time that the Giants would boast a 300-yard passer, a 100-yard runner, and two 100-yard receivers in the same game.

The Giants got off to a fast start by scoring the first three times they got the ball in the first quarter—on a field goal, a run by Montgomery, and a 61-yard touchdown pass from Collins to Toomer. On the key touchdown pass, Collins and Toomer gave an indication that they were going to make a dangerous combination when they made a slight adjustment to the defensive coverage at the line. Toomer broke off his route and ran a quick slant. Collins hit him precisely on his right shoulder, allowing Toomer to

> **A**ny time you can step on the field and have the opportunity to make things happen, you do it. I think today I just had the opportunity. The quarterback is making me look good. It's a combination of things when I have a game like this.
>
> **—AMANI TOOMER**

Amani Toomer outpaces linebacker Marvin Jones on his way to a 61-yard touchdown in the first quarter of Toomer's breakout game against the Jets. He would go on to set scores of Giants career receiving records. *(Photo courtesy of AP Images)*

Amani Toomer

At long last, this three-touchdown performance was Amani Toomer's coming-out party. Toomer was a second-round pick out of Michigan in 1996, but he spent his first three seasons as a punt returner who could not get on the field as a receiver. He showed big-play ability by returning three punts for scores—including two in his first six games—but was unreliable on offense because he did not run precise routes and seemed lackadaisical.

In his fourth season, Toomer finally won a starting job and was averaging four catches a game for the first 10 games of the season, then upped that to six catches a game once Kerry Collins took over. At 6'3" with deceptive, long-striding speed, Toomer began working to develop his natural talent, and he became a sure-handed deep threat opposite shifty possession receiver Ike Hilliard. With the passage of time and the coming of Plaxico Burress, Toomer smoothly made the transition from deep threat to smart veteran possession receiver. In both guises, he has used his speed and size to be a willing and effective downfield blocker for the Giants' running game.

As a rookie, Toomer tore the anterior cruciate ligament in his right knee, and he tore the ACL in his left knee in 2006, at age 32. However, he returned in 2007 as Eli Manning's reliable third-down target. By 2007, Toomer was the Giants' all-time leader in receptions, receiving yards, receiving touchdowns, and 100-yard receiving games.

Amani Toomer races past Marcus Coleman and Victor Green for an 80-yard touchdown in the Giants' 41–28 victory over the Jets.

GAME DETAILS

New York Giants 41 • New York Jets 28

Date: December 5, 1999

Location: The Meadowlands

Attendance: 78,200

Significance: Crosstown rival Jets and Bill Parcells returning to the Meadowlands to face the Giants

Box Score:

Jets	0	7	0	21	**28**
Giants	17	10	7	7	**41**

Scoring:

NYG Blanchard 41-yard FG
NYG Montgomery 4-yard run (Blanchard PAT)
NYG Toomer 61-yard pass from Collins (Blanchard PAT)
NYJ Johnson 13-yard pass from Lucas (Hall PAT)
NYG Collins 1-yard run (Blanchard PAT)

NYG Blanchard 31-yard FG
NYG Toomer 9-yard pass from Collins (Blanchard PAT)
NYJ Green 10-yard pass from Lucas (Hall PAT)
NYJ Chrebet 10-yard pass from Lucas (Hall PAT)
NYG Toomer 80-yard pass from Collins (Blanchard PAT)
NYJ Chrebet 5-yard pass from Lucas (Hall PAT)

Team	FD	YDS	RUSH	PASS	RTN	A-C-I	Sacked	PUNT	FUM	PEN
Jets	18	291	12-15	276	132	48-31-0	2-8	6-48	4-0	4-50
Giants	25	490	45-152	338	166	29-17-0	1-3	3-31	3-1	3-67

Jets: Lucas 284P
Giants: Montgomery 111R, Collins 341P, Toomer 181C, Hilliard 121C

spin away easily from corner Aaron Glenn and race upfield for the touchdown.

At the half, the Giants were up 27–7, and they added another touchdown pass to Toomer in the third quarter. The Jets managed a couple of fourth-quarter scores, but still trailed 34–21 with less than four minutes to go. Payton caught the attention of the offense by still going full throttle, with Collins throwing a jump-ball bomb to Toomer, who outleaped Marcus Coleman for the ball and again strode for the end zone. Tiki Barber said after the game,

"Here we are leading late in the game and Sean is [calling for] bombs. I was flabbergasted, but I was impressed."

Toomer had a breakout game, with six catches for 181 yards and three scores, while the other starting receiver, Ike Hilliard, caught six for 121 yards in an impressive aerial assault. The Giants would go on to lose three of their last four games and finish 7–9, but in 2000 they would go to the Super Bowl behind the passing of Collins, the receiving of Toomer and Hilliard, and the multidimensional skills of Barber.

December 3, 1939

REDSKINS' HOPES BOOTLESS

Giants Win Eastern Title on Controversial Kick

The Giants and the Redskins became bitter rivals in the 1930s during their annual battles for supremacy in the East. On the final day of the 1937 season, Washington pounded New York 49–14 to clinch the Eastern crown, while in the 1938 finale, the Giants upended the Redskins 36–0 and went on to win the NFL title over the Packers the following week. In 1939, Washington owner George Preston Marshall literally marched into New York, leading a 150-man marching band and bringing 12,000 Redskins fans along with him. Those 12,000 Redskins rooters helped kick the Polo Grounds attendance over 62,000, the highest level for any game since Red Grange's New York debut in 1925. With both teams 8–1–1, this game would determine the Eastern Conference champion.

The Giants scored first on a 40-yard field goal by Ward Cuff, set up by Cuff's 27-yard reverse. Later in the opening period the Redskins intercepted a pass, but Bo Russell, in a bit of foreshadowing, missed the field-goal try from the 35-yard line. In the second quarter, the Giants scored again on a three-pointer. This time it was Ken Strong from 19 yards.

The Redskins threatened after a 37-yard Dick Todd punt return and three pass receptions—two by Todd and one by Bob Masterson—took them to the Giants' 1-yard line. But Tuffy Leemans intercepted Frankie Filchock's pass in the end zone.

In the third quarter, Ward Cuff missed a 21-yard field-goal attempt, but got a second chance after Hank Soar intercepted Sammy Baugh and returned the ball 25 yards. Cuff made good from the 15, and

> I wasn't even watching. I was too busy talking to a man sitting behind me. Halloran had the best view. Why argue with him?
>
> —STEVE OWEN

GAME DETAILS

New York Giants 9 • Washington Redskins 7

Date: December 3, 1939

Location: Polo Grounds, New York

Attendance: 62,530

Significance: Season finale to determine the Eastern Conference title

Box Score:

Redskins	0	0	0	7	**7**
Giants	3	3	3	0	**9**

Scoring:
NYG Cuff 40-yard FG
NYG Strong 19-yard FG

NYG Cuff 15-yard FG
WSH Masterson 20-yard pass from Filchock
(Masterson PAT)

Team	FD	YDS	RUSH	PASS	RTN	A-C-I	PUNT	FUM	PEN
Redskins	8	202	38	164	25	27-14-4	6-41	2-0	4-20
Giants	10	164	117	47	48	12-6-2	7-42	2-0	3-15

the Giants held a 9–0 lead going into the fourth quarter.

Redskins tackle Willie Wilkins got Washington back in the game by blocking Len Barnum's punt at the 19, and Filchock quickly capitalized with a 20-yard strike to Masterson with 5:34 left to play. Trailing 9–7, the Redskins got still another big play from Dick Todd when he returned a punt 30 yards to the 47-yard line. A mix of runs and passes moved the ball to the 5.

After a delay-of-game penalty on Washington, Bo Russell came onto the field to attempt a 15-yard field goal with 45 seconds left in the game. The snap came to Filchock, who placed the ball squarely, and Russell booted it high over the upright. As the Redskins began to celebrate what they thought was a good kick, they saw referee Bill Halloran signaling "no good." Led by their coach Ray Flaherty, whose jersey had been retired by the Giants to honor his playing career in New York, the Redskins stormed the field to protest the call, but to no avail. Halloran ruled that the ball indeed went over the upright, but that it needed to be entirely within the plane of the uprights to be good.

WARD CUFF

While the Redskins' Bo Russell made only one of six field-goal attempts in 1939, his reliable Giants counterpart, Ward Cuff, led the NFL with seven field goals that year. It was one of four seasons in which the versatile Giants back led the league in three-pointers.

Cuff was a fourth-round pick out of Marquette in 1937 who had never place-kicked before coming to New York. Steve Owen saw his potential and trained him so well that when Cuff left New York nine years later, he was the Giants' all-time leading scorer with 305 points. Owen often called the five-time All-Pro "the greatest Giants back of all time." Cuff was a wingback in Owen's A-formation and was especially skilled as a blocker and receiver, in addition to being a scourge on defense and a top kicker. It was only later in his career that he was called upon to do much running, and he ultimately proved himself more than able as a ball carrier, leading the league in rushing average in 1943.

Cuff was known as a quiet, placid, pleasant man who always had a smile on his face on and off the field. In training camp, he roomed with Wellington Mara, three years his junior, and the two remained friends the rest of their lives. In 1945, the Giants traded Cuff to the Chicago Cardinals at his request so he could be closer to his Milwaukee home. Cuff spent one season with the Cardinals and a final season in Green Bay before retiring in 1946. Both he and Mara lived to be 89.

Giants great Ward Cuff kicked New York to victory against the Redskins in 1939. *(Photo courtesy of AP Images)*

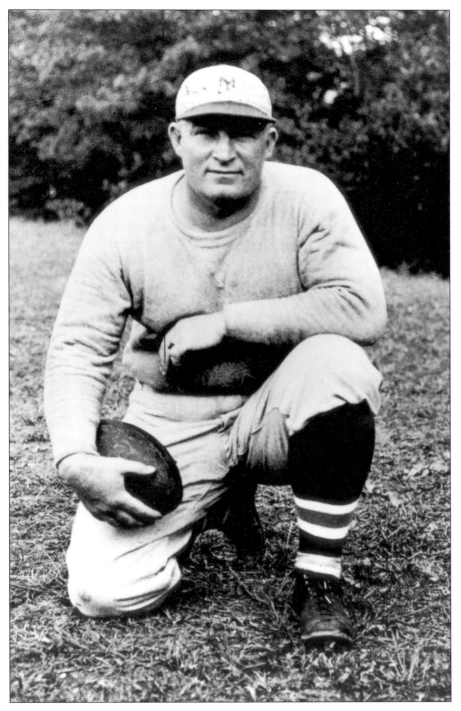

The Giants ran out the clock, but the action didn't end there. Fist-fights broke out on the field between players and fans. The Redskins' Ed Justice went after Halloran and just missed him with a punch. New York police and Giants players helped escort Halloran off the field, and the drama shifted to the league office, which was prepared to fine and ban Justice for hitting an official. A few days later, though, Halloran reported that he had not been struck by Justice, and the angry Redskins player was spared.

Both Halloran and the Giants went on to Milwaukee the next week for the title game with the Packers. It would be the fifth Giants game he refereed in 1939. On that day, the Giants were overwhelmed by the Packers' two-armed passing attack of Arnie Herber and Cecil Isbell and they lost 27–0 in the first ever championship game shutout.

It wasn't even close. It was plenty inside. All the players said so. Every cop in back of the goal posts said it was good. If Halloran has a conscience, he'd never again sleep an untroubled night.

—RAY FLAHERTY

Head coach Steve Owen led his Giants to a controversial win over the Washington Redskins in the 1939 season finale.

September 20, 1964

TITTLE TOPPLED
Steelers and Age Conquer Giants

From 1961 through 1963, the Giants lost one of the first two games of the season and recovered to win the East handily each year. So when New York dropped its 1964 opener to a blitzing Eagles team that sacked quarterback Y. A. Tittle five times—causing him to fumble three times and throw two interceptions—it was cause for concern but not panic. After all, Allie Sherman's teams had never lost two in a row. After the next game, though, against the Steelers, it was time to admit the obvious: the dynasty was crumbling.

All appeared well at the outset of this September day. Thirty-five-year-old Steelers quarterback Ed Brown got off to a slow start, throwing two interceptions in his first five passes. Erich Barnes returned one for a touchdown and a quick Giants lead. A 64-yard pass from 38-year-old Y. A. Tittle to 29-year-old Del Shofner led to a touchdown run by 33-year-old Alex Webster and a 14–0 first-period lead.

However, the second quarter brought devastation.

As halftime approached, Tittle called an ill-fated screen pass from deep in his territory. While Tittle looked left for Joe Morrison, Steelers defensive end John Baker slipped by second-year tackle Lane Howell and came free. Baker crashed full-bore into Tittle's right side, with his forearm hitting Y. A. in the mouth and knocking off the quarterback's helmet. The force of the blow lifted Tittle off the ground as he floated a wounded-duck pass that defensive tackle Chuck Hinton gathered in at the 8-yard line and ran in for the score.

A dazed Tittle knelt in the end zone with a bloodied head and no helmet. This sad image was captured by local photographer Morris Berman, who won a National Headliner Award for the affecting shot. Tittle was unable to breathe and was helped to the locker room with bruised ribs.

> This is a moment I have dreaded. I don't want to come back and be a mediocre football player again. I was one last fall.
>
> —Y. A. TITTLE, FOUR MONTHS LATER AT HIS RETIREMENT

John Baker unloads a devastating hit on Y. A. Tittle, which caused Tittle to throw an interception on which Chuck Hinton scored. *(Photo courtesy of AP Images)*

Perhaps the most famous photograph in pro football history, the image of a bloody Tittle captures the rough, violent nature of the game. Ironically, the *Pittsburgh Post-Gazette* chose not to run the picture at the time because there was not enough action in it. It now hangs in the Pro Football Hall of Fame. *(Photo courtesy of AP Images)*

ANDY ROBUSTELLI

In retrospect, Andy Robustelli must have regretted his decision to reverse his announced retirement in 1964 and line up at defensive end for one more pursuit of a championship. Allie Sherman was remaking the Giants in his own image. Sam Huff was replaced by Lou Slaby and Dick Modzelewski by Andy Stynchula. Robustelli was slated to be supplanted by the forgettable Bob Taylor when Sherman implored his defensive coach to slap on the pads for one more try behind Y. A. Tittle, who, as it turned out, was running on empty. Several other teammates were also feeling the full effects of age, and their replacements were not worthy of the Big Blue uniform.

Robustelli was a 19th-round draft choice of the Rams out of tiny Arnold College in 1951. He seemed an unlikely bet to make the roster of the defending Western champs, let alone become a seven-time All-Pro elected to the Hall of Fame after a 14-year NFL career. The Rams, in fact, thought he was already too old after five seasons and traded him to New York for a first-round pick in 1956.

As a Giants player, Andy captained the defense and never missed a game in nine years as the team went to six title games. For his career, Robustelli appeared in eight NFL title games and won two championship rings. Not only was he quick, agile, and especially noted for his pass rushing, but Andy was a brainy leader who was considered a coach on the field.

When Tom Landry left for Dallas, the speculation was that Robustelli or Harland Svare were most likely to succeed him. Svare got the initial appointment, but two years later when he left for the Rams head coaching job, Andy became a playing coach. In each of his last three seasons, he announced he would be retiring as a player, but twice was talked out of it. When he finally retired after the 1964 season, he also quit as defensive coach to pay more attention to his business concerns.

Ten years later, Wellington Mara brought Robustelli back as director of football operations to try to restore the floundering franchise. In five years under Robustelli, the Giants made slow, steady progress but were still not winning, and he resigned. His replacement, George Young, completed the rebuilding job in the next decade, but Robustelli's front-office role should be remembered with appreciation. His on-the-field contribution will never be forgotten.

> It looked like my head was hurting, but it was actually my rib cage. I pulled cartilage there. My head was bleeding because my helmet cut it when I hit the ground.
>
> —Y. A. TITTLE, QUOTED IN *THE NEW YORK TIMES*

GAME DETAILS

New York Giants 24 • Pittsburgh Steelers 27

Date: September 20, 1964

Location: Pitt Stadium, Pittsburgh

Attendance: 35,053

Significance: Symbolic end of an era

Box Score:

Giants	14	0	7	3	**24**
Steelers	0	13	7	7	**27**

Scoring:

NYG Barnes 26-yard interception return (Chandler PAT)

NYG Webster 2-yard run (Chandler PAT)

PIT Hinton 8-yard interception return (Clark kick failed)

PIT Johnson 2-yard pass from Brown (Clark PAT)

PIT Brown 2-yard run (Clark PAT)

NYG James 2-yard run (Chandler PAT)

PIT Brown 1-yard run (Clark PAT)

NYG Chandler 22-yard FG

Team	FD	YDS	RUSH	PASS	A-C-I	PUNT	FUM	PEN
Giants	24	356	38-147	209	34-14-2	3-47	0	40
Steelers	14	214	42-137	77	10-5-2	5-43	0	64

Giants: Tittle 132P, Wood 107P

The Steelers missed the extra point and kicked off to the Giants, who were now led by rookie scrambler Gary Wood. With a minute to go in the half, Wood was picked off by corner Brady Keys, which led to a second Pittsburgh score right before the intermission.

Both teams engineered long scoring drives in the third quarter to keep the game close. Pittsburgh's Brady Keys then set up the winning score in the final period with a 90-yard punt return. Keys was knocked out at the 1, but Ed Brown scored from there to put the Steelers up

27–21. Don Chandler added a 22-yard field goal, but he also missed one from the 37 to go with his two 42-yard misses from the first half.

New York was now 0–2 with an injured quarterback who suddenly looked old and feeble. Tittle would relieve Wood the following week against Washington and spark a victory, but he was injured again in the process. Although Tittle gamely would play in every game in 1964, the team finished the season 2–10–2. The championship run was over.

November 9, 1958

GIANTS BEAT BALTIMORE 24-21

Frank's Fling Fuels Feat

The Giants began the 1958 season struggling; they split their first four games before winning two in a row to take them to midseason with a 4–2 record, just one game behind Cleveland in the East. In the Western Conference, the Colts started the season 6–0, but they lost starting quarterback Johnny Unitas to a rib injury in a costly 56–0 win over Green Bay. Behind backup quarterback George Shaw, Baltimore came to Yankee Stadium for what would turn out to be an exciting prelude to the 1958 NFL Championship Game.

The Giants began the game with a cannon blast, courtesy of one of their favorite plays. On the first play from scrimmage at the Giants' 24-yard line, Frank Gifford took the pitch from Charley Conerly, rolled right, stopped, and threw the halfback option pass downfield. End Bob Schnelker caught the pass over his shoulder at the Giants' 45 and began to rumble. Andy Nelson dove and missed Schnelker at the Colts' 45 as Nelson cut back toward the left sideline. Finally, 32 yards downfield, cornerback Milt Davis wrestled Schnelker down at the 13, ending

a 63-yard pass play. Four plays later, Alex Webster went over for the touchdown from the 5, and the Giants had a 7–0 lead three minutes into the contest.

Late in the first quarter, Baltimore was stopped on fourth down at the Giants' goal line, but then forced New York to punt. Taking over at the Giants' 47, the Colts scored the tying touchdown in two plays—an 11-yard run by Alan Ameche and a 36-yard strike from Shaw to Lenny Moore in the end zone. Shaw added a 23-yard touchdown pass to Raymond Berry in the second quarter, and Baltimore led 14–7 at the half.

New York began double-teaming both Moore and Berry in the second half and held the Colts scoreless in the third period, while Conerly led the Giants to two touchdowns. The first touchdown was set up by the sort of improvisation later made famous by fellow Mississippian Brett Favre. Conerly was sandwiched by two Colts blitzers, Bill Pellington and Don Shinnick, but he managed to shove the ball forward to halfback Phil King, who darted for a first

GAME DETAILS

New York Giants 24 • Baltimore Colts 21

Date: November 9, 1958

Location: Yankee Stadium, New York

Attendance: 71,163

Significance: Midseason preview of the 1958 NFL Championship Game

> Our planning is done before ballgames. Our offense is given to the boys Wednesday. However, we don't use one-third of the plays we agree on. Everything agreed upon before the game is based on the particular defense we will face and if that defense is different, we can be expected to change.
>
> —VINCE LOMBARDI

Box Score:

Colts	7	7	0	7	**21**
Giants	7	0	14	3	**24**

Scoring:

NYG Webster 5-yard run (Summerall PAT)
BAL Moore 36-yard pass from Shaw (Myhra PAT)
BAL Berry 23-yard pass from Shaw (Myhra PAT)
NYG Rote 25-yard pass from Conerly (Summerall PAT)
NYG Gifford 13-yard run (Summerall PAT)
BAL Moore 4-yard pass from Shaw (Myhra PAT)
NYG Summerall 28-yard FG

Team	FD	YDS	RUSH	PASS	A-C-I	PUNT	FUM	PEN
Colts	19	384	32-146	238	30-12-1	2-37	2	81
Giants	18	341	39-167	188	20-13-1	4-43	1	91

Colts: Moore 101C

down. He then hit Kyle Rote in the corner of the end zone for the score. Gifford ran a 13-yard sweep for the second touchdown, which lifted New York to a 21–14 lead. Early in the final period, though, the unstoppable Moore got loose for a 47-yard reception and then scored on a four-yard toss from Shaw to tie the score.

In the closing minutes, the Giants drove down the field once more, getting to the Colts' 21, where they faced a fourth-and-three. Pat Summerall came in and kicked the game-winning 28-yard field goal with 2:40 to play, and the Giants defense protected the lead for the remainder of the game. The next time these two teams faced each other, Unitas would be back, and New York would find it much more difficult to protect a three-point lead in the last two minutes.

THE HALBACK OPTION

The base play of Vince Lombardi's offense, in both New York and Green Bay, was the power sweep with two pulling guards. One reason the play was so effective was that with Frank Gifford in New York and Paul Hornung in Green Bay, Lombardi had a skilled passer to further transform the play into a halfback option pass. This halfback option play against the Colts, however, features straight-ahead line blocking and no pulling. After taking the pitch from Charley Conerly (42), Gifford (16) had three options against the Colts on this play: one, pass to Bob Schnelker (85) who was running a deep out; two, pass to halfback Alex Webster (29) who was running a shorter out; and three, run the ball around the end if the defensive backs stay back. On this play, the Colt cornerbacks charged to defend the run, so Gifford took option number one and hit Schnelker for a 63-yard gain on the first play of the game.

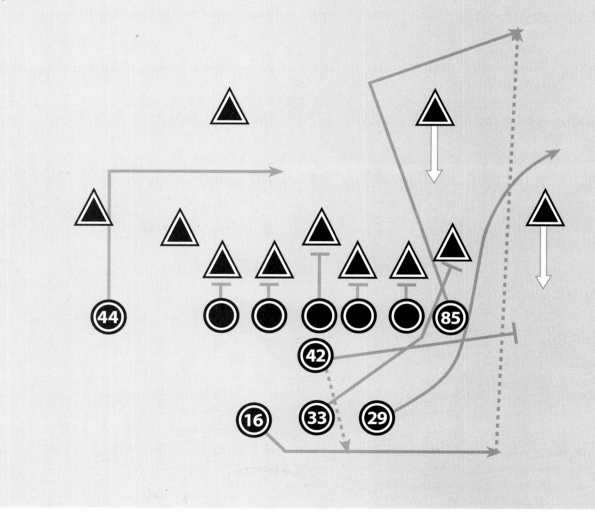

VINCE LOMBARDI

The play that set the tone for this game right from the start was a variant of the play that set the tone for the Giants' offense under offensive coach Vince Lombardi: the sweep with the option to pass. The play took full advantage of the versatility of left halfback Frank Gifford; it was a play the Giants would run right and left in the five seasons Lombardi spent on the Giants sideline.

Lombardi was one of the famed "seven blocks of granite" line at 1930s football power Fordham, at the same time that Wellington Mara was a student there. Vince began his career as a high school teacher and coach in New Jersey and progressed slowly through the assistant coaching ranks from Fordham to West Point to—finally—the New York Giants in 1954. In New York, he teamed with Tom Landry under head coach Jim Lee Howell during the late 1950s to give the Giants probably the best set of offensive and defensive coaches in league history.

Giants players originally looked at the emotional, exuberant Lombardi dubiously and mocked him, but Vince was smart enough to go to veteran leaders like Conerly, Rote, and Gifford and enlist their help in developing plays that would work in the NFL. Soon Lombardi's teaching methods and ideas brought respect and even devotion. While the offense lacked speed, Lombardi's power game took

advantage of the skills on hand, and the team won the title in 1956 and nearly won it in 1958.

The 1958 championship game was the last game Lombardi would coach for New York. Green Bay hired him in 1959, and his five-title tenure in Wisconsin made him the most legendary coach in NFL history. The Super Bowl trophy was even named in his honor after his early death to cancer. After Jim Lee Howell retired in 1960, native New Yorker Lombardi investigated getting out of his contract to succeed Howell, but the Packers and Commissioner Pete Rozelle would not allow that. History had a different course for both teams.

Frank Gifford and Vince Lombardi used the option pass to top the Colts in a midseason preview of the 1958 NFL Championship Game.

November 20, 1938

HEIN'S HEIST AND TUFFY'S TORRENT

Big Plays Key Big Win over Packers

By a quirk of scheduling, when the 8–2 Green Bay Packers rolled into the Polo Grounds in 1938 for their season finale against the 6–2 Giants, New York still had three games to play. The two teams topped their respective conferences, though, and would meet again in the same ballpark three weeks later to decide the NFL championship. While the Packers would gain 20 first downs that day to the Giants' six, this defensive battle between evenly-matched rivals would be decided by big plays. Without receiver Don Hutson, Green Bay found itself at a disadvantage, even though the Giants would throw just four passes on the afternoon.

The hard-fought scoreless first half was highlighted by the Giants' defense continu-

ally rising to the occasion. Four times in the first two periods, Green Bay penetrated inside the New York 30-yard line and came away with no points. For the game, Green Bay had seven drives reach deep into Giants territory: two ended in interceptions, two ended in missed field goals, two ended by turning the ball over on downs, and one resulted in a field goal.

The Giants got on the scoreboard on the opening play of the second half. Packers fullback Clarke Hinkle fumbled the kickoff at the 4, recovered his bobble, but then was corralled in his own end zone by a wave of Giants tacklers, led by Johnny Dell Isola, for a safety. Green Bay answered with a field goal to make the score 3–2 in the third quarter, setting up the first of the two big plays by the Giants.

> The Giant captain took the ball on the dead run and sped over the turf like a Jesse Owens. Fear of pursuit put wings on his feet. Mel never had run so swiftly in his life as he flashed for the touchdown.
>
> —ARTHUR DALEY IN *THE NEW YORK TIMES*

Mel Hein (center) and Tuffy Leemans (right) teamed up with head coach Steve Owen (left) to defeat the Green Bay Packers 15–3 in 1938. *(Photo courtesy of AP Images)*

MEL HEIN

Mel Hein's 50-yard interception return in this game was the only touchdown this great lineman would ever score in his 15-year career. Hein played center on offense and linebacker on defense and was team captain for 10 seasons. For the first 50 years of the franchise, this charter member of the Hall of Fame was indisputably the greatest of all Giants. The team retired his No. 7 jersey.

Hein was not approached by any pro teams at the conclusion of his college career at Washington State, so he took the initiative and wrote to a few offering his services. The Providence Steamroller offered $125 a game and Hein returned a signed contract, but then the Giants wrote offering $150 a game. Hein then wired the Providence postmaster to request the return of his letter. Luckily for the Giants, the Providence contract was returned.

In New York, Mel was an eight-time All-Pro, played on seven conference champs, and won two NFL titles. In the championship year of 1938, the 6'3", 230-pound Hein was even named NFL MVP, the only time an interior lineman has ever been so honored.

During World War II, Hein was known as the "Sunday Center" because he coached at Union College in upstate New York during the week and came into the city on Sunday to play for the Giants. After he finally did retire, he spent 20 years as a line coach with the Rams, the New York Yankees of the AAFC, and the USC Trojans. He finished his football career as the supervisor of officials in the AFL and then in the AFC from 1965 to 1974. Only Michael Strahan, who announced his retirement in June 2008, played as long in a Giants jersey.

TUFFY LEEMANS

Tuffy Leemans's 75-yard gallop in this game was the longest run of his career. As his nickname suggests, Tuffy was noted not for his speed and elusiveness, but for his toughness. As a Giants player, he also passed, called signals, blocked, and played defense.

Alphonse "Tuffy" Leemans was personally scouted and signed by the 20-year-old Wellington Mara in 1936; he was the second player ever drafted by New York. As a rookie, Leemans led the NFL in rushing with 830 yards, but he would never again come within 350 yards of that total in his eight-year career.

He was a reliable pro who took on the team's play-calling and passing responsibilities after the retirement of Ed Danowski in 1940. In 1941, Leemans led the Giants in both passing and rushing. The Giants honored him with Tuffy Leemans Day on December 7, 1941, but the Pearl Harbor attack upstaged the tribute. During the war, a football injury kept Tuffy out of the military and on the playing field.

Leemans was a two-time All-Pro who five times gained more than 100 yards in a game and twice led the league in rushing average. While he gained just 3,142 yards rushing, his No. 4 jersey was retired by the Giants, and Tuffy was elected to the Hall of Fame in 1978 shortly before his death.

GAME DETAILS

New York Giants 15 • Green Bay Packers 3

Date: November 20, 1938

Location: Polo Grounds, New York

Attendance: 48,279

Significance: Preview of NFL title game three weeks later

Box Score:

Packers	0	0	3	0	**3**
Giants	0	0	9	6	**15**

Scoring:

NYG Hinkle tackled in end zone for safety
GB Engebretsen 22-yard FG
NYG Leemans 75-yard run (Cuff PAT)
GB Hein 50-yard interception return (Cuff kick failed)

Team	FD	YDS	RUSH	PASS	RTN	A-C-I	PUNT	FUM	PEN
Packers	20	307	173	134	48	19-9-5	5-53	1-0	2-10
Giants	6	187	180	7	23	6-2-1	8-50	2-2	5-22

Giants: Leemans 159R

From their 25, Tuffy Leemans took a direct snap while the Giants' front wall collapsed the Packers' line. Leemans raced around the right end, cut back inside Packers Cecil Isbell and Milt Gantenbein, and broke a tackle by Buckets Goldenberg at the 33. After Tuffy got by Hank Bruder, he cut back outside at the 42 to avoid Joe Laws and ran untouched to the end zone for a 75-yard touchdown and a 9–3 lead.

The Giants' second big play occurred on the first play of the fourth quarter and clinched the victory. Packers passer Cecil Isbell dropped back from his own 40, and under a heavy rush from John Mellus and Frank Cope, he tossed a wobbly pass to the sideline well behind Hinkle, the intended target. Center/linebacker Mel Hein leaped in, grabbed the ball at midfield, and outraced Baby Ray for the 50-yard touchdown that iced the game for New York. Hein, who played 57 minutes of the game, earned himself a $10 bonus from coach Steve Owen for the pick-six play of the game. The Giants went on to earn an impressive victory over their chief rivals for the NFL title.

December 22, 2002

SHOCKEY STAMPEDES THE COLTS

Giants Tight End Leads Team to Victory with Swagger

In a late-season drive for the playoffs, one wouldn't expect a rookie to lead the charge, but Jeremy Shockey was no ordinary rookie. The 8–6 Giants and the 9–5 Colts were desperately trying to stay afloat in 2002's tight playoff races as they came into this inter-conference battle in the next-to-last week of the season. One player who was ready for action was the aptly named Shockey, New York's flamboyant first-year tight end.

The Giants got onto the scoreboard first with a field goal following a blocked punt and then mounted a long drive later in the first quarter, after Dhani Jones intercepted a Peyton Manning pass at the Giants' 37-yard line. This drive and the New York offense were sparked by a screen pass to Shockey with the Giants facing a second-and-16 from the Colts' 38 on the first play of the second quarter. Shockey grabbed the pass and then began rumbling downfield. At the 25, Colts safety David Gibson, who had been widely quoted before the game describing Shockey as "just another player," got set to make the tackle.

Shockey saw Gibson, lowered his shoulder, and headed right for him. Shockey trampled over Gibson as if he were a Styrofoam cup and continued toward the end zone before the Colts finally lassoed him and brought him down at the 14. Shortly thereafter, Tiki Barber scored from the 4 and the Giants led by 10.

New York put the game away in the third quarter, starting with the first play from scrimmage. On a flea flicker, Barber took the handoff from Kerry Collins and flipped it back to him, and Collins unleashed the bomb to Amani Toomer for an 82-yard touchdown with the victimized David Gibson in fruitless pursuit. The Giants scored two more touchdowns in the third period and went into the fourth quarter leading 30–6.

Collins added two more touchdown passes to Toomer in the final 15 minutes, while Peyton Manning led the Colts to three meaningless touchdowns to narrow the final score to 44–27. For the day, Kerry Collins achieved a perfect 158.3 passer rating and threw for 366 yards and four touchdowns.

Jeremy Shockey steamrolled Colts safety David Gibson on his way to 116 receiving yards that quieted the boasts of the talkative Gibson, who had downplayed Shockey's impact before the game.

Toomer caught 10 passes for 204 yards and three scores, and Shockey caught seven for 116 yards. Although Shockey would also fumble inside the Colts' 10 on a later drive, his electric play inspired the entire team, and the Giants would go on to beat the Eagles in the last game of the season to make the playoffs as a wild card.

JEREMY SHOCKEY

In a game in which veteran receiver Amani Toomer caught 10 passes for 204 yards and three touchdowns, the unforgettable moment was still Jeremy Shockey's first-quarter catch and run, in which he rumbled over safety David Gibson like an 18-wheeler mashing a rabbit on the highway. It was the signature play for this vocal, vociferous rookie and will forever be the lead on his highlight reel.

Shockey grew up in Oklahoma and dreamed of going to the University of Oklahoma, but was rejected by the Sooners as too small. In junior college, Shockey grew two inches and put on 30 pounds. Now the Sooners wanted Shockey, but he didn't want them. Instead, Shockey went to the University of Miami, and in his second year there won a national title and was named All-American. He declared early for the 2002 NFL Draft, and the Giants grabbed him with the 14th pick in the first round. Jeremy made his presence known right away in training camp by sparking a fight in the dining hall about singing his school song. Surprisingly, coach Jim Fassel's reaction to the fight was, "My man has arrived," because he so loved Shockey's battling spirit.

While off the field Shockey's dating and nightclub exploits have been notorious, on the field he is the total tight end. He is a solid blocker and a powerful runner with the ball in his hands. At times he will drop a pass, but that never stops his drive—or his mouth.

His mouthiness isn't limited to opponents, but is also extended to teammates and even to his coaches—most notably, when he told the media after a loss to

> **H**e won't be saying nothing else about me, I don't think.
>
> —JEREMY SHOCKEY, AFTER THE GAME

Seattle in 2006 that the Giants were "outplayed and we got outcoached." A subsequent apology to Tom Coughlin smoothed over that situation, but Shockey remains a loose cannon on a team that can be remarkably undisciplined. However, in 2007, he became the Giants' all-time leader in receptions by a tight end—in just his sixth season.

Tight end Jeremy Shockey brought plenty of swagger to the Giants as a rookie in 2002.

GAME DETAILS

New York Giants 44 • Indianapolis Colts 27

Date: December 22, 2002

Location: RCA Dome, Indianapolis

Attendance: 56,579

Significance: Both teams were headed for a wild-card berth

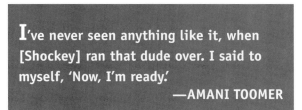
Box Score:

Giants	3	7	20	14	**44**
Colts	0	3	3	21	**27**

Scoring:

NYG Bryant 20-yard FG

NYG Barber 4-yard run (Bryant PAT)

IND Vanderjagt 20-yard FG

NYG Toomer 82-yard pass from Collins (Bryant PAT)

NYG Stackhouse 18-yard pass from Collins
   (Bryant missed kick)

IND Vanderjagt 27-yard FG

NYG Barber 1-yard run (Bryant PAT)

IND Wayne 21-yard pass from Manning
   (run for two-point conversion failed)

NYG Toomer 21-yard pass from Collins (Bryant PAT)

IND Harrison 25-yard pass (Pollard two-point conversion
   pass from Manning)

IND Wayne 40-yard pass from Manning (Vanderjagt PAT)

NYG Toomer 27-yard pass from Collins (Bryant PAT)

Team	FD	YDS	RUSH	PASS	RTN	A-C-I	Sacked	PUNT	FUM	PEN
Giants	24	469	36-103	366	121	29-23-0	0-0	3-39	3-3	5-33
Colts	20	399	19-50	349	216	46-30-2	2-16	6-34	0-0	7-59

Giants: Collins 366P, Toomer 204C, Shockey 116C

Colts: Manning 365P, Harrison 128C, Wayne 104C

November 18, 1985

41 Taylor Takes Out Theismann

Redskins Lose Quarterback, Giants Lose Game

This 1985 *Monday Night Football* battle for supremacy in the East featured one of the most gruesome plays in NFL history, in which the Redskins lost their veteran starting quarterback Joe Theismann but still won the game. With the help of several trick plays, coach Joe Gibbs led Washington to victory over New York behind an untried backup quarterback who had already failed at professional baseball before hooking on with the Redskins.

The Redskins scored first after a fake punt by Steve Cox kept their drive alive, and Theismann hit tight end Don Warren for the touchdown. The Giants evened the score in the first quarter on a two-play, 80-yard drive that consisted of a 24-yard interference call on the Redskins' Vernon Dean and a 56-yard run by Joe Morris on a trap play.

On the second play of the second period, Gibbs dialed up another trick play, but he would forever regret this one. Theismann handed off to John Riggins near midfield, and Riggins flipped the ball back to Theismann for a flea flicker, but the Giants were not fooled. Harry Carson

was in on Theismann immediately, but Joe eluded him. From behind, Lawrence Taylor jumped on Theismann's back. As the quarterback went down, his right leg got caught in an awkward position and bent the wrong way. From the other side, Gary Reasons hit Theismann low while Jim Burt came in over the top. Theismann's lower tibia and fibula snapped like kindling.

Taylor and Burt immediately realized what had happened and began signaling furiously to the Washington bench for medical assistance. Taylor held his head in his hands and thought to himself, *What have I done?*

Theismann was wheeled off the field. His career was over, but the game continued on, with rookie Jay Schroeder taking over at quarterback. Schroeder's first pass went for a 44-yard gain, but a Redskins fumble ended that drive, leaving the game 7–7 at the half.

Washington opened the second half with an onside kick by Steve Cox, who recovered it himself. John Riggins scored four plays later to take the lead. The Giants rebounded, with Joe Morris scoring two

Redskins quarterback Joe Theismann is carted off the field after having his leg broken by Giants linebacker Lawrence Taylor in one of the most memorable moments in *Monday Night Football* history.

HARRY CARSON

As Joe Theismann was being wheeled off the field this ugly night, he turned to his longtime, respected adversary, 10-year veteran linebacker Harry Carson, and said, "I hear you're thinking about retiring."

Carson replied, "Yeah, I am."

Theismann continued, "Well, don't you go retiring, because I'm coming back."

Carson told him, "That may be the case, but it ain't going to be tonight."

The stalwart Carson would continue playing for another three seasons, despite a painful chronic shoulder injury, and would finally get to play on a championship team in New York.

> You could just see it. It was like the foot was just hanging there.
>
> —HARRY CARSON

The Giants drafted Carson out of South Carolina State as a defensive end in the fourth round in 1976. Converted to middle linebacker by position coach Marty Schottenheimer and then to an inside linebacker in the 3-4 defense in 1979, Harry played between Brad Van Pelt and Brian Kelley until 1984, when both were traded. Harry walked out of training camp soon after.

Bill Parcells tweaked him by telling the press that he hoped Carson was going to the library to look up the word *leadership*, and Harry returned two days later. In truth, Parcells relied heavily on Carson and defensive end George Martin as veteran leaders, and those two teammates would retire together in 1988.

A nine-time Pro Bowl player, Harry was a premier run stuffer who once made 20 tackles in a game against the Packers in 1982. As he stated simply in his autobiography, *Point of Attack*, "My job is knocking people down. I'm a linebacker in the National Football League. And I'm good at my job...I rarely do anything spectacular. I hardly ever blitz the quarterback. I stop the run. I wrap running backs up and lay them down."

After six unsuccessful campaigns as a Hall of Fame finalist, the proud old linebacker wrote to the selection committee in 2005, saying he no longer wanted to be considered for election. The following year, Harry was elected and dropped his public reluctance because he knew how much Wellington Mara had wanted to see him enshrined. Harry Carson indeed understood leadership; he was the heart and soul of the New York Giants for more than a dozen years.

Linebacker Harry Carson was a leader on defense and was eventually elected to the Pro Football Hall of Fame.

GAME DETAILS

New York Giants 21 • Washington Redskins 23

Date: November 18, 1985

Location: RFK Stadium, Washington, D.C.

Attendance: 53,371

Significance: Joe Theismann injured on *Monday Night Football*

Box Score:

Giants	7	0	14	0	**21**
Redskins	7	0	7	9	**23**

You could see that those guys were as upset as we were.

—CLINT DIDIER

Scoring:

WSH Warren 10-yard pass from Theismann (Moseley PAT)
NYG Morris 56-yard run (Schubert PAT)
WSH Riggins 1-yard run (Moseley PAT)
NYG Morris 41-yard run (Schubert PAT)
NYG Morris 8-yard run (Schubert PAT)
WSH Moseley 28-yard FG
WSH Didier 14-yard pass from Schroeder
(Moseley kick failed)

Team	FD	YDS	RUSH	PASS	RTN	A-C-I	Sacked	PUNT	FUM	PEN
Giants	12	253	24-152	101	8	18-9-1	4-37	7-42	1-0	7-40
Redskins	22	356	41-98	258	24	31-21-0	4-24	6-38	4-3	5-49

Giants: Morris 118R, Simms 138P
Redskins: Schroeder 221P, Monk 130C

more touchdowns in the third quarter on a 41-yard trap play and an eight-yard run following a fumble recovery, to retake the lead 21–14.

Washington staged a comeback in the final period on a Mark Moseley field goal followed by a second Steve Cox onside kick with more than 11 minutes to play. Again, the Redskins recovered the kick and this time drove down to score on a Schroeder pass to tight end Clint Didier. The Giants were unable to mount any more offense, and the Redskins held on for the Pyrrhic victory.

The Giants, the Redskins, and the Cowboys all would end the season at 10–6, but Washington lost out on the playoffs because of tiebreakers. The talkative Theismann naturally moved into the broadcasting booth, while Taylor would later say of the nightmarish game, "It's not a moment I want to remember or ever see again."

40

HEADS-UP HAINES HOODWINKS BEARS

Giants Beat Chicago for First Championship

In 1927, the NFL had been around for a scant eight years and Timothy Mara's Giants were in just their third. It requires a leap of imagination to envision just how different pro football was in those early days. Longtime Giants coach Steve Owen told Barry Gottehrer in *The Giants of New York*, "Football was a different game then. The ball was bigger and harder to pass, you couldn't pass from closer than five yards behind the line of scrimmage, and in 1927, they moved the goal posts back 10 yards from the goal line. But the big difference was the way we played the game. We were pretty much a smash-and-shove gang. We were bone-crushers, not fancy Dans." However, it was a clever trick play that helped secure the team's first NFL title that year in a late-season showdown against the Bears.

People often refer to the style that Bill Parcells's Giants played in the 1980s as "smash-mouth football." In the 1920s, the players weren't as big or as fast, but they were the true smash-mouth players because of the way the game was played. Primarily, the game was about field position, with

the punter featured as a prominent part of the attack as teams tried to pin their opponents deep in their own end and hoped to capitalize on fumbles. The seven men on the line stood shoulder-to-shoulder against the seven on the opponent's line in a relentless power game. Passes were rare and scores were low. The Giants averaged just five or six passes a game. Their large, powerful line was the key element in a league-leading defense that gave up just 20 points for the *entire* 13-game season, with 10 shutouts.

On November 27, the 7–2–1 Bears came to the Polo Grounds to face the 8–1–1 Giants in a showdown for first place. Early in the game, the Bears mounted a drive that gave them a first-and-goal from the 5-yard line. With their backs to the goal line, the Giants line produced a massive stand, stopping each of the Bears' four line thrusts. New York took over at the 1, and Chicago expected them to punt the ball immediately out of danger. Hinkey Haines, New York's signal caller, shouted to Mule Wilson to be careful to avoid stepping on the end line for

GAME DETAILS

New York Giants 13 • Chicago Bears 7

Date: November 27, 1927

Location: Polo Grounds, New York

Attendance: 15,000

Significance: Battle for first place between the 7–2–1 Bears and the 8–1–1 Giants

> It was the best football team of its time. Their line beat the hell out of you and wore you down, and their backs could move the ball. But they would have been passed off the field by the top teams of the '30s.
>
> —RED GRANGE,
> IN *THE GIANTS OF NEW YORK* BY BARRY GOTTEHRER

Box Score:

Bears	0	0	0	7	**7**
Giants	0	0	13	0	**13**

Scoring:
NYG McBride 2-yard run (McBride missed kick)
NYG McBride 1-yard run (McBride PAT)
CHI Walquist pass to J. Sternaman (J. Sternaman PAT)

a safety when he punted. Hinkey then asked for a towel from the official to clean the mud off the ball. When the ball was snapped, however, Haines took the snap and threw a quick pass to end Chuck Corgan, who ran it out to the 40, shifting the entire momentum of the game. Haines's trickery was the play of the day.

There was no scoring in the first half, but the Giants drove 60 yards after taking the third-quarter kickoff and scored on a short Jack McBride run. New York later drove for a second McBride touchdown in the period to go up 13–0. The Bears finally got on the board on a pass to Joey Sternaman early in the fourth quarter to make the score 13–7.

The final 10 minutes of the game were fiercely fought, as Chicago struggled desperately to even the score. Steve Owen, who played tackle for the Giants in this game, later called it the hardest game he ever played in. He played 60 minutes against wrestler Jim McMillen of the Bears; at the final gun, the two of them just sat on the ground, too tired to move for several minutes. After all, this was the game in which aging Hall of Fame back Joe Guyon went back to pass for the Giants and was pursued by George Halas of the Bears. Just as Halas was about to unload on Guyon, Joe let go of the pass and whirled around to greet Halas with a knee that broke several of Papa Bear's ribs. Now *that's* smashmouth football.

HINKEY HAINES

Hinkey Haines was the first star back of the Giants; he joined the team at its inception in 1925. He was a speedy all-around back who called signals, ran the ball, caught passes, returned kicks, threw an occasional pass, and played defense. After graduating from Penn State, Haines was signed by the Yankees to play pro baseball and even appeared in the 1923 World Series. He was the first athlete to play for championship teams in both Major League Baseball and the NFL. Coincidentally, Haines's target on the fake punt, Chuck Corgan, also played in the major leagues.

As the Giants' first star, he inspired this bit of devoted doggerel from an anonymous sportswriter in 1926:

> Oh Hinkey Haines, Oh Hinkey
>   Haines!
> The New York Giants' football brains.
> He never loses, always gains.
> Oh Hinkey Haines, Oh Hinkey
>   Haines!

Haines scored twice in the Giants' very first victory in 1925, one of which was the very first touchdown pass in Giants history. After the victory over the Bears, the Giants still had two games left in the season, both against Red Grange's New York Yankees. The Giants won each game by shutout, and Haines returned a kickoff 75 yards for a touchdown in the first and uncorked a 60-yard touchdown gallop in the second.

After he retired, Haines spent 20 years as an NFL referee. Steve Owen named him to his personal All-Time Giants team in 1952.

Hinkey Haines trick play led the Giants to a grueling victory over the Bears in 1927.

CAL HUBBARD

The key to the Giants' smothering defense was man-mountain Cal Hubbard, a 6'2", 250-pound Missouri farm boy in his first year as a pro. Hubbard played end for the Giants and even caught an occasional pass on offense, but he was especially noted for his toughness. On defense, he was often able to collapse one side of the opposing line all by himself. He was something of an innovator who often played like a roving linebacker by backing out of the line so he could better pursue ball carriers across the field. Giants tailback Harry Newman later compared Hubbard's intensity to that of 1960s Bears wild man Dick Butkus.

Hubbard chose to move on after just two years in New York because he yearned for the small-town atmosphere that he found in Green Bay. Cal's arrival in Green Bay coincided with three consecutive Packers titles, from 1929 to 1931. In the first two of those championships, the Giants finished second, and they lost four of five games against the Packers in those years. Perhaps if Cal had stayed a Giant in name as well as form, New York would have earned a couple more titles.

Cal returned to the Giants in 1936 to finish up his Pro Football Hall of Fame career while he began a new Hall of Fame career as an umpire in Major League Baseball. Hubbard is the only person who is a member of the Halls of Fame for both sports, not to mention his enshirement in the College Football Hall of Fame. Hubbard was chosen as the all-time greatest NFL tackle on the league's 50th anniversary team and was named to the league's two-way team for the NFL's 75th anniversary.

Cal Hubbard, one of the most feared lineman of his era, was named the all-time greatest tackle on the NFL's 50th anniversary team.
(Photo courtesy of WireImages)

December 27, 1997

Sure-Handed Calloway Lets Season Slip Through His Fingers

Vikings Oust Giants in Playoffs

In Jim Fassel's first year as coach, the Giants surprised everyone by rebounding from a 6–10 season to become 10–5–1 division champs in 1997. The team's success was built on a solid defense and a careful ball-control offense that relied on a committee of runners made up of Charles Way, Tiki Barber, and Tyrone Wheatley. In the playoffs, these overachievers were done in by mistakes and a loss of poise in a sloppy game in which the Vikings scored 10 points in the final 90 seconds.

At the outset, it was Minnesota making mistakes, but the Giants failed to fully capitalize. Two Randall Cunningham fumbles in the first quarter were recovered by the Giants and led to field goals. In the second quarter, a short punt by Minnesota gave New York good field position, and they drove 56 yards to score on a two-yard pass from Danny Kanell to tight end Aaron Pierce. Cunningham was then intercepted by Jason Sehorn, and that led to another field

goal and a 16–0 lead with five minutes left in the first half. An Amani Toomer fumbled punt allowed Minnesota to get on the board with a field goal in the last two minutes. However, when Mitch Berger's kickoff went out of bounds, the Giants had great field position. Brad Daluiso then kicked a 51-yard field goal to end the half up 19–3.

In the second half, the Giants began to implode. A Tiki Barber fumble on the New York 4-yard line led to a Vikings touchdown on the next play late in the third quarter, but the Giants still led by nine. A 14-yard Brad Maynard punt led to another Minnesota field goal at the start of the fourth quarter. Even more disturbing was an on-field argument between Giants defensive backs Phillippi Sparks and Conrad Hamilton in the midst of that drive that led to a physical confrontation between Sparks, Hamilton, and linebacker Jesse Armstead on the sideline. Meanwhile, defensive ends Michael Strahan and Keith Hamilton were going at it themselves, both on the field and off. New York still answered that field goal with the best drive of the day—13 plays covering 74 yards—and Daluiso nailed his fifth field goal to restore the nine-point lead, 22–13, with seven minutes left.

A few minutes later, a 26-yard punt by Brad Maynard gave Minnesota the ball on the New York 49. Two Cunningham passes—19 yards to Cris Carter and a 30-yard score to Jake Reed—pulled the Vikings within two. With the onside kick coming, the Giants put their best ball handlers on the field for what proved to be the most disappointing play of the game. Kicker Eddie Murray dribbled the ball to

Giants defensive lineman Keith Hamilton sits dejectedly on the sideline after the Giants loss to the Vikings. *(Photo courtesy of AP Images)*

DANNY KANELL AND THE QUARTERBACK MARKET

Jim Fassel said after the Minnesota game that Danny Kanell was his starter for the next season: "Danny managed the game well, and I expect him to take that to the next level." That was wishful thinking. One of the hidden reasons that the Giants lost to the Vikings was that they could not do any better than field goals, even with Minnesota's mistakes in the first half. On the first score, Kanell twice overthrew open receivers in the end zone before settling for the three-pointer. But how much could be expected of a fourth-round draft pick? The only reason that Kanell was the starter was that former first-round pick Dave Brown was a total flop.

The Giants have spent a number-one draft pick on a quarterback a total of five times. Philip Rivers was traded, but of the other four who stayed with the team, only Phil Simms was a success; Brown, Travis Tidwell, and Lee Grosscup were all busts. As a matter of fact, of the 10 other starting quarterbacks the Giants have drafted over the years, only third-rounders Jeff Hostetler and Don Heinrich have had any success. Kanell, Jesse Palmer, Randy Dean, Scott Brunner, Kent Graham, Bobby Clatterbuck, Jerry Golsteyn, and Gary Wood are all best forgotten.

The Giants have had much more luck in trading for quarterbacks. Since World War II, New York has obtained Frankie Filchock, Charley Conerly, Y. A. Tittle, Earl Morrall, Fran Tarkenton, and Eli Manning through trades. Of course, not all trades can be winners; other deals brought in lesser lights Norm Snead, Craig Morton, Jim Del Gaizo, George Shaw, Ralph Guglielmi, Milt Plum, Dick Shiner, and Randy Johnson.

The other avenue for quarterbacks—free agency—has also proven a mixed bag, bringing to New York Joe Pisarcik from the CFL, Kerry Collins and Tommy Maddox from the scrap heap, and Kurt Warner from a heroic recent past.

Vikings kicker Eddie Murray celebrates his game-winning field-goal as Giants defensive back Percy Ellsworth walks dejectedly off the field. Ellsworth was one of two New York players who failed to recover Murray's onside kick a few moments earlier.
(Photo courtesy of AP Images)

GAME DETAILS

New York Giants 22 • Minnesota Vikings 23

Date: December 27, 1997

Location: The Meadowlands

Attendance: 77,710

Significance: Wild-card playoff game

Box Score:

Vikings	0	3	7	13	**23**
Giants	6	13	0	3	**22**

Scoring:

NYG Daluiso 43-yard FG

NYG Daluiso 22-yard FG

NYG Pierce 2-yard pass from Kanell (Daluiso PAT)

NYG Daluiso 41-yard FG

MIN Murray 26-yard FG

NYG Daluiso 51-yard FG

MIN Hoard 4-yard run (Murray PAT)

MIN Murray 26-yard FG

NYG Daluiso 22-yard FG

MIN Reed 30-yard pass from Cunningham (Murray PAT)

MIN Murray 24-yard FG

Team	FD	YDS	RUSH	PASS	RTN	A-C-I	Sacked	PUNT	FUM	PEN
Vikings	16	293	28-106	187	144	36-15-1	2-16	6-39	4-2	3-21
Giants	13	266	36-76	190	90	32-16-0	1-9	6-38	2-2	4-28

Vikings: Cunningham 203P

Giants: Kanell 199P

his left. New York's best and most sure-handed receiver, Chris Calloway, had the first shot at the ball 10 yards downfield, but shockingly, he let it bounce off his chest, and in the ensuing scramble the Vikings recovered it.

The Giants were reeling and continued to lose their composure, allowing Minnesota to drive down the field on seven plays, aided by an interference call on Sparks. Murray kicked the game-winning 24-yard field goal with 10 seconds remaining, and the Giants' season was over.

The internal squabbling would continue as a theme for the rest of Fassel's inconsistent seven-year tenure, although he would lead New York to one Super Bowl. Sadly, this spectacle was the last game for two Giants heroes. On the field, all-time leading rusher Rodney Hampton gained a paltry 18 yards in his final appearance; watching from a booth above was the man responsible for the turnaround of the Giants franchise over the last two decades, retiring general manager George Young.

October 30, 2005

WELL DONE, MR. BARBER
Giants Rip Redskins in Tribute to Mara

Tiki Barber was at Wellington Mara's bedside to say good-bye to the dying team owner on the Monday before this game. Barber, like so many Giants players over the years, had grown close to Mara, and was distressed at his death on Tuesday.

Barber led his teammates into a packed St. Patrick's Cathedral on Friday for the emotional funeral services, which were attended by many former players as well as such former coaches as Bill Parcells, Bill Belichick, John Fox, Romeo Crennell, and Charlie Weis. All returned to honor the memory of a great man who touched many lives in and out of football. On Sunday, though, there was still a game against traditional rival Washington at Giants Stadium, and New York was ready.

The most important play of this game was the very first one from scrimmage: Tiki Barber took a handoff from Eli Manning, slipped around the left end, and sprinted down the sideline for 57 yards. Barber's initial burst set the dominating tone for the game, and it would not be his last. That first run led to a field goal, and the Giants added a second three-pointer later in the quarter to go up 6–0.

Early in the second quarter, Barber cut back to the left again and raced 59 yards before he was dragged down from behind at the 1-yard line. Two plays later, Brandon Jacobs powered in for the touchdown and the rout was on. New York added two more field goals in the period and went into halftime with a 19–0 lead, having outgained Washington 261 yards to 34 in the first half.

Jeremy Shockey caught a touchdown pass to open the third quarter and Jay Feely added a fifth field goal to increase the lead to 29–0, but there was one more piece of unfinished business to make the day perfect. From the Redskins' 4, Barber took the handoff and scampered into the end zone for his own six-point tribute to Mara. Barber had promised Mara's grandson Tim McDonnell, who for many years worked as a ballboy in Giants training camps, that he would score a touchdown for his grandfather. Barber tossed the ball to McDonnell and told him, "This one was for the Duke."

In the locker room after this 36–0 victory, Eli Manning presented the game ball to Wellington's son and heir, John. The Giants had outgained the Redskins, 386 yards to 125, and had gained 262 yards on the ground—206 of them from Barber. It was a game that old Wellington would have loved.

> The emotion and circumstance of last week, to be able to have my best day on this day, was something I'll never forget. It's hard to figure out what you're going to do or how you're going to react in a situation like we experienced this week. We did what Mr. Mara would have wanted us to do, which was carry on.
>
> —TIKI BARBER

Tiki Barber bid a fond farewell to the late Wellington Mara with 206 yards on the ground against Washington.

WELLINGTON MARA

Wellington Mara spent his whole life with the Giants. Once his father bought the franchise in 1925, when Wellington was nine, it became the family business destined to be passed down to the sons. Wellington got his nickname, "Duke," from the players, and the official NFL ball was christened Duke in his honor in 1941. The youngest Mara watched most games from the bench until 1951, and he used his first movie camera to shoot the team's first game films. When he moved up to the press box in the 1950s, Wellington would take Polaroid shots of the opposing team's formations and drop them down to the bench in a weighted sock.

Wellington scouted college players for the Giants and ran the personnel side of the team, while his older brother Jack ran the financial side. It was a fruitful partnership for several years, with Wellington building the team through astute drafts and trades. In the mid-1960s, though, the system developed cracks. Wellington allowed the team to get old, and his brother Jack died, leaving him with added responsibilities. The team suffered, and so did Wellington's popularity with players, fans, and ultimately with Jack's son Tim, who owned the other 50 percent of the Giants. The Maras' bitter feud contributed to the team's decline on the field.

Once George Young turned the team around on the field, Wellington began to be viewed as one of the patriarchs of the league again. Indeed, his league-first attitude had been instrumental in assuring such necessary developments as revenue sharing and the merger with the AFL.

At Super Bowl XXI, team leader Harry Carson delighted in throwing his beloved boss in the shower to share in the celebration of the long-awaited championship. That was one of six titles the Giants won in Mara's life. For his lifelong contributions to pro football, Wellington was elected to the Hall of Fame in 1997, where he joined his deceased father, Tim Mara.

Wellington Mara cared deeply about three things throughout his life: family, church, and the Giants. When he died, his loss was mourned by millions of Giants fans.

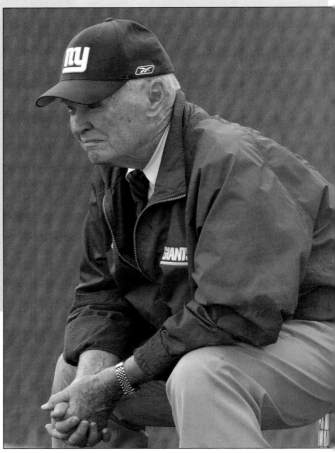

The passing of owner Wellington Mara in 2005 was mourned by millions of Giants fans.
(Photo courtesy of AP Images)

GAME DETAILS

New York Giants 36 • Washington Redskins 0

Date: October 30, 2005

Location: The Meadowlands

Attendance: 78,630

Significance: First Giants game after the death of beloved owner Wellington Mara

Box Score:

Redskins	0	0	0	0	**0**
Giants	6	13	17	0	**36**

Scoring:

NYG Feely 39-yard FG
NYG Feely 50-yard FG
NYG Jacobs 3-yard run (Feely PAT)
NYG Feely 33-yard FG

NYG Feely 39-yard FG
NYG Shockey 10-yard pass from Manning (Feely PAT)
NYG Feely 44-yard FG
NYG Barber 4-yard run (Feely PAT)

Team	FD	YDS	RUSH	PASS	RTN	A-C-I	Sacked	PUNT	FUM	PEN
Redskins	7	125	13-38	87	118	34-14-1	5-40	8-43	3-3	10-88
Giants	19	386	45-262	124	83	31-12-1	2-22	4-43	2-0	9-73

Giants: Barber 206R, Manning 146P

Actress Kate Mara, granddaughter of Wellington Mara, sings the national anthem before the Giants took on the Redskins two days after the funeral services of the Giants' longtime owner and patriarch.

Morrison Flies Past Flattened Eagles

Giants Crush Birds 37–14

The two-time defending Eastern Conference champion Giants came into this game against the Eagles off a 31–0 drubbing by the Steelers, in which New York was led by backup quarterback Ralph Guglielmi. That loss to Pittsburgh dropped the Giants to 1–1 and Guglielmi was cut, leaving only rookie Glynn Griffing behind 37-year-old starter Y. A. Tittle. When Tittle returned to action against Philadelphia on this day, it was more obvious than ever just how important he was to the Giants' success.

With the wily Tittle back at the controls, the offense righted itself and swamped the overmatched Eagles. Tittle tossed two touchdown passes in the first half and led New York to three more scores in the first 11 minutes of the third quarter, putting the game out of reach at 30–0. The Giants defense intercepted five Eagles passes—four off Sonny Jurgensen and one off King Hill—and recovered a fumble as well in this easy victory.

On this day, versatile utility man Joe Morrison stepped in at fullback for the injured Alex Webster and had a career rushing day, running for 120 yards on 12 carries and three touchdowns. The third touchdown came in the fourth quarter after the Eagles had punched in a couple of meaningless touchdowns to make the score more respectable, and it was the sweetest play of the day.

Morrison's final score came on a simple end run from the Giants' 29-yard line. He took the handoff and went right, while both guards and left tackle Rosey Brown all pulled to run interference. Right guard Ken Byers brush-blocked Eagles linebacker Bob Harrison in the backfield, and Harrison could only get a hand on Morrison. Next, left guard Darrell Dess mostly whiffed in trying to block Tom Brookshier, but Morrison broke the tackle at the 35. Finally, with three Eagles closing in from the left, All-Pro tackle Brown clobbered defensive end Jerry Mazzanti at the 38 and sent him backwards like a skittering bowling pin into teammates Don Burroughs and Jimmy Carr, knocking all three to the ground.

GAME DETAILS

New York Giants 37 • Philadelphia Eagles 14

Date: September 29, 1963

Location: Franklin Field, Philadelphia

Attendance: 60,671

Significance: Early-season match with a conference rival

Box Score:

Giants	0	14	16	7	**37**
Eagles	0	0	7	7	**14**

Scoring:

NYG Walton 43-yard pass from Tittle (Chandler PAT)
NYG Shofner 10-yard pass from Tittle (Chandler PAT)
NYG Morrison 9-yard run (Chandler kick failed)
NYG Chandler 12-yard FG

NYG Morrison 1-yard run (Chandler PAT)
PHL Retzlaff 11-yard pass from Brown (Clark PAT)
PHL McDonald 19-yard pass from Hill (Clark PAT)
NYG Morrison 71-yard run (Chandler PAT)

Team	FD	YDS	RUSH	PASS	A-C-I	PUNT	FUM	PEN
Giants	17	352	27-176	176	25-15-0	5-47	0	2-10
Eagles	18	316	30-125	191	28-18-5	3-43	1	4-40

Giants: Morrison 120R, Tittle 185P
Eagles: Hill 140P

> **I**t's called a dive end run, and we must run it thousands of time in practice. Alex [Webster] has made this play go for years. The two guards pulled out and when Kenny Byers blocked their cornerback out, I cut inside and had a clear field. It's a nice feeling, I'll tell you.
>
> —JOE MORRISON

It was as perfect a block as has ever been delivered, and the deliberate Morrison was untouched the rest of the way to the end zone, accompanied by an escort of receivers Joe Walton and Del Shofner. That touchdown closed the scoring at 37–14 and gave a textbook example of why Rosey Brown is in the Hall of Fame.

JOE MORRISON

Joe Morrison never again came close to running for 71 yards from scrimmage on one play, but that's not a surprise. He was too slow and too small to accomplish most of what he did in his long Giants career. However, when he retired after 14 years, only Mel Hein had played more seasons in New York and only Charley Conerly had played as many. When he retired, no one had caught more passes as a Giants player, and only Frank Gifford had scored more touchdowns or gained more yards receiving. Joe Morrison was smart, steady, and determined; he was a pro.

He became a Giant by accident. Scout Ed Kolman went to a University of Cincinnati game to watch Tulsa's Ron Morris, but he fell in love with Morrison, the Bearcats' quarterback, instead. New York drafted Joe in 1959 and switched him to halfback as a rookie. In his third year, he was forced to play safety because of injuries at the end of the season, and by 1963, he was the starting fullback on the Eastern Conference champs despite weighing only 210 pounds. The following season, he switched to wide receiver; he would play flanker and split end for the rest of his career. On occasion, he even lined up at tight end and at one point was the club's emergency quarterback. His versatility and dedication were the major reasons he lasted so long in the NFL.

Of the 11 Giants who have had their number retired by the team, Morrison is the most inexplicable. He was never a great player, just a reliable one. The story goes that coach Alex Webster, Morrison's former teammate, was conducting a retirement news conference in which Morrison was to be presented with his jersey, but got confused and remarked that it was "great to retire Joe's number." Thus, the accidental Giant had his number retired accidentally.

Joe Morrison stepped in for injured running back Alex Webster and rushed for 120 yards against the Eagles in 1963.

ROSEY BROWN

The remarkable triple block that Rosey Brown threw to spring Joe Morrison in this game was emblematic of his talents and his style of play. First, Brown had the speed and mobility to pull from the left side and get in front of the ball carrier to lead a run over the right side. Very few offensive tackles in NFL history have been quick enough to pull and lead running plays. Second, Rosey had the power and technique to obliterate his man and clear the way. At 6'3" and 250 pounds, he was a good-sized tackle for his time and a preeminent downfield blocker.

Because Rosey's uncle had died playing football, Brown's father made him play in the marching band in high school. He had to sneak onto the football team during his senior year while his father was away. In college at Morgan State, he competed in wrestling, baseball, and football and twice was named to the Black All-America Football Team. As an unscouted,

lowly 27th-round draft choice out of a small black school in 1953, Rosey was not expected to make the team. However, he played for the Giants for 13 years and then stayed with the team for another 38 years as an assistant coach and scout. During his playing career, he was named All-NFL eight times and played in the Pro Bowl nine times.

Brown played left tackle on the Giants, and therefore was entrusted with guarding his quarterback's blind side on passing downs. He had the intelligence, balance, and muscle to excel at pass blocking. The Giants also took advantage of his size and power by using him on defensive goal-line stands in his early years. This all-time great lineman was named to the NFL's 75th Anniversary team and was elected to the Hall of Fame in 1975; he was just the second pure offensive tackle ever enshrined.

Rosey Brown (kneeling) was the anchor of the Giants' offensive line for 13 years and pioneered the 7-10 split block, in which he sent one tackler careening into two others, knocking down all three.

October 17, 1965

MORRALL HITS HOMER DEEP

Giants Blast Eagles 35–27

After the debacle of the 1964 season, the Giants could only get better in 1965. Things were looking up as they went into their fifth game with a 2–2 record. Against the Eagles this day, a new star receiver and a veteran journeyman quarterback would emerge as leaders, and a new scoring celebration would be born.

The Eagles scored first on an Earl Gros run after a long drive, and they were driving again when Gros fumbled in the first quarter. Quarterback Earl Morrall, whom the Giants had obtained from Detroit in September, quickly capitalized with a 71-yard touchdown pass to Aaron Thomas, who beat Eagles corner Nate Ramsey. Just a few minutes later, Morrall burned Ramsey and the Eagles a second time with a 46-yard strike to Joe Morrison.

Three minutes later came the play of the day. From the Giants' 11-yard line, Morrall took a straight drop back and at the 4, let the ball fly. Down the sideline sped Homer Jones, who had caught just five passes so far in his two-year career. Jones had two steps on corner Irv Cross, but the ball was behind him, and Jones had to slow down at the 45 to catch it at midfield.

Jones wheeled to the sideline, while Cross stumbled trying to tackle him at the 35. Jones rocketed into the end zone for an 89-yard touchdown bomb and then punctuated his very first touchdown with the very first spike in NFL history.

Eagles quarterback King Hill began to get desperate, and he threw four interceptions in his next five passes over an 11-minute period. Linebacker Jerry Hillebrand returned one for a touchdown, and the Giants led at the half 28–7. New York extended its lead to 35–7 in the third quarter after a Ramsey interference penalty led to a two-yard touchdown pass to Bobby

> **I** knew Homer was fast. I've never been able to overthrow him in practice. So I thought I'd hang one up there and see if he could go get it. As it was, he had to wait for the ball.
>
> **—EARL MORRALL**

GAME DETAILS

New York Giants 35 • Philadelphia Eagles 27

Date: October 17, 1965

Location: Yankee Stadium, New York

Attendance: 62,815

Significance: First touchdown for Homer Jones and first end-zone spike for the NFL

Box Score:

Eagles	7	0	13	7	**27**
Giants	7	21	7	0	**35**

Scoring:
PHL Gros 1-yard run (Baker PAT)
NYG Thomas 71-yard pass from Morrall (Stynchula PAT)
NYG Morrison 46-yard pass from Morrall (Stynchula PAT)
NYG Jones 89-yard pass from Morrall (Stynchula PAT)
NYG Hillebrand 25-yard interception return
    (Stynchula PAT)
NYG Crespino 2-yard pass from Morrall (Stynchula PAT)
PHL Brown 45-yard pass from Hill (Baker kick failed)
PHL Retzlaff 9-yard pass from Hill (Baker PAT)
PHL Brown 24-yard pass from Hill (Baker PAT)

Team	FD	YDS	RUSH	PASS	A-C-I	PUNT	FUM	PEN
Eagles	21	440	28-129	311	41-23-4	1-46	1	90
Giants	14	398	33-111	287	5-10-0	3-37	1	61

Eagles: Hill 321P, Retzlaff 133C
Giants: Morrall 296P, Thomas 145C, Jones 102C

Crespino and a 35–7 lead. Hill threw for three second-half touchdowns and more than 300 yards, but it was all too little, too late. Morrall, meanwhile, completed just 10 of 15 passes, but they went for 287 yards and four scores. Jones had served notice that his two-year apprenticeship on the taxi squad was over.

For the season, the Giants improved from 13th to 10th in points scored and from 14th to 10th in points allowed; they finished 7–7. However, they allowed 68 points more than they scored in 1965, and they dropped back to awful in 1966. Fran Tarkenton would replace Morrall in 1967, and Jones would go to the Pro Bowl twice catching passes from the scrambler, but the team would be lost in the wilderness of mediocrity for the next 15 years.

The Fly Pattern

This 89-yard touchdown came off a simple fly pattern run by the Giants' flyer, Homer Jones (45). Joe Morrison (40) and Aaron Thomas (88) run short routes, but they were just decoys. Earl Morrall (11) took a seven-step drop and aired out the long bomb, aiming to hit the speeding Jones in stride. In the execution, though, Jones had outraced the ball and had to come back for it. As Irv Cross, the defensive back, tried to scramble back into the play, he stumbled—and Jones was gone for six.

> **I** didn't want to run out from under the ball. And looking back into that sun is tough, too. But that is my favorite play in football.
>
> **—HOMER JONES**

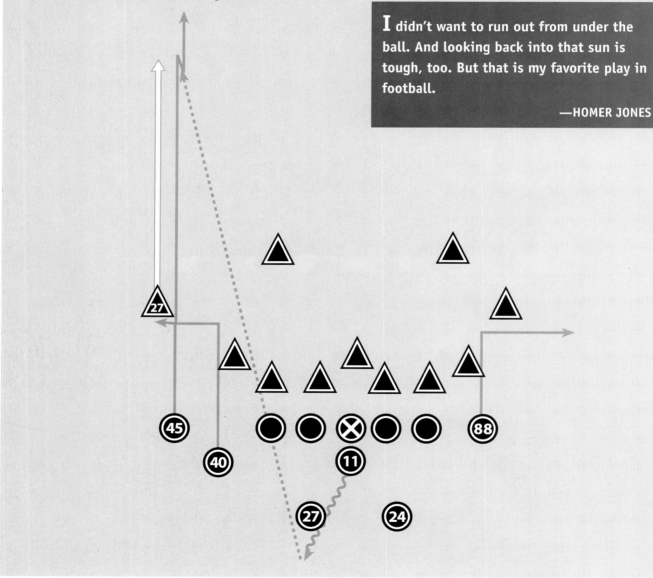

HOMER JONES

The 89-yard touchdown bomb that Homer Jones caught for his very first NFL touchdown doubled as the NFL's very first spike. Jones wanted to do something special for his first score, like throw the ball into the stands. But since he didn't want to have to pay the fine that would result, he improvised. As he crossed the goal line, he flung the ball down behind himself, although with far less force than he would on future spikes. The unknown speedster had made a name for himself twice in one play.

Jones was a 20th-round pick out of Texas Southern in 1963, but he signed with the AFL's Oilers instead. Houston cut him in training camp because he had a knee injury. The Giants then brought him to New York, helped him rehab his knee, and assigned him to the taxi squad, where he spent two seasons. Jones was 6'2" and 220 pounds and could run the 100 in 9.3 seconds. He had enormous hands, but had trouble catching the ball—he dropped nine balls in a row in the pre-game warmup on this momentous day—and was originally known as "Question Mark." That nickname quickly changed to "Rhino" when he became a starter because his hard-charging style was about power, not elusiveness.

Jones was known for taking some plays off and was unpredictable as a route runner, but he was an amiable player who got along well with his teammates. The fly pattern was his favorite, and he was an unstoppable deep threat. He caught the longest pass in Giants history, 98 yards, from Morrall in 1966, during a game in which he also caught a 75-yard score. In another game, he caught touchdowns of 74 and 72 yards. Fran Tarkenton once said that throwing to Jones was like "throwing to a man riding a motorcycle holding a butterfly net." No passer could overthrow him.

The Giants traded the mercurial Jones to the Browns for runner Ron Johnson in 1970. New York won that deal when knee problems ended Homer's career after one season in Cleveland. When Jones retired, he was third in Giants history in receiving yards and first in NFL history in yards per catch, at 22.3.

Sadly, no Giants wide receiver has been to the Pro Bowl since Jones went in 1967 and 1968. Although he never caught more than 49 passes in a year, he went over 1,000 yards receiving in three different seasons, and he led the NFL with 13 touchdowns in 1967; roughly one of every six passes he caught as a Giant went for six points.

Receiver Homer Jones punctuated his 89-yard touchdown pass in 1965 with the first spike in NFL history. *(Photo courtesy of WireImages)*

October 14, 1951

MR. OFFENSE ON DEFENSE CUTS CARDS WITH PUNT RETURNS

Giants Win Home Opener 28–17

After the Giants' 1950 revival, the team came into the 1951 season with high hopes of upending Cleveland in the East. New York began the season by tying the Steelers and beating the Redskins, while Cleveland lost their first game to the 49ers before rebounding to beat the Rams in Week 2. The lowly Cardinals offered the Giants a great opportunity to open their home schedule with a win on this October day.

All-Pro defensive tackle Arnie Weinmeister got New York off to a great start when he recovered a Don Paul fumble at the Cardinals' 13-yard line in the first quarter. Four plays later, Eddie Price punched in the touchdown from the 1 to give the Giants the lead. The Cardinals got that score back in the second period when they capped a

seven-play, 65-yard drive with a 34-yard touchdown strike from Frank Tripucka to Don Paul. Four minutes later, a Giants fumble led to a Cardinals field goal and a 10–7 lead.

Once again, a big play gave the Giants the lead before the quarter ended. Throughout the game, Emlen Tunnell gave a convincing demonstration of why he was "Mr. Offense on Defense" for the Giants, but never more than on the most exciting play of the day. He caught a Cardinals punt at his 18 and wove upfield through the Chicago punt team, using his teammates' blocks to elude every defender and score a touchdown to put the Giants back on top. New York's lead would prove short-lived, though, as the Cardinals drove right back and scored on a 34-yard

> I never saw the equal of [Tunnell's] performance returning kicks against the Cards. Whew, 178 yards on four kicks. And the way he made use of his downfield blockers!
>
> —COLUMBIA COACH LOU LITTLE TO HIS FRIEND STEVE OWEN, IN *THE NEW YORK TIMES*

EMLEN TUNNELL

Emlen Tunnell was known to Giants fans as "Mr. Offense on Defense" because of days like this one against the Cardinals. His combined total of 790 interception, punt, and kickoff return yards for 1951 would compare favorably to the leaders in rushing yards for that season. In fact, Tunnell's 924 return yards in 1952 exceeded the rushing total of league leader Dan Towler by 30 yards. In 1953, Tunnell would add another 819 return yards. He was also a scoring threat, bringing back four returns for touchdowns in 1951, eight in his first four years in the NFL, and 10 for his 14-year career.

Tunnell played football for Toledo before World War II and for Iowa after, but he went undrafted by any NFL team. So the 26-year-old took matters into his own hands and hitchhiked from his home in the Philadelphia suburbs to the Giants' office one day, offering his services as a player. The Giants were familiar with his college record and gave him a tryout. With his versatility and nose for the ball, he made the team.

He was the first black player on a Giants team that employed a fair number of southern players, yet he fit in from the start with his sunny personality and exciting play. In turn, Tunnell loved conservative coach Steve Owen like a father. Owen turned Tunnell loose as a brilliant punt returner. The sure-handed Tunnell caught punts in his unique basket-catch, and the open field was the perfect stage for Em's elusive, cut-back running style.

Tunnell was a free-roaming safety whose style was not fully attuned to defensive coach Tom Landry's design, but it was hard to argue with the results. Em

used his speed and anticipation to become the all-time leading NFL interceptor, with 79, by the time he retired in 1961. At that point, he continued blazing a trail as the first black assistant coach in the NFL, under Allie Sherman. Tunnell went to nine Pro Bowls and notched two Hall of Fame firsts in 1967: he was the first black inductee and the first pure defensive player enshrined.

Defensive back Emlen Tunnell put on an offensive display against the Cardinals, totaling 178 yards and a touchdown on four kick returns.
(Photo courtesy of AP Images)

GAME DETAILS

New York Giants 17 • Chicago Cardinals 28

Date: October 14, 1951

Location: Polo Grounds, New York

Attendance: 28,095

Significance: Home opener against a conference rival

Box Score:

Cardinals	7	7	0	14	**28**
Giants	0	17	0	0	**17**

Scoring:

NYG Price 1-yard run (Poole PAT)

CHI Paul 34-yard pass from Tripucka (Yablonski PAT)

CHI Yablonski 11-yard FG

NYG Tunnell 82-yard punt return (Poole PAT)

CHI Paul 24-yard pass from Trippi (Yablonski PAT)

NYG Price 25-yard run (Poole PAT)

NYG Price 12-yard run (Poole PAT)

Team	FD	YDS	RUSH	PASS	RTN	A-C-I	PUNT	FUM	PEN
Cardinals	17	283	72	211	32	41-19-2	6-39	3-2	6-60
Giants	16	265	149	116	178	22-8-5	4-40	3-3	6-40

Giants: Price 107R

pass from Charley Trippi to Paul, over Tunnell's head, to go up 17–14 at the half.

The third quarter brought no scoring, and in the fourth quarter New York changed from Charley Conerly leading a double-wing attack to Travis Tidwell directing Steve Owen's old A-formation. Another whirling punt return by the slippery Tunnell—for 31 yards this time—led to the go-ahead 25-yard touchdown gallop by Price. Price scored a third touchdown late in the game after an interception to make the final score 28–17.

For the day, Tunnell totaled 178 yards and one touchdown on four returns; he was so exhausted that he was taken to the hospital after the game. He returned to practice later in the week, though, and would score three more times on kick returns during the season.

In actuality, returns were a third of the anemic Giants attack in 1951. During the season, New York would score 11 touchdowns on passes, 10 on runs, and 10 more on returns from punts, kickoffs, interceptions, and fumbles. The Giants and the Browns had the best defenses in the league, but the Browns had a markedly better offense and ultimately would beat out New York again in 1951.

ARNIE WEINMEISTER

Arnie Weinmeister's fumble recovery in this game was the sort of big play that the rangy defensive tackle delivered on a regular basis. He only played four years in the NFL, but he was All-Pro each year and was elected to the Hall of Fame because of his speed, quickness, strength, and often-spectacular play.

Weinmeister was drafted by the long-forgotten Boston Yanks in 1948, but he signed instead with the New York Yankees of the All-America Football Conference. He was All-AAFC in 1949 and then came to the Giants in the player dispersal after the AAFC merged with the NFL in 1950. The 6'4", 240-pound Weinmeister immediately became a key member of Steve Owen's new umbrella defense. Although he continually found himself double-teamed, he was still a terror rushing the passer. Among the Yankees, only sprinter Buddy Young could outrun him, and no one on the Giants could, although rookie ends were often matched against him in training camp races.

Weinmeister squabbled continually with the Giants over money issues in the days before there was a players association, and he eventually signed with the CFL for a healthy raise in 1954. The Giants sued him for breach of contract but lost the case because they had not properly exercised the contract's option clause. Weinmeister spent two seasons in Canada before retiring; he went on to serve as an elected official and contract negotiator with the Teamsters Union for the rest of his life. His break with the Giants

had been bitter, but after he was elected to Canton in 1984—with lobbying from his former teammate Tom Landry as a decisive factor—he and the Mara family reconciled at Pro Bowl festivities in Hawaii that year.

Lineman Arnie Weinmeister was elected to the Pro Football Hall of Fame despite playing just four seasons in the NFL.

December 15, 1963

GIANTS SCRAP STEELERS 33–17 FOR EASTERN TITLE

Giff's Single-Handed Scoop Is Decisive

Four teams battled throughout the 1963 season for the Eastern Conference lead. By Week 14, the Cleveland Browns and the St. Louis Cardinals had been eliminated, but the remaining two contenders would meet in the final game of the year at Yankee Stadium.

Coach Buddy Parker had built the roughhouse Pittsburgh Steelers by trading draft choices for veterans, and they came into the game against the Giants with an odd record of 7–3–3. However, because ties did not count in the standings at the time, a victory over the 10–3 Giants would give Pittsburgh the crown by virtue of a slightly higher winning percentage.

Despite having lost to Pittsburgh 31–0 in Week 2 when quarterback Y. A. Tittle was injured, New York came into the game as a seven-point favorite. On a frozen home field in windy, 25-degree conditions, the Giants came out fast and ran up a 16–0 lead—on a field goal by Don Chandler, a 41-yard bomb from Tittle to Del Shofner,

and a three-yard lob to Joe Morrison. Chandler missed the first extra point, but all Pittsburgh could manage in the first half was a field goal, leaving them trailing 16–3 at the intermission.

The Steelers continually derailed their own momentum in this game, with three interceptions and two lost fumbles; their quarterback, Ed Brown, had a miserable day. It was the first time he had returned to Yankee Stadium since losing the 1956 championship game as the Bears' quarterback seven years before.

Finally, though, Pittsburgh appeared to be rolling in the third quarter. They scored quickly on a touchdown pass to Gary Ballman and had the Giants in a third-and-eight hole at the New York 24-yard line. Both coaches later cited the Giants' conversion of this vital third down as the turning point of the game, because of the spectacular way it was accomplished.

Flanker Frank Gifford had been running sideline patterns against corner Glenn Glass

Although it wasn't quite as spectacular as his one-handed scoop catch in the same game, Frank Gifford catches a pass in front of Dick Haley (27) in the Eastern Conference clincher against the Steelers on the final day of the 1963 season. Note that both teams are wearing sneakers on the frozen field. *(Photo courtesy of AP Images)*

THE WING ZIG-IN

All game long, flanker Frank Gifford had been running sideline patterns against corner Glenn Glass. At this key juncture in the third quarter, Y. A. Tittle (14) called a wing zig-in play. Gifford (16) ran straight for Glass (43) and dipped his shoulder as if he were running another out, but when Glass bit on the fake, Gifford headed across the middle of the field. Tittle's pass was low, but Gifford scooped it up and made the first down. The Giants went on to score the clinching touchdown on this drive.

> **T**hat third-down pass to Gifford did it. If he doesn't make that play, they have to kick. We can come back and score again, the way we're going, and take the lead. Maybe take the game. Who knows?
>
> —STEELERS COACH BUDDY PARKER

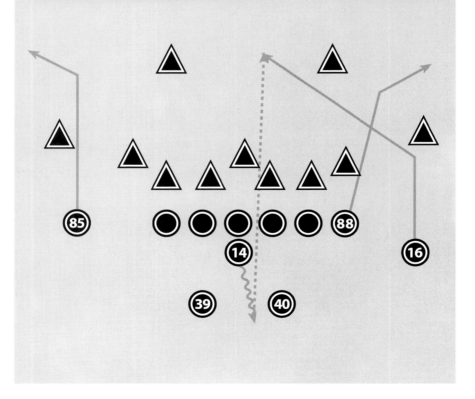

throughout the contest. At this key moment of the game, Y. A. Tittle called a wing zig-in play. Gifford faked running another out and instead headed across the middle of the field, leaving Glass going in the wrong direction. Tittle's pass was low, but Gifford bent over and scooped it up at his knees with just one hand and scurried upfield. Glass caught up to Gifford at the Pittsburgh 47 and tackled him after a 29-yard gain. Tittle went back to Gifford on the next play, for 25 yards. He then shot a short pass to fullback Joe Morrison, who ran down the sideline for a 22-yard touchdown.

Three minutes later, Morrison scored his second touchdown of the day on a short plunge, and New York had a commanding 30–10 lead. Pittsburgh added another touchdown on a bomb to Buddy Dial, and Chandler would close out the scoring in the final period with a field goal that gave him the NFL scoring title.

As a team, the Giants led the league in points by a wide margin, averaging five points per game more than their nearest competitor. In the NFL title game, though, they would meet the Bears—who that year had set a new record for fewest points allowed in a 14-game season—and fall short behind a hobbled Tittle in their last hurrah.

GAME DETAILS

New York Giants 33 • Pittsburgh Steelers 17

Date: December 15, 1963

Location: Yankee Stadium, New York

Attendance: 63,240

Significance: Winner goes to the NFL Championship Game

Box Score:

Steelers	0	3	14	0	**17**
Giants	9	7	14	3	**33**

Scoring:

NYG Chandler 34-yard FG

NYG Shofner 41-yard pass from Tittle (Chandler kick failed)

NYG Morrison 3-yard pass from Tittle (Chandler PAT)

PIT Michaels 27-yard FG

PIT Ballman 21-yard pass from Brown (Michaels PAT)

NYG Morrison 22-yard pass from Tittle (Chandler PAT)

NYG Morrision 1-yard run (Chandler PAT)

PIT Dial 40-yard pass from Brown (Michaels PAT)

NYG Chandler 41-yard FG

Team	FD	YDS	RUSH	PASS	A-C-I	PUNT	FUM	PEN
Steelers	17	400	38-188	212	33-13-3	5-35	2	35
Giants	21	423	36-143	280	26-17-1	5-44	3	61

Steelers: Johnson 104R, Brown 217P, Ballman 104C

Giants: Tittle 308P, Shofner 110C

> **I** thought Gifford would catch it all along, but I didn't realize I had thrown it so low until he reached for it.
>
> —Y. A. TITTLE

> **I**t was the biggest catch I ever made. All I was trying to do was bat the ball up in the air, and it stuck in my hand.
>
> —FRANK GIFFORD

Don Chandler

With the final field goal in this game, Don Chandler became just the third Giants player to lead the league in scoring (after Ken Strong in 1934 and Choo Choo Roberts in 1949). No Giants player has managed the feat since. The 1963 season was Chandler's second as a place-kicker, but his eighth as the team's punter, and he performed both jobs well.

Chandler was a triple-threat back at the University of Florida who was drafted by the Giants in the fifth round in 1956 and converted into a punting specialist. Chandler had initial doubts about professional football, and he left camp before being intercepted at the airport by an enraged Vince Lombardi, who brought him back. Chandler rewarded that faith by leading the NFL in punting in 1957; Dave Jennings and Sean Landeta are the only other Giants punters to lead the league. When Pat Summerall retired in 1962, Chandler took over the place-kicking duties as well. After scoring more than 100 points in his first two years as a kicker, Chandler had an off year in 1964, and Allie Sherman traded him to Vince Lombardi's Packers for a third-round pick, which the Giants used on Bob Timberlake.

While Timberlake was hitting just one of 15 field-goal attempts and then vanishing from the league, Chandler joined Green Bay in time for its late 1960s three-peat. He kicked the controversial 1965 playoff field goal against the Colts that led to the uprights being raised 20 feet the following year. Two years later he scored 15 points in his final game, Super Bowl II. Chandler played in nine title games in 12 seasons and won four championship rings, including ones in both his first and last seasons.

Kicker Don Chandler led the NFL in scoring in 1963—no Giants player has done so since.

December 19, 1981

IN THE HUNT FOR THE PLAYOFFS AFTER 18 YEARS
Key Pick Leads to Overtime Win

The Giants went into their 1981 season finale against the 12–3 Dallas Cowboys with an 8–7 record. It was the third season for general manager George Young and head coach Ray Perkins, and it was time for the team to produce. A win over the vaunted Cowboys would not only mean just the third winning season in the past 18 for the Giants, but it would also keep their hopes alive for ending an 18-year playoff drought. Although it may not have been clear at the time, 1981 was a turning-point season for New York—it was Lawrence Taylor's rookie year, and it marked the return of Bill Parcells to the Giants as defensive coordinator. That pairing would bring a renaissance to the franchise in the coming decade.

The fired-up Giants came out smoking on this clear, 25-degree Saturday with the wind gusting to 23 miles an hour, and they held Dallas to just 41 yards of total offense in the first half. However, two potential Giants scoring drives ended in missed field goals into the wind by the usually reliable Joe Danelo: a 21-yarder was wide left and a 27-yarder was wide right. Danelo also plunked one off the upright, but that was erased by a penalty.

Finally, with five minutes to go in the third quarter, a 20-yard touchdown pass from Scott Brunner to Tom Mullady capped a six-play, 62-yard drive and gave New York the first lead. Dallas then took the ensuing kickoff and drove 80 yards in 11 plays to tie the game on a three-yard lob to Doug Cosbie. On the Giants' next possession, Brunner was intercepted by Michael Downs, and Dallas kicked a field goal to take a 10-7 lead with nine minutes to play.

As has often been the case in Giants history, it was the defense to the rescue, forcing turnovers on the Cowboys' last three possessions of the game. With 2:08 left, rookie linebacker Byron Hunt knocked loose a pitchout to Tony Dorsett and defensive end George Martin recovered it on the

Joe Danelo's overtime field goal gave the Giants a 13–10 victory over the Dallas Cowboys at Giants Stadium in 1981. *(Photo courtesy of AP Images)*

THE LINEBACKERS

This game was another example of Giants linebackers coming up with big plays that led to victory. New York has been blessed with some of the very best sets of linebackers ever to play professional football, right from the start of the 4-3 defense that Tom Landry implemented in New York in 1956. That first linebacker group included Hall of Famer Sam Huff in the middle, flanked by All-Pros Harland Svare and Bill Svoboda. Svare would give way to Tom Scott and Svoboda would be replaced by Cliff Livingston and then Bill Winter, but for eight seasons, Giants linebackers defined excellence.

In 1976, New York assembled another great threesome when Hall of Famer Harry Carson was converted

to middle linebacker in his rookie season. He was surrounded by fourth-year veterans Brad Van Pelt and Brian Kelley. Van Pelt was a five-time All-Pro, while Kelley was an 11-year starter and the defense's signal caller. The team was terrible, but the linebacking was as good as anywhere in the league.

When Ray Perkins became coach in 1979, he saw the strength at the linebacker position and instituted the 3-4 defense. The transition was complete in 1981, with Bill Parcells coaching the linebackers and Hall of Famer Lawrence Taylor joining the team. With Taylor on the outside, Kelley moved to the inside where he was better suited. Parcells, as head coach in 1984, wanted more youth and speed, so he replaced aging veterans Van Pelt and Kelley with Byron Hunt and Gary Reasons. Linebackers coach Bill Belichick took the 3-4 base and introduced a heady mix of variations that called for linebackers quick both of foot and of mind. As Banks once told *The New York Times*, "One thing we do is be around the ball. That's demanded of us."

The inconsistent Hunt was beaten out by All-Pro Carl Banks two years later. Three years after that, All-Pro Pepper Johnson replaced the retiring Harry Carson, with Reasons taking over as signal caller. The linebacking during this golden era was so good that backups such as Hunt, Andy Headen, Johnie Cooks, and Steve DeOssie would have started on many teams throughout the NFL.

Consistent across all eras, though, was the aggressive intensity of Giants linebackers, best expressed by Lawrence Taylor on the sideline during one game: "Let's go out there like a bunch of crazed dogs."

Byron Hunt picked off a Danny White pass to set up Joe Danelo's game-winning field goal in 1981.

GAME DETAILS

New York Giants 13 • Dallas Cowboys 10

Date: December 19, 1981

Location: The Meadowlands

Attendance: 73,009

Significance: The Giants needed to beat division leader Dallas to make the playoffs

Box Score:

Cowboys	0	0	0	10	0	**10**	
Giants	0	0	7	3	3	**13**	

Scoring:

NYG Mullady 20-yard pass from Brunner (Danelo PAT)

DAL Cosbie 3-yard pass from White (Septien PAT)

DAL Septien 36-yard FG

NYG Danelo 40-yard FG

NYG Danelo 35-yard FG

Team	FD	YDS	RUSH	PASS	RTN	A-C-I	Sacked	PUNT	FUM	PEN
Cowboys	16	254	34-90	164	7	33-17-1	4-36	7-40	5-2	8-70
Giants	15	297	40-139	158	31	27-13-1	1-5	5-40	4-1	5-42

Cowboys: White 200P

Giants: Brunner 163P

Dallas 45-yard line. After converting a fourth-and-13 on a 21-yard pass to John Mistler, New York was in position for a field goal, and Danelo tied the game with a 40-yarder with 30 seconds to play in regulation.

On Dallas's first possession in the overtime period, Dorsett bobbled another pitchout. Lawrence Taylor engulfed him and came away with the football at the Dallas 40. Brunner ran a bootleg on an audible and got all the way to the 17, but Danelo bounced another kick off the upright on his 33-yard try into the wind. Two plays later came the play of the game. On second down, Lawrence Taylor blitzed Danny White and forced him to scramble. White unwisely unloaded a weak pass toward Butch Johnson, but Hunt glided over, snagged the interception at the 31, and returned it to the 24. Three plays later, at 6:19 of the overtime period, Danelo knocked

one straight and true from 35 yards out to give the Giants the 13–10 victory. Coach Perkins was so excited that he helped carry his kicker off the field.

The Giants had their winning season. The next day at the Meadowlands, the Jets beat the Packers, sending the Giants to the postseason for the first time since 1963. New York upset the defending NFC champion Eagles the next week on the road, but ran into the eventual Super Bowl champion 49ers in the divisional round and were overmatched. There was still a lot of building to be done, but the 1981 Giants proved they were on the way back at last.

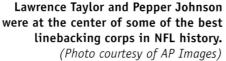

Lawrence Taylor and Pepper Johnson were at the center of some of the best linebacking corps in NFL history.
(Photo courtesy of AP Images)

December 17, 1933

32 Sleight of Hand, Misdirection, and Who's Got the Ball?

Giants Come Up One Trick Short Against the Bears

The very first NFL Championship Game in 1933 has seldom been equaled in the ensuing 75 seasons of title games and Super Bowls. The game featured six lead changes, and all five touchdowns were set up or scored on passing plays, highly unusual for this ground-oriented era. During the season, New York scored the most points and the Bears gained the most yards in the league, and both won their conference crown by at least three games. They were the two best teams in the NFL by far, and they proved it on this cold, misty day in Wrigley Field.

Early on, the Giants set the quirky tempo for this game with the trickiest play of the day. They lined up with only an end to the left of center Mel Hein. Before the ball was snapped, that end dropped back into the backfield as a wingback, while the wingback on the right side shifted up to the line. According to the rules of the time, Hein was now an eligible receiver. Hein hiked the ball to Harry Newman, who slid the ball right back to the center. Pretending

to have the ball, Newman dropped back to pass and the Bears defense followed. When George Musso tackled Newman, he bellowed, "Where the hell's the ball?" Meanwhile, Hein hid the ball under his shirt and started slowly downfield, but he quickly got impatient and began running. Bears safety Keith Molesworth saw through the trick and brought Hein down after a gain of several yards.

That drive led to no points, though. Instead, the Bears got on the board first after a Bronko Nagurski interception in the first quarter led to a Jack Manders field goal. The Bears then got a second field goal after another drive in the second quarter. The Giants finally answered with a drive of their own that ended with a 29-yard touchdown pass from Newman to Red Badgro for the first lead change of the day. Manders missed a short field-goal try just before halftime, and the Giants went to the locker room leading 7–6.

Manders kicked his third field goal in the third period to take the lead back, but

No amount of offensive trickery could push the Giants past Bill Hewitt (lateraling) and the Bears in the 1933 NFL Championship Game.

THE HIDDEN-BALL TRICK

Although the hidden-ball trick is a staple in movies such as *Little Giants,* it is too outlandish for any NFL team to try, right? The Giants not only tried it in a game, they tried it in the very first NFL Championship Game in 1933. The Giants came out and set up in a very unbalanced line, with only an end to the left of center Mel Hein. Before the ball was snapped, that end, Red Badgro (17), dropped into the backfield as a wingback while the wingback on the other side, Dale Burnett (18), shifted to the line. This made Mel Hein an eligible receiver, since he was now on the end of the line. Harry Newman (12) took a direct snap from Hein and surreptitiously slipped the ball right back to him. Newman faded back to pass and drew the charge of the Bears defense, while Hein stuffed the ball under his shirt and started walking downfield. Once Hein started to run, though, safety Keith Molesworth spotted the trick and tackled him.

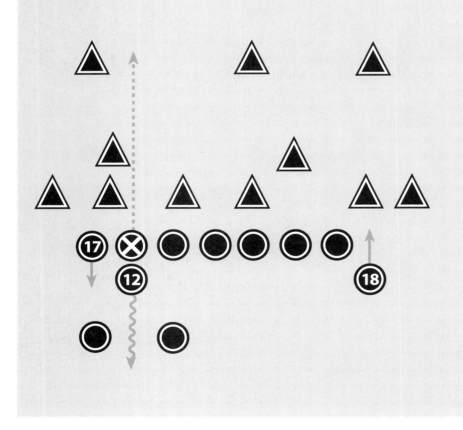

Newman's passes to Dale Burnett, Kink Richards, and Max Krause brought New York to the Chicago 1-yard line. Krause punched it in from there to put the Giants in the lead again, 14–9.

On their next possession, the Bears used a trick play of their own. George Corbett faked a punt and instead threw a pass to quarterback Carl Brumbaugh; the play traveled 67 yards to the Giants' 8. From there, Nagurski threw a jump pass to Bill Karr for the touchdown and a 16–14 lead at the end of three quarters.

The Giants continued passing and got to the Bears' 8, where a broken play produced another touchdown and lead change. Ken Strong took a handoff from Newman and tried to head around the left end. Seeing nothing but Bear defenders, Strong improvised and tossed the ball back to a surprised Newman. As the Bears charged for Newman, Strong drifted into the end zone, where the retreating Newman spotted him and hit him for a touchdown in an unplanned flea flicker.

Trailing in the closing minutes of the game, Chicago got the ball in great field position after a poor punt by Strong. After a couple of runs, Nagurski tried another jump pass and completed it to Bill Hewitt, who then lateraled the ball to a trailing Bill Karr at the 19. Karr went in for

GAME DETAILS

New York Giants 21 • Chicago Bears 23

Date: December 17, 1933

Location: Wrigley Field, Chicago

Attendance: 26,000

Significance: Very first NFL Championship Game

Box Score:

Giants	0	7	7	7	**21**
Bears	3	3	10	7	**23**

Scoring:

CHI Manders 16-yard FG
CHI Manders 40-yard FG
NYG Badgro 29-yard pass from Newman (Strong PAT)
CHI Manders 28-yard FG

NYG Krause 1-yard run (Strong PAT)
CHI Karr 8-yard pass from Nagurski (Manders PAT)
NYG Strong 8-yard pass from Newman (Strong PAT)
CHI Karr 19-yard lateral from Hewitt after 14-yard pass from Nagurski (Brumbaugh PAT)

Team	FD	YDS	RUSH	PASS	RTN	A-C-I	PUNT	FUM	PEN
Giants	13	307	25-99	208	39	20-14-1	13-29	0-0	3-15
Bears	12	311	49-161	150	44	16-7-1	10-40	0-0	8-40

Giants: Newman 201P

the winning score. The strange thing was that the lowly Philadelphia Eagles had utilized the very same hook-and-lateral play for a touchdown against the Giants just one week before. New York should have been prepared for it.

The Giants still had time left for two plays, and they tried two more tricks. On the first, they lined up as they had for Hein's earlier hidden-ball play. However, this time Newman took the snap and pitched out to Dale Burnett.

As the Bears pursued Burnett, Hein sped downfield as a wide-open receiver, but Burnett was quickly swarmed over and his weak pass was batted down. On the final play, New York tried their own hook-and-lateral play, but the Bears' Red Grange wrapped up receiver Red Badgro so that he was unable to lateral the ball to the trailing Burnett. The game was over; the Bears were champions, but the Giants could hold their heads high and plan for a better outcome next year.

HARRY NEWMAN

The hidden-ball play the Giants ran in this first NFL Championship Game originated, oddly enough, with the nieces of tailback Harry Newman. He was watching them play a touch football game in which they had the quarterback hand the ball back to the center, and that got Harry thinking. He discussed it with coach Steve Owen, and they sprung the trick play on the Bears.

Harry grew up in Detroit and attended Benny Friedman's summer camp, where Friedman taught him how to pass and recommended him to his alma mater, the University of Michigan. Newman enrolled there and became an All-American, just like his predecessor. In his tenure at Ann Arbor, the Wolverines lost just one game in three years, and Newman was the MVP of the Big Ten. The Giants signed the 5'8" passer upon his graduation in 1933, and he was once again following in Friedman's footsteps.

Newman negotiated a smart deal with New York that included a percentage of the gate, and all went well in his rookie season. He led the league in passing yards, with 973, and in touchdowns, with 11—as well as in attempts, completions, and yards. He also finished sixth in the NFL in rushing. In the championship game, he threw for 201 yards, an astonishing total for the time. The rookie sensation fell victim to a sophomore slump, though, falling to just one touchdown pass and averaging just four yards per completion in 1934. His second season ended early when his back was injured by the crush of the Bears' pass rush during a regular-season game. Ed Danowski took over as tailback, led the Giants to the title, and then kept the starting job the following season.

When the Giants weren't willing to meet Newman's contract demands in 1936, Harry helped form the new American Football League. However, after two lackluster seasons, the league went under and Newman retired. Newman went on to have a successful career as a private businessman and lived vibrantly to the age of 90. This early Giants player will always be remembered as a pioneer of the passing game and a master of the trick play.

There may have been unusual plays, but in terms of drama, why, there were six lead changes. Both teams were magnificent. The winning touchdown came with less than three minutes to play. But the game still could have been won on the last play. I'd say it was a classic game, one of the greatest ever.

—GEORGE HALAS, IN *THE NFL'S TOP 40* BY SHELBY STROTHER

Mel Hein's hidden-ball trick momentarily fooled the Chicago Bears during the first NFL Championship Game.

December 7, 1958

SVARE SWATS LIONS AWAY

Blocked Field Goal Seals Giants Win

The surging second-place Giants came to Detroit in Week 11 of the 1958 season to face the struggling defending champion Lions. New York needed a victory to keep alive their hopes of overtaking the Browns for the Eastern crown. On a gray, 15-degree Michigan day that featured several unlikely plays, the Giants toughed out a win.

New York scored twice in the opening period. First, defensive end Jim Katcavage dumped Lions runner Gene Gedman in the end zone for a safety, and then Pat Summerall added a field goal for a 5–0 lead. Safety Jimmy Patton set up the Giants' third score by recovering a Lions fumble at the 19-yard line in the second quarter. Charley Conerly hit Alex Webster for a six-yard touchdown to extend the lead to 12–0, but Detroit's Jim Martin booted a field goal before the half to narrow the lead.

In the third quarter, Detroit gained control of the game. Quarterback Tobin Rote—cousin to the Giants' Kyle Rote—led the Lions to the Giants' 2 and then hit Ken Webb with a touchdown pass. Soon after, Conerly fumbled in trying a handoff to Mel Triplett at his own 34; linebacker Wayne Walker scooped up the ball and ran it in for another touchdown and the lead, 17–12.

Lions head coach George Wilson derailed his team's momentum early in the fourth quarter. Facing a fourth-and-21 from his own 44, Wilson ordered a fake for punter Yale Lary. Lary took off running but was collared by Cliff Livingston on a diving tackle after gaining just a yard, drawing

> **N**othing doing. I'll block the kick. You have a better blocking angle than I will. You drive him inside.
>
> **—HARLAND SVARE TO ANDY ROBUSTELLI, QUOTED IN *THE NEW YORK TIMES***

Linebacker Harland Svare was the defense's coach on the field and eventually succeeded Tom Landry on the sideline as defensive coach in 1960.

Game Details

New York Giants 19 • Detroit Lions 17

Date: December 7, 1958

Location: Briggs Stadium, Detroit

Attendance: 50,115

Significance: Beginning of the late-season push for the conference title

Box Score:

Giants	5	7	0	7	**19**
Lions	0	3	14	0	**17**

Scoring:

NYG safety, Gedman tackled by Katcavage
NYG Summerall 18-yard FG
NYG Webster 6-yard pass from Conerly (Summerall PAT)

DET Martin 39-yard FG
DET Webb 2-yard pass from Rote (Martin PAT)
DET Walker 34-yard fumble recovery (Martin PAT)
NYG Gifford 1-yard run (Summerall PAT)

Team	FD	YDS	RUSH	PASS	A-C-I	PUNT	FUM	PEN
Giants	13	251	48-116	135	17-6-2	5-39	1	55
Lions	13	154	31-140	14	20-6-2	6-45	2	65

hearty booing from the stands. This play call appeared so fishy that afterward NFL commissioner Bert Bell was called on to defend it and deny it was influenced by gambling interests.

On the next play, Conerly hit Bob Schnelker for a 34-yard gain to the Lions' 11. On fourth-and-one from the 2, the Giants went for it. Conerly handed off to Frank Gifford, and he punched in the lead-changing score over right tackle.

Down 19–17, Tobin Rote drove the Lions down the field in a two-minute drill that stalled at the Giants' 18. On fourth down, Jim Martin and the field-goal unit came onto the field with 1:21 to play. With the season in the balance, Giants veterans Andy Robustelli and Harland Svare discussed the situation and decided the best approach was for Robustelli to drive Lions lineman Gerald Perry inside, giving Svare an angle to shoot in and get his arms up. When the ball was snapped, Robustelli took Perry out and Svare shot through the gap. Svare didn't even have to dive as he blocked Martin's kick with his left wrist, and the game and season were saved. On this great play, the steadfast Giants defense had risen to the occasion once again.

Dee-Fense

Defensive coach Tom Landry had warned defensive end Jim Katcavage that he needed to line up wide to defend against Tobin Rote's rollouts. That tip put him in position to drop Gene Gedman for a first-quarter safety that provided the winning margin in the game. This was just the sort of play that Giants fans came to expect in the late 1950s, when their "Dee-Fense" chants echoed throughout Yankee Stadium and inspired the first truly celebrated defense in the sport's history during the Giants' championship run from 1956 through 1963.

It was also the first 4-3 defense in pro football, a base defense devised by Landry that is still the base scheme for most NFL teams 50 years later. Landry's defense took full advantage of the immense talent on hand. The four-man defensive line was the very first "fearsome foursome." Ends Katcavage and Andy Robustelli were rangy and quick, and Katcavage was also noted for his aggressiveness. Robustelli was very bright and would later become the team's defensive coach on his way to the Hall of Fame. Tackles Roosevelt Grier and Dick Modzelewski were a study in contrasts: Rosey was a gentle giant who tended to play just as well as he needed to, while the stumpy Modzelewski was more fiery and plugged the line with as much desire and smarts as talent.

The 4-3 was crafted to funnel plays to the middle linebacker position, where Sam Huff was a hard tackler and natural leader with a reputation for playing mean. On his flanks were clever outside linebackers Harland Svare and Cliff Livingston. Svare was like a coach on the field; he would replace Landry as the Giants' defensive coach in 1960. On the field, he would be replaced by veteran Tom Scott. Livingston was a free spirit on and off the field and was the brother of former Giants player Howie Livingston. He succeeded Bill Svoboda in 1958 and would be succeeded by Bill Winter in 1962.

The secondary was anchored by ball-hawking safeties Emlen Tunnell and Jimmy Patton. The aging Tunnell was too much of a freelancer for Landry's tastes and would give way to former Giants corner-back Dick Nolan in 1959. The cornerbacks of 1958, Ed Hughes and Carl Karilivacz, were supplanted by Lindon Crow and Dick Lynch in 1959, and Crow was replaced by Erich Barnes in 1961. Barnes and Lynch were risk-takers who made a lot of big plays.

The years of 1956 to 1963 were a great period in Giants history, and their aptly feted defense was a major reason why.

Tom Landry's 4-3 defense and a key field-goal block by Harland Svare (left, kneeling) led the Giants to a win over the Lions in 1958.
(Photo courtesy of AP Images)

October 31, 1999

TRICK OR TREAT

Strahan Completes Halloween Comeback with Overtime Touchdown

Ultimately, 1999 would not be a playoff year for either New York or Philadelphia, but at the midway point of the season, the Giants had hope. They were still in the hunt. With some luck and opportunistic play on this Halloween Sunday, they would head into their bye week with a promising 5–3 record.

By contrast, the Eagles were coming off a 3–13 season and were a slapdash, bumbling bunch under first-year coach Andy Reid in 1999. Yet at halftime, they led the Giants 17–3 on the strength of Duce Staley's 83 rushing yards and an 84-yard touchdown strike from the weak-armed Doug Pederson to Torrance Small, who had slipped by cornerback Jason Sehorn.

The Giants were being beaten soundly and not by giants on the other side of the field. When the players hit the locker room, Jim Fassel tore into their pathetic display with an expletive-laced tirade that caught the attention of the team, and they tightened up their play in the second half.

Midway through the third quarter, the Giants launched a 16-play, 83-yard, nine-minute drive that ended with runner LeShon Johnson going in from the 2-yard line to put New York within a touchdown of the lead. The plodding Kent Graham–led offense could not add to that, though.

Pederson then got the Eagles in position for a 33-yard field goal with less than eight minutes to play. However, defensive tackle Christian Peter got his hand up and blocked the attempt, preserving the one-score deficit. Again, the Giants could not move the ball. They were forced to punt,

> The big guys on a team are supposed to make the big plays. There comes a time in every game when somebody has to step up or go home with a loss. That time came for us and the guys did what they had to. And we get on the bus and go home winners.
>
> —JESSE ARMSTEAD

Head coach Jim Fassel watches as the Eagles' fourth-quarter field-goal attempt is blocked by lineman Christian Peter. *(Photo courtesy of AP Images)*

GAME DETAILS

New York Giants 23 • Philadelphia Eagles 17

Date: October 31, 1999

Location: Veterans Stadium, Philadelphia

Attendance: 66,481

Significance: Two division rivals playing for pride in a down year

Box Score:

Giants	3	0	0	14	6	**23**
Eagles	3	14	0	0	0	**17**

Scoring:
PHL Johnson 28-yard FG
NYG Blanchard 28-yard FG
PHL Staley 21-yard run (Johnson PAT)

PHL Small 84-yard pass from Pederson (Johnson PAT)
NYG Johnson 2-yard run (Blanchard PAT)
NYG Mitchell 7-yard pass from Graham (Blanchard PAT)
NYG Strahan 44-yard interception return

Team	FD	YDS	RUSH	PASS	RTN	A-C-I	Sacked	PUNT	FUM	PEN
Giants	20	298	24-91	207	163	42-26-0	3-8	8-42	0-0	5-40
Eagles	15	360	31-112	248	131	30-19-2	5-33	5-42	2-1	3-15

Giants: Graham 240P
Eagles: Pederson 256P, Small 119C

but they got another break when Eagles punt returner Allen Rossum let the punt bounce at the 15 and it rolled all the way to the 3.

Penned up on third-and-11 from the 2, Staley took the handoff, was hit immediately by Keith Hamilton and Lyle West, and dropped the ball. New York recovered on the 5, and Graham hit Pete Mitchell for a touchdown to tie the score with two minutes to play. Regulation play ended with the score knotted at 17–17.

In overtime, Christian Peter and Michael Strahan combined for the game-winning play. After a Giants punt, the Eagles were driving, having reached the New York 45. Pederson dropped back to pass, and once again Peter stuck his hand up to deflect the pass. The ball shot straight up in the air. Strahan, who had thus far had a quiet day, found himself in the right place at the right time and made the most of the opportunity. He grabbed the ball and took off 44 yards for the end zone and the winning score, with only heavy-footed linemen in futile pursuit. There, in ground-level end-zone seats of the hostile Veterans Stadium, he found a group of Giants fans, and it was high fives all around.

MICHAEL STRAHAN

Michael Strahan scored three times during his 15 years in New York and was a bulwark of strength on defense. In the locker room, his signature gap-toothed smile was ever-present, and he was always a receptive interview for the media, win or lose. His league-wide stature was evident in the aftermath of the 9/11 terrorist attack, when he was in the forefront of the group of players who successfully pushed to cancel the following week's games out of respect for the dead.

The son of a career military man, Strahan was a solid but opinionated citizen after coming to the NFL as a second-round pick out of Texas Southern in 1993. That year, he and fellow rookie Jesse Armstead got to send off Lawrence Taylor and Phil Simms and assume the mantle of team leadership.

However, Strahan was also a moody and overly sensitive player. His teammate Glenn Parker once sarcastically told Mike Freeman of *The New York Times* that he had seen grapes with thicker skin than Strahan. When Tiki Barber publicly criticized Strahan for his contract demands, it created a rift between the two that would never heal.

Even in his moment of greatest triumph, when he set a new single-season sack record with 22.5 in 2001, Strahan engendered criticism because Brett Favre allowed himself to be sacked at the end of the game so that Strahan could break the record. Strahan sacked more than 60 different quarterbacks during his career; he passed Lawrence Taylor as the Giants' all-time leading sacker in 2007. A seven-time Pro Bowl selection, Strahan twice led the NFL in sacks.

While he used a host of different pass-rushing techniques, he was primarily a bull rusher who took advantage of his great strength to push past offensive

> **I** was thinking, *It's too good to be true.* It was moving in slow motion. I knew I had to catch it or everyone in New York would hate me right now. But I have good hands. I grabbed it and ran. If you're going to end a game coming back from 14 points down, that's the way to end it.
>
> —MICHAEL STRAHAN

linemen. Even so, he was equally adept at stopping the run and was the most complete defensive end in the league since Hall of Famer Reggie White. Strahan announced his retirement in June 2008.

Michael Strahan celebrates his game-winning overtime interception return in a Halloween matchup against the Eagles in 1999.
(Photo courtesy of AP Images)

Choo Choo Chugs 85 Yards with Game-Winner

Giants Nip Bears 35–28

In a wild game that featured more than 600 yards of passing by the two teams, the Giants pulled out a victory over the Bears in the closing minutes on an exciting 85-yard screen pass by speedy Giants halfback Gene "Choo Choo" Roberts. Played before a disappointing crowd of just 30,000—since 38,000 other football fans were across the river at Yankee Stadium watching an AAFC game between the Yankees and the 49ers—it was the most points ever scored by the Giants against the Bears in the regular season. It has not been topped since in the 80-year-old series.

The Giants controlled matters early, with Charley Conerly hitting Roberts for a 31-yard score in the first quarter and finding Bill Swiacki in the second quarter for 35 yards and a 14–0 halftime advantage. When safety Emlen Tunnell intercepted a Johnny Lujack pass in the third quarter and returned it 53 yards for a third score, the game was beginning to look like a mismatch.

Lujack then drove the Bears to touchdowns on their next two possessions to draw closer, but Conerly hit Roberts again with a short pass that Choo Choo converted into a 62-yard touchdown to end the third period with the Giants up 28–14.

Once again Lujack went to the air and drove the Bears to two more touchdowns, knotting the score at 28–28. George Blanda's kickoff went into the end zone for a touchback, and the Giants started at their 20-yard line. Conerly was sacked for a five-yard loss on first down by the fired-up and hardcharging Bears.

On second down, with less than five minutes to play, he countered the angry Bears rush with a simple screen pass. It turned out to be the screen pass of the year. As the Bears' rushers pursued the retreating Conerly, he floated a pass to the fleet-footed Roberts by the left sideline. With a wall of Giants in front of him, Roberts took off and motored untouched

Quarterback Charley Conerly and Gene "Choo Choo" Roberts hooked up for an 85-yard touchdown pass against the Bears in 1949.

GAME DETAILS

New York Giants 35 • Chicago Bears 28

Date: October 23, 1949

Location: Polo Grounds, New York

Attendance: 30,587

Significance: Great performance against an old rival

Box Score:

Bears	0	0	14	14	**28**
Giants	7	7	14	7	**35**

Scoring:

NYG Roberts 31-yard pass from Conerly (Agajanian PAT)

NYG Swiacki 35-yard pass from Conerly (Agajanian PAT)

NYG Tunnell 53-yard return of pass intercepted from Lujack (Agajanian)

CHI Keane 2-yard pass from Lujack (Lujack PAT)

CHI McAfee 11-yard run (Lujack PAT)

NYG Roberts 62-yard pass from Conerly (Agajanian PAT)

CHI Gulyanics 3-yard pass from Lujack (Lujack PAT)

CHI Rykovich 7-yard run (Lujack PAT)

NYG Roberts 85-yard pass from Conerly (Agajanian PAT)

Team	FD	YDS	RUSH	PASS	RTN	A-C-I	PUNT	FUM	PEN
Bears	28	431	77	354	87	59-34-2	6-44	2-1	6-60
Giants	10	367	94	273	97	15-8-0	8-39	0-0	4-46

Bears: Lujack 319P, Keane 189C

Giants: Conerly 273P, Roberts 201C

for an 85-yard touchdown, putting the Giants up by seven again.

The game was not over yet. Lujack once again drove his Bears downfield, completing six passes to take them to the Giants' 16. In the closing seconds, though, Tunnell and Moon Mullins each batted away passes in the end zone, preserving the upset victory for the Giants.

Conerly, who had not practiced all week because of a sore arm, ended up with 273 yards on just eight completions—that's 34 yards per completion. Lujack put the ball up 59 times and threw for more than 300 yards in defeat. His number-one target, Jim Keane, caught 14 balls for 198 yards, but he was overshadowed by Roberts, who had 201 yards receiving for three scores and the game-winner.

Young Charley Conerly, his back pressed not too far from his own goal line, took the ball from center and fled backward in apparent disorder. Licking their chops in bloodthirsty eagerness, the Bears swarmed in on him. The cool kid from Mississippi waited until they were about to hammer him into the turf and wheeled quickly to his left. He threw. Out by the left sideline lurked Gene Roberts, the Chattanooga Choo Choo, and the engine was all stoked up. Conerly's pass shot into Roberts's arms on the 15-yard line. It seemed as though every Giant in the park was in front of him, mopping up any stray Bears they could find as Choo Choo chugged 85 yards to the winning touchdown.

—ARTHUR DALEY, *THE NEW YORK TIMES*, DECEMBER 2, 1949

CHOO CHOO ROBERTS

Gene Roberts had a short but spectacular career with the Giants, in which he set several records that would stand for decades. Roberts was a speedy back from Kansas who could run the 100 in 9.8 seconds. He was drafted in the eighth round of the 1946 draft, but he stayed at the University of Tennessee–Chattanooga (hence, the "Choo Choo" nickname) for another season, in which he scored 18 touchdowns in 10 games.

Roberts's third and greatest year in New York was 1949. He finished fourth in the NFL in rushing, with 634 yards; fourth in receiving yards, with 711; first in touchdowns, with 17; and first in points, with 102. He became the first back to have two games of more than 200 yards receiving. He also had two games in which he gained more than 100 yards rushing; the Giants went 4–0 in those four games but 2–6 the rest of the year.

Choo Choo was a home-run hitter who had touchdown runs of 62 and 63 yards and touchdown catches of 49, 68, and 85 yards. In 1950, he set the NFL single-game rushing mark with 218 yards against the Cardinals, in a game in which Steve Owen brought back his old A-formation.

Roberts announced he was retiring to his Brazilian ranch in April 1951. He was traded to the Packers on July 23 of that year, but he signed with Montreal of the Canadian Football League the following day. He spent four seasons in Canada, leading the CFL in scoring in 1953.

His Giants records have been slowly erased over the years: Del Shofner had 269 receiving yards in a 1962 game; Joe Morris scored 21 touchdowns in 1985; and Tiki Barber had games of 220 and 234 yards rushing in 2005 and 2006. However, Choo Choo should be remembered as the pass-catching halfback prototype that Gifford and Barber followed.

December 30, 2001

LAMBUTH SPECIAL STOPPED SHORT OF THE PLAYOFFS

Time Runs Out for Giants Against Eagles

A spectacular play the Giants hadn't practiced since training camp nearly kept their expiring postseason hopes alive on the final play of a hard-fought battle with division rival Philadelphia—but it fell a few yards short of the mark. After 2000's surprising Super Bowl appearance, the play called "86 Lambuth Special" served as a fitting metaphor for the Giants' disappointing, oh-so-close 2001 season, in which they missed the playoffs by losing three games in the last minutes by a total of just five points to the Eagles and the Rams.

Going into this 15th game of the year, 7–7 New York trailed the 9–5 Eagles by two games, but a victory in Philadelphia would keep the Giants' postseason hopes alive. October's 10–9 loss to the Eagles at the Meadowlands had broken the Giants' nine-game winning streak over Philadelphia; it was the first time Jim Fassel had lost to the Eagles or to their coach, Andy Reid.

With control of the division on the line the night before New Year's Eve, tempers were short and players from the opposing teams got into a scuffle during warm-ups, 45 minutes before the game even started. The Eagles opened the game with a 72-yard drive that culminated in a five-yard touchdown pass from Donovan McNabb to Chad Lewis. The remainder of the first half was a hard-hitting defensive contest, in which Michael Strahan continued his mastery over Eagles tackle Jon Runyan by constantly harrassing McNabb. Strahan had 3.5 sacks in the first half and had many big plays throughout the game.

The Giants evened the score at the outset of the second half with a flea flicker in which Tiki Barber took a handoff from Collins and tossed the ball back to the quarterback, who then hit Amani Toomer for a 60-yard touchdown. Later in the quarter, a 30-yard Ron Dayne run led to a 25-yard field goal, giving the Giants a 10–7 lead going into the exciting fourth quarter.

The Eagles took the lead back in the first minute of the final quarter on a 57-yard bomb from McNabb to speedster James Thrash. The Giants answered with a field goal to draw within a point; they then drove 81 yards and scored on a 16-yard run by Dayne. New York went for two, and Tiki Barber's successful two-point conversion gave the Giants a 21–14 lead with 2:43 to play.

McNabb responded by driving the Eagles 67 yards in six plays, including a 32-yard reception by Thrash, with Lewis again catching the scoring pass with 1:49 remaining. Philadelphia used all their time-outs and forced a three-and-out from the Giants. Starting at their 29-yard line with

58 seconds left, the Eagles marched 54 yards in seven plays to the Giants' 17, where David Akers kicked a 35-yard field goal to take the lead with seven seconds to play. The key plays on the drive were a 25-yard strike to Thrash and a clock-stopping five-yard delay-of-game penalty against Michael Strahan for not letting Donovan McNabb get up after Strahan tackled him just one play before the field goal.

Down 24–21 with seven seconds left, it appeared the Giants had no hope after the touchback on the ensuing kickoff gave them

Tiki Barber's lateral to Ron Dixon on the 86 Lambuth Special wasn't enough to save the Giants against the Eagles in the 2001 regular-season finale.

GAME DETAILS

New York Giants 21 • Philadelphia Eagles 24

Date: December 30, 2001

Location: Veterans Stadium, Philadelphia

Attendance: 65,885

Significance: Giants needed a win over rival Eagles to stay alive for the playoffs

Box Score:

Giants	0	0	10	11	**21**
Eagles	7	0	0	17	**24**

Scoring:

PHL Lewis 5-yard pass from McNabb (Akers PAT)
NYG Toomer 60-yard pass from Collins (Andersen PAT)
NYG Andersen 25-yard FG
PHL Thrash 57-yard pass from McNabb (Akers PAT)

NYG Andersen 32-yard FG
NYG Dayne 16-yard run (Barber run)
PHL Lewis 7-yard pass from McNabb (Akers PAT)
PHL Akers 35-yard FG

Team	FD	YDS	RUSH	PASS	RTN	A-C-I	Sacked	PUNT	FUM	PEN
Giants	18	408	26-119	289	128	39-22-0	2-12	6-36	2-1	6-73
Eagles	21	354	23-113	241	125	39-21-1	4-29	7-37	2-1	3-25

Giants: Collins 301P
Eagles: McNabb 270P, Thrash 143C

the ball at their own 20. Fassel ordered the 86 Lambuth Special, named after the small Tennessee school that speedster Ron Dixon had attended. The Lambuth Special is nothing more than a variation on the old hook-and-lateral play that has been around since the dawn of pro football. Kerry Collins took the snap and threw a seven-yard pass to Tiki Barber on the left. As Barber and his blockers headed right, Ron Dixon crossed behind Barber from the right and took a lateral at the 40, headed in the opposite direction from the Eagles' pursuit.

With all the Eagles defenders out of position, Dixon took off down the sideline with the end zone in his sights. As Dixon got closer to the sideline, he slowed down a bit, looking for a cutback lane, and was caught at the 6-yard line by the only Eagles player with a shot at him, safety Damon Moore. As Dixon was knocked out of bounds, the Giants looked up at the clock to see the sad sight of 0:00. The game—and the season—were over. General manager Ernie Accorsi summed it up by saying, "For what it meant and how we lost it, it was heartbreaking."

THE 86 LAMBUTH SPECIAL

The Giants' 86 Lambuth Special is designed so that Ike Hilliard (88) lines up on the left and catches a pass over the middle heading right. He then laterals to a trailing Tiki Barber (21). Meanwhile, Ron Dixon (86) lines up on the right and heads left, where he crosses behind Barber and takes a second lateral headed in the opposite direction, away from the defensive pursuit, with blockers Joe Jurevicius (84) and Amani Toomer (81) in front of him. Since Hilliard was held up at the line, Kerry Collins (5) threw the ball to Barber, who lateraled to Dixon, who traveled all the way to the 6-yard line before being knocked out of bounds by safety Damon Moore (43) on this 74-yard play.

> **W**hen Ron got to the 30, I thought he had a chance to go all the way, but he got knocked out of bounds.
>
> —KERRY COLLINS

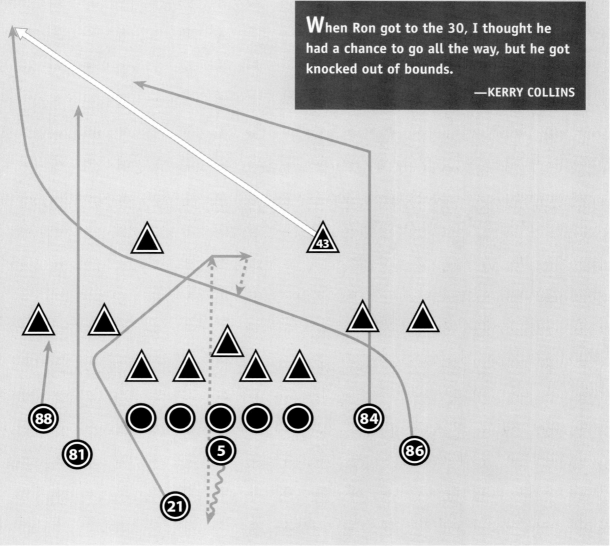

Linebacker Jesse Armstead was a team leader and one of coach Jim Fassel's favorite players during his years with the Giants.

JESSE ARMSTEAD

Jesse Armstead manfully and correctly stated after the game, "I had no idea where [Dixon] was because I was still so pissed off. If something happened, if he scored a touchdown, great. But I was still so mad at how we came up short, I didn't really care. If I had an extra leg, I'd be kicking myself."

Armstead was so mad because not only had the Giants given up 17 fourth-quarter points, but 10 of them came in the last 1:49. The defense let the game slip away.

Armstead was one of three linebackers who came out of the University of Miami in 1993 and became quality NFL starters; his Miami teammates Darrin Smith and Michael Barrow were drafted in the second round by Dallas and Houston, respectively. Armstead was only an eighth-round draft pick of New York, though, because he weighed just 220 pounds. In New York, he bulked up to 240 pounds as he advanced from special-teams demon to Pro Bowl linebacker. Armstead was a playmaker known for his intelligence, speed, and ball-hawking instincts during his nine years as a Giant.

Armstead was also a team leader who did not hesitate to publicly criticize the team's inept offense in 1999, before Kerry Collins took over at quarterback. In a public tiff during a contentious season, Fassel told him to mind his own business. In the off-season, Armstead met with Fassel and cleared the air. The Giants went to the Super Bowl that year with Fassel calling Armstead one of his favorite players.

This loss to the Eagles, though, would be Armstead's next-to-last game in blue. The aging veteran who correctly diagnosed the defense's weakness left for Washington as a free agent. After two years, Armstead re-signed with New York and immediately retired, a Giant forever.

> This is our [the defense's] loss. We like to say it when we're good, but we didn't make a stand to win the game when we could have. That's on us.
>
> —JESSE ARMSTEAD

THE HIT HEARD 'ROUND THE WORLD

Gifford and Giants Fall to Eagles

Having won three of four Eastern Conference titles, the Giants looked well-positioned to make another run in Week 8 of the 1960 season. The 6–1 Eagles were in town for a first-place showdown with the 5–1–1 Giants, and New York got off to a good start with a 10–0 halftime lead on a Joe Morrison touchdown run and a Pat Summerall field goal. At the half, the Giants had 12 first downs versus four for the Eagles, and Philadelphia quarterback Norm Van Brocklin was under constant pressure from the Giants defense, which held him to just one completion in six attempts.

To stabilize the Eagles' front line, veteran linebacker Chuck Bednarik replaced rookie center Bill Lapham for the second half, telling Giants linebacker Sam Huff that the "men were taking over now." This would be the first of several games in which Bednarik would play both ways during the Eagles' stretch drive. The bolstered Eagles offense evened up the game on a 35-yard touchdown pass to Tommy McDonald in the third quarter and a Bobby Walston field goal in the fourth quarter.

With the score tied at 10–10, the Giants got the ball back behind quarterback George Shaw, who was subbing for an injured Charley Conerly. Facing a third-and-inches at their 38-yard line, Shaw handed off to fullback Mel Triplett, but the exchange was shaky and when Triplett was hit by Bednarik at the line of scrimmage, the ball popped up in the air. Safety Jimmy Carr snatched it and raced untouched into the end zone for a 17–10 Eagles lead with 2:33 to play.

With the situation now desperate, Shaw hit Gifford for a 33-yard gain to midfield. Shaw overthrew Gifford on his next pass and then sent Bob Schnelker deep on second down. Schnelker was open and Shaw was on target, but the normally reliable receiver let the ball fall right through his hands.

Now came the play of the day. Needing a first down on third-and-10, Shaw went back to the team's leader, Gifford, and hit him near the right hash mark at the Eagles' 35. With two Eagles converging from the front and Bednarik circling from behind, Gifford attempted to cut back behind Bednarik.

In perhaps the most famous tackle in NFL history, Bednarik hit Gifford hard and high, knocking him backwards off his feet so that his head bounced off the frozen field, rendering Gifford unconscious. In the process, Gifford fumbled and Chuck Weber of Philadelphia recovered the ball. When Bednarik saw that, he leaped in the air to celebrate winning the game, but all the Giants and their fans saw was a cocky brute taunting their fallen star. The Giants' 5'5" team doctor screamed expletives at Bednarik, and quarterback Conerly called him a "cheap-shot artist," but the hit was clean and brutal.

In a bit of quirky scheduling, the teams met again the following week in Philadelphia. Once again, the Giants got off to a lead—17–0 in the first quarter this time—but could not hold it. The Eagles were in the midst of a magical season in which six of their 10 victories would be comeback wins. The Giants, by contrast, were headed to a 6–4–2 third-place finish and were starting to look old. A new coach, quarterback, and wide receiver would turn the club around in 1961, but Frank Gifford would retire and spend that season as a team scout while he began his broadcasting career.

> **I**t sounded like a rifle shot.
> —RILEY GUNNELS, IN *THE 1960 PHILADELPHIA EAGLES* BY ROBERT GORDON

Eagles linebacker Chuck Bednarik knocks Frank Gifford unconscious in one of the most famous and brutal plays in football history.

GAME DETAILS

New York Giants 10 • Philadelphia Eagles 17

Date: November 20, 1960

Location: Yankee Stadium, New York

Attendance: 63,571

Significance: Late-season game for the division lead

Box Score:

Eagles	0	0	7	10	**17**
Giants	7	3	0	0	**10**

Scoring:
NYG Morrison 1-yard run (Summerall PAT)
NYG Summerall 26-yard FG
PHL McDonald 35-yard pass from Van Brocklin
(Walston PAT)

PHL Walston 12-yard FG
PHL Carr 38-yard fumble recovery (Walston PAT)

Team	FD	YDS	RUSH	PASS	A-C-I	PUNT	FUM	PEN
Eagles	14	264	30-61	203	24-13-0	7-40	0	35
Giants	17	348	40-154	204	25-12-1	2-46	3	50

Eagles: Van Brocklin 203P, Walston 119C
Giants: Shaw 204P

> **I** hit him good, and I hit him clean. In this game, a man can get hurt.
>
> —CHUCK BEDNARIK

> **I** actually don't remember any of this.... My memory of that play—and most of that day and night—has been blurred by having seen the 'hit' replayed on TV shows more times than the Hindenburg disaster.
>
> —FRANK GIFFORD, *THE WHOLE TEN YARDS*

FRANK GIFFORD

Chuck Bednarik knocked Frank Gifford clear into another season with his concussion-inducing smackdown. The 30-year-old Gifford went into retirement in 1961, but he missed the action and was eager to return in 1962, when he replaced his old teammate Kyle Rote as the Giants' dependable flanker for three more years.

Handsome and stylish, Gifford was an early pop-culture icon who moved easily in the bright lights on and off the field. He inspired hero worship from many fans—most notably troubled writer Frederick Exley, whose novel *A Fan's Notes* used Gifford and the Giants as a prism through which he viewed his own life.

Gifford was a Southern California native who starred as an All-American tailback at USC, and he also did some acting. He was the top pick of New York in 1952, but Giants coach Steve Owen was suspicious of Gifford and primarily used him on defense. Under new offensive coach Vince Lombardi, though, Gifford's career changed course in his third year. Lombardi valued Gifford's "versatility and alertness" and used his running, receiving, and passing abilities as the centerpiece of New York's offense. In 1956, the Giants won the title and Gifford won the league MVP award.

When he retired for good in 1964, Gifford was first in team history in points, touchdowns, and receiving yards and second in receptions and rushing yards. He had been selected for the Pro Bowl five times as a running back, once as a flanker, and once as a defensive back—three different positions in all. He had thrown 14 touchdown passes on the halfback option play.

Gifford was elected to the Hall of Fame in 1977 and had his number retired by the Giants in 2000. In a high-profile second career, he spent more than 30 years as a broadcaster, most notably on *Monday Night Football* with Howard Cosell and Don Meredith.

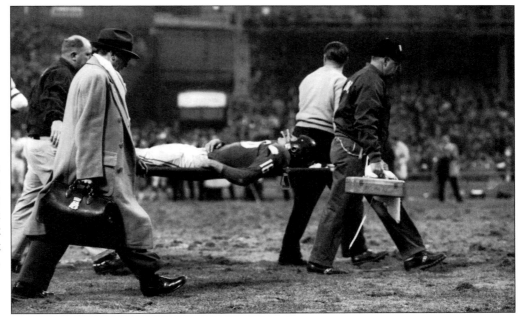

Frank Gifford was taken off the field on a stretcher after being knocked out by Chuck Bednarik. Gifford spent a year in retirement because of the injury.

November 8, 1970

26 TARKENTON'S LATE COMEBACK CLIPS COWBOYS

Johnson Scores Twice to Top Dallas

After losing the first three games of the 1970 season, the Giants got on a roll and won the next four to post a winning record for the first half of the year. One of the losses was to the Cowboys, a perennial power who came into Yankee Stadium on November 8 bearing a 5–2 record, tied for first with the Cardinals.

The first half of the game went pretty much as expected, with the Cowboys taking a 17–6 lead on two bombs from Craig Morton to Bob Hayes, one for 38 yards and the other for 80. All the Giants could manage were two Pete Gogolak field goals, and Gogolak missed a 55-yard try shortly before halftime. However, New York got a lift at the end of the half when they moved to the Dallas 47-yard line with 16 seconds left. This time, Gogolak was true, making a 54-yard kick to draw the Giants three points closer.

Dallas extended its lead to 20–9 with a field goal in the third quarter, but the Giants responded with a 71-yard drive on which star runner Ron Johnson carried the ball on seven of the 10 plays for 54 yards, including the last four for the score. The Giants recovered the ensuing surprise onside kick, and Johnson carried the ball five more times to get them into field-goal range. But Gogolak missed the 29-yard chip shot.

The Giants were still trailing 20–16 when they got the ball in the final minutes of the game. Fran Tarkenton completed passes to Johnson and Clifton McNeil—who was playing with a broken nose—to move the ball to the 17. A scramble got four yards and left New York facing a third-and-six.

> **I** can see us gaining confidence each week.
>
> —FRAN TARKENTON

Fran Tarkenton

The thrilling fourth-quarter comeback in this game encompassed why the Giants acquired Fran Tarkenton: to provide excitement, star power, and wins to an ailing franchise being challenged for fan interest by the crosstown New York Jets (led by Broadway Joe Namath). Tarkenton was the son of a minister and could not compete with Namath's charisma, but he was confident and feisty and gave life to the struggling Giants. This comeback was one of 15 he would lead in his five seasons in New York.

Tarkenton was drafted in the third round in 1961 by Minnesota. With the Vikings, he was a dynamic leader who ultimately had a falling-out with abrasive coach Norm Van Brocklin. New York gave up too much to obtain Tarkenton in 1967 (two first-round picks and two second-round picks), but he brought electricity, professionalism, and steadiness to a lousy team.

In his first year as a Giant, Fran threw for 29 touchdowns and 3,000 yards. He had a weak arm, but he was a clever quarterback and was able to compensate with an effective short passing offense that took him to four Pro Bowls for New York. Simply stated, he made the Giants better. While the team's record was an unimposing 33–37 in his five years in New York, it was 10–29–3 in the three years before he arrived and 12–29–1 in the three years after he left.

In 1971, Tarkenton got into a contract dispute with the Giants because he wanted a business loan from the team. Things turned so sour that he was pointlessly kept out of the season finale—the first game he had missed in his 11 years as a professional. New York traded him back to Minnesota for a first- and a second-round draft pick and three nondescript players; Fran led the Vikings to three Super Bowls in his second tour as a Vikings player.

In retirement, he remained visible as a broadcaster on *Monday Night Football* and *That's Incredible*. Additionally, he was an infomercial pitchman in his second career as an entrepreneur.

Acquired from the Vikings in 1967, quarterback Fran Tarkenton brought spirit and steadiness to a struggling New York franchise.

GAME DETAILS

New York Giants 23 • Dallas Cowboys 20

Date: November 8, 1970

Location: Yankee Stadium, New York

Attendance: 62,938

Significance: Giants victory tied them with the Cowboys for second in the East

Box Score:

Cowboys	10	7	3	0	**20**	
Giants	3	6	7	7	**23**	

Scoring:

DAL Clark 28-yard FG
NYG Gogolak 40-yard FG
DAL Hayes 38-yard pass from Morton (Clark PAT)
NYG Gogolak 42-yard FG
DAL Hayes 80-yard pass from Morton (Clark PAT)

NYG Gogolak 54-yard FG
DAL Clark 22-yard FG
NYG Johnson 4-yard run (Gogolak PAT)
NYG Johnson 13-yard pass from Tarkenton (Gogolak PAT)

Team	FD	YDS	RUSH	PASS	RTN	A-C-I	PUNT	FUM	PEN
Cowboys	9	263	25-102	161	0	22-10-0	7-44	0	51
Giants	10	334	41-202	136	22	25-15-0	4-44	3	30

Cowboys: Morton 191P, Hayes 129C
Giants: Johnson 140R, Tarkenton 170P

On the game-winning play, Tarkenton sent Johnson circling out of the backfield. Ron was picked up by All-Pro cornerback Mel Renfro, but he beat Renfro to the goal post, where Tarkenton hit him for the touchdown with three minutes remaining. Dallas had plenty of time to come back, but the Giants defense rose up and stopped the Cowboys on downs to preserve the win.

With the win, New York was tied with Dallas at 5–3, and both teams went into the final week with 9–4 records. The Giants hosted Los Angeles and got smoked 31–3 by the Rams, missing the playoffs. Meanwhile, the Cowboys won their last game easily and ultimately ended up in the Super Bowl, where they lost to the Colts.

RON JOHNSON

This stirring comeback win over the Cowboys was achieved largely because of the multidimensional skill set of running back Ron Johnson, who ran for 140 yards and caught four passes—including the game-winner—for 59 more yards. Johnson and Fran Tarkenton meshed perfectly in 1970 and gave the undermanned Giants a real chance to win each week.

Johnson was the first-round draft choice of the Browns in 1969, but they were disenchanted with his rookie season; they also needed a wide receiver to replace Paul Warfield, whom they had traded. So Johnson and two other Browns were packaged to the Giants for end Homer Jones. Johnson became the first Giants runner to exceed 1,000 yards rushing in a season in 1970, and he duplicated that feat in 1972.

In fact, the only two winning seasons for the Giants from 1964 to 1981 were the two years that Johnson ran for 1,000 yards. He was a fast, elusive, slashing runner, a dependable receiver out of the backfield, and the workhorse centerpiece of New York's offense.

Unfortunately, Johnson needed knee surgery in 1971 and missed most of that season. In 1973, he played through a host of injuries and was not himself, although he did gain more than 900 yards. By 1974, he was a worn-down shadow of the player he had been. He retired after the 1975 season, second only to Alex Webster in career rushing yards for the Giants. He later achieved great success as a local businessman.

Running back Ron Johnson scored twice in a 1970 victory over the Dallas Cowboys.
(Photo courtesy of WireImages)

TAYLOR TURNS LIONS INTO TURKEYS

97-Yard Interception Return Wins Thanksgiving Game

The 1982 NFL season featured an ugly players strike, during which Weeks 3 through 9 were canceled. The NFL returned on Sunday, November 21, and the Giants promptly lost to the Redskins, falling to 0–3 just one season after making the playoffs for the first time in 18 years. Even worse, Lawrence Taylor, the team's second-year superstar linebacker, was listed as doubtful with a sprained knee for the next game—just four days later on Thanksgiving Day, against the Lions.

Indeed, Taylor did not start, and the Lions scored twice on field goals set up by interceptions to take a 6–0 lead in the second quarter. Drawn by the needs of his team and the national stage of the annual Turkey Day contest, Taylor replaced Byron Hunt in the second quarter. In the third quarter, he started to impose his will on the

Lions, and the game became the Lawrence Taylor Show.

Early in the second half, Taylor blitzed and forced Lions quarterback Gary Danielson to get off an ill-advised, hurried pass that Harry Carson picked off and returned to the Detroit 41-yard line. Six plays later, kicker Joe Danelo made the score 6–3. On the first play after the ensuing kickoff, Taylor exploded on Lions ball carrier Billy Sims and knocked the ball loose. Brad Van Pelt recovered it at the Detroit 18. Although the inept Giants offense, led by Scott Brunner, still could not move the ball, Danelo came on to kick another field goal to tie the game.

The next time the Lions had the ball, Taylor blitzed again, grabbed Danielson by the jersey with one hand, and tossed him to the ground, forcing a punt.

> The running back cut outside, and the quarterback should have recognized that Taylor had him.
>
> —BILL PARCELLS

Despite an ailing knee, Lawrence Taylor converted a 97-yard interception return for a touchdown against the Lions.
(Photo courtesy of WireImages)

GAME DETAILS

New York Giants 13 • Detroit Lions 6

Date: November 25, 1982

Location: Silverdome, Pontiac, Michigan

Attendance: 64,348

Significance: The Lawrence Taylor Show comes to a national stage

Box Score:

Giants	0	0	6	7	**13**
Lions	3	3	0	0	**6**

Scoring:

DET Murray 46-yard FG
DET Murray 44-yard FG

NYG Danelo 34-yard FG
NYG Danelo 40-yard FG
NYG Taylor 97-yard interception return (Danelo PAT)

Team	FD	YDS	RUSH	PASS	RTN	A-C-I	Sacked	PUNT	FUM	PEN
Giants	10	206	27-88	118	135	28-12-2	2-18	4-41	2-1	6-36
Lions	19	321	38-171	150	16	32-15-3	1-14	5-40	1-1	8-86

Giants: Brunner 136P
Lions: Sims 114R, Danielson 125P

In the fourth quarter, the Lions finally got a drive going and moved to the New York 4. At this critical moment in a tie game, Lawrence Taylor made the biggest play of the day. On third down, running back Horace King and tight end David Hill ran crisscrossing routes to confuse Taylor and fellow linebacker Brian Kelley. Kelley followed Taylor's original man, Hill, as he was supposed to do. To bait Danielson, Taylor faked that he was staying with Hill, but he then closed on his new man, King, with the pass in the air. L.T. caught the ball at the 3 and went into a sprint down the sideline, sore knee notwithstanding. At the 50, Taylor noticed defensive coordinator Bill Parcells on the sideline motioning to keep running, and he did, with Danielson and Dexter Bussey in distant pursuit. Although there was a penalty on the play, it was against King for offensive pass interference, so the touchdown stood.

The 97-yard interception return was the third longest in team history. It proved to be the winning score and only touchdown in the Giants' 13–6 defensive victory. New York would end the season 4–5 and out of the playoffs, but 1982 remains memorable for the Thanksgiving game that Lawrence Taylor won all by himself.

LAWRENCE TAYLOR

Lawrence Taylor terrorized quarterbacks primarily as a pass rusher. This interception against the Lions was one of only nine he would record in his 13 years in the NFL. He was the definition of an impact player, and he forced opponents to gameplan against him. Coach Joe Gibbs of the division-rival Redskins devised the H-back—a combination tight end and offensive lineman—as a direct counter to the havoc Taylor wrought. Washington's formations were always crafted to try to get two blockers on Taylor, and other teams followed suit.

Taylor was the second player taken in the 1981 draft; he proved his value by recording 133 tackles and 9.5 sacks in that first season. For that, he was named both Rookie of the Year and Defensive Player of the Year. Taylor would go on to be named Defensive Player of the Year three more times; he also won the NFL MVP Award in 1986. For seven consecutive seasons, he recorded double-digit sack totals, leading the league with 20.5 sacks in 1986.

During his career, Taylor was named to 10 Pro Bowls, recorded 142 sacks, forced 33 fumbles,

> **The ball in my hand took care of all the pain from the injury.**
>
> **—LAWRENCE TAYLOR**

and recovered 11 more. He was a ferocious tackler and unrelenting in pursuit of the play. L.T. combined the speed of a back and the strength of a lineman, along with quickness, agility, and intensity.

Off the field, Taylor had outsized appetites that put him in and out of rehab several times, both during and after his playing career. This sordid side caused some controversy when he became eligible for the Hall of Fame, but no one could deny his greatness on the football field. He was enshrined in Canton in 1999.

Some consider him the greatest defensive player in NFL history; most would concede he was the finest linebacker. Without question, he is the greatest player the Giants have ever had, and his No. 56 jersey has been retired.

Coach Bill Parcells's motivational skills helped Lawrence Taylor become arguably the greatest linebacker in NFL history. *(Photo courtesy of WireImages)*

GIANTS' 87-YARD PASS PLAY FALLS SHORT

Colts Capture Title in Sudden Death

It has come to be known as "The Greatest Game Ever Played," but it was never that, especially not for Giants fans. The 1958 NFL Championship Game was the first title game to end regulation play in a tie and force a sudden-death overtime period, and thus it had an exciting conclusion. However, the game between the Giants and the Baltimore Colts was filled with fumbles and miscues on both sides and was hardly the best game played by either team that season. What captivated a national television audience was the expert execution of the two-minute offense by a young Johnny Unitas to tie the game, and then his relentless march in overtime for the win.

Despite having beaten the Colts seven weeks before, the Giants were 3.5-point underdogs on this mild December day at Yankee Stadium. New York boasted the NFL's best defense, but Baltimore had the second-best defense to go with the highest-scoring offense in the league. The Giants were just ninth in points scored and were worn down from having to win a playoff game over the Browns the week before to get to the championship game.

The two starting quarterbacks, Unitas and Don Heinrich, traded fumbles in the first quarter and then Unitas was intercepted by Carl Karilivacz, but New York was forced to punt. The Colts' offense could be explosive, and Unitas proved that by quickly hitting Lenny Moore for a 60-yard bomb. However, the Giants defense stiffened, and Colts kicker Steve Myhra missed a 26-yard field goal.

The Giants followed the unusual practice of keeping Charley Conerly on the sideline at the outset of games to observe, as backup quarterback Heinrich probed the opposing defense. Conerly now entered the game and led the Giants into Colts territory for Pat Summerall to kick a 36-yard field goal with two minutes left in the first period.

Early in the second quarter, Frank Gifford lost a fumble at his own 20-yard line, and the Colts capitalized to take a 7–3 lead. The Giants were forced to punt from

It was the greatest game I've ever seen.
—NFL COMMISSIONER BERT BELL

Colts back Alan Ameche scores the winning touchdown in overtime of the 1958 NFL Championship Game, also known as "The Greatest Game Ever Played." *(Photo courtesy of AP Images)*

ALEX WEBSTER

It wasn't surprising that Alex Webster was in the right place at the right time on the spectacular 87-yard pass play that got the Giants going in the third quarter. The tough New Jersey native was someone his teammates could always depend upon to make the big play at crunch time.

Webster was an 11th-round draft pick of the Redskins in 1953; they tried him on defense before cutting him. Webster headed to Montreal, where he became a star and led the CFL in rushing in 1954. The Giants noticed him when they were scouting Montreal quarterback Sam Etcheverry. They signed Alex in 1955.

The determined Webster led the team in rushing as a rookie halfback. He had an effective, gliding running style and used his blocks very well, and he would fight for every yard when the blocking disappeared. He also had a determined nose for the goal line; until recent years, his 56 touchdowns rushing and receiving were only exceeded by Giants Frank Gifford and Joe Morrison.

Shoulder and leg injuries from 1958 through 1960 nearly got Webster cut in training camp in 1961. However, after being switched to fullback by Allie Sherman, Webster had his two biggest seasons before he began to show the signs of age in 1963, at age 32. He led the Giants in rushing three times and retired as their all-time leading rusher. A popular figure with the fans, Webster went on to coach the team in the post-Sherman era with limited success, finishing with a 29–40–1 record.

midfield on their next possession, but Baltimore's Jackie Simpson fumbled on the return and the Giants had the ball on the Colts' 10. Once again, Frank Gifford lost the handle. Baltimore got the ball back and drove 86 yards in 15 plays to score on a 15-yard pass to Raymond Berry. The Giants went to the locker room at the half trailing 14–3 and having been outgained 198 yards to 86.

After an exchange of punts to begin the third quarter, the Colts mounted another drive. With a first-and-goal at the New York 3, it looked as if the game were about to turn into a rout. After three dive plays moved the ball just two yards, however, Unitas tried something different on fourth-and-goal from the 1. He pitched out to Alan Ameche, who had the option to pass the ball to tight end Jim Mutscheller. Instead, instinctive linebacker Cliff Livingston dragged Ameche down at the 5.

The Giants took possession and moved the ball to the 12 on runs by Gifford and Webster, setting the stage for the Giants' play of the day. Conerly faked a pitch to Gifford and dropped back to pass under a heavy rush by Gino Marchetti. Conerly hit an open Kyle Rote crossing the 35. Rote broke a tackle by Carl Tasseff at the 48 and kept running until Andy Nelson grabbed him at the Colts' 40. With help from Ray Brown, Nelson wrestled Rote to the ground at the 35 as the ball came flying out.

While those three players scrambled to their feet, Alex Webster came rushing in from behind, scooped up the ball at the 25, and headed for the flag—but a hustling Tasseff knocked Alex out at the 1. On the next play after this 87-yard miracle, Mel Triplett dove in for the score, and the Giants were alive.

Baltimore could not move the ball, but Conerly was sharp on the Giants' next possession. Passes to Schnelker

GAME DETAILS

New York Giants 17 • Baltimore Colts 23

Date: December 28, 1958

Location: Yankee Stadium, New York

Attendance: 64,185

Significance: First sudden-death NFL Championship Game

Box Score:

Colts	0	14	0	3	6	**23**
Giants	3	0	7	7	0	**17**

Scoring:

NYG Summerall 36-yard FG
BAL Ameche 2-yard run (Myhra PAT)
BAL Berry 15-yard pass from Unitas (Myhra PAT)

NYG Triplett 1-yard run (Summerall PAT)
NYG Gifford 15-yard pass from Conerly (Summerall PAT)
BAL Myhra 20-yard FG
BAL Ameche 1-yard run (no PAT)

Team	FD	YDS	RUSH	PASS	RTN	A-C-I	Sacked	PUNT	FUM	PEN
Colts	27	453	38-139	314	10	40-26-1	4-35	4-51	2-2	3-15
Giants	10	266	31-88	178	32	18-12-0	3-22	6-46	6-4	2-22

Colts: Unitas 349P, Berry 178C, Moore 101C
Giants: Conerly 187P

moved the ball down the field, and a 15-yard strike to Gifford gave the Giants a 17–14 lead in the fourth period. The Colts missed another field goal, and the Giants had the ball with less than five minutes to play. They picked up one first down and were faced with a third-and-five from their 39 when they handed off to Gifford, who appeared to make the first down. However, Gino Marchetti's leg had been broken when teammate Big Daddy Lipscomb fell on the pile.

In the ensuing confusion of removing Marchetti on a stretcher, New York got a bad spot and faced fourth down. The players and offensive coach Vince Lombardi wanted to go for the first down, but Jim Lee Howell decided to punt. The rest is legend: a 62-yard drive in 1:53 for the tying field goal and a 13-play, 80-yard touchdown drive in overtime for the Colts victory.

The Colts were champions, and Johnny Unitas won a car as the game's MVP. Had Frank Gifford made that disputed first down, that car would have gone to Charley Conerly.

KYLE ROTE

The man who traveled the furthest with the ball on that 87-yard play from the 1958 championship game was receiver Kyle Rote, who caught the pass and went 52 yards before losing the ball on a rare fumble. Rote was a big-play receiver for New York. His mark of 48 receiving touchdowns held up as the team record for 47 years, until Amani Toomer exceeded it in 2007.

Rote got his first national recognition as a junior at Southern Methodist, when he substituted for All-American Doak Walker and nearly beat the heavily favored Notre Dame single-handedly. In his senior year, Kyle was runner-up for the Heisman Trophy. The Giants nabbed him as the bonus pick at the top of the 1951 draft.

As a rookie, the running back tore up his knee in training camp and played little. He showed promise in his second season, but then he tore up his other knee in 1953, and his career as a running back was over practically before it began. Tom Landry noted how well Rote ran pass patterns, though, and suggested Kyle switch to end. That move rescued his career. Rote

> **I** didn't really fumble. The guy pulled the ball away. But there it was on the goddamn ground, and I just went numb. You know what? Thank God for Alex Webster.
>
> —KYLE ROTE, IN *THE GAME OF THEIR LIVES* BY DAVE KLEIN

was slow but shifty, with great moves and hands.

Rote would play in four Pro Bowls. He had his greatest years at the end of his career, when Allie Sherman began to open up the offense. Rote caught the most passes of his 11-year tenure as a Giant in his final season, with 53 in 1961. He finished as the all-time leader in receptions and receiving yards for the Giants. He was an intelligent, talented man who was so universally admired by his teammates that many of them named sons after him. After retiring as a football player, he had a long, successful career in broadcasting.

Frank Gifford (left), Mel Triplett (33), and Alex Webster (29) combined for an 87-yard pass play and subsequent touchdown run—unfortunately for the Giants, it wasn't enough to top the Colts.

December 11, 1938

Danowski to Soar for Winning Score

Giants Beat Packers for Title 23–17

In 1938, the Giants were the Eastern representatives in the NFL title game for the fourth time in six years. They allowed the fewest points in the league by a wide margin, and they scored the second most. They had beaten the top-scoring Green Bay Packers just three weeks before. Yet the Packers were favored in this game on the strength of their spectacular passing offense and the sheer size of their line—they outweighed the New York line by an average of 10 pounds per man.

The championship game was an exciting, hard-hitting contest in which the teams moved up and down the field despite having had their stars flattened. Mel Hein, who never missed a game in his career, sustained a concussion. Johnny Dell Isola and Ward Cuff had to leave the field. Of most significance for Green Bay, Don Hutson—who had missed the regular-season game against New York with a knee injury—reinjured the knee and limped off early in the second quarter.

The Giants took the lead early when end Jim Lee Howell blocked Clarke Hinkle's punt. Four plays later, Ward Cuff converted a 14-yard field goal. Just four minutes after that, Jim Poole, the Giants' other end, blocked a punt by Cecil Isbell, and the Giants had the ball at the Packers' 28-yard line. A series of runs culminated with Tuffy Leemans's six-yard cutback for the touchdown. Johnny Gildea missed the extra point, but New York had a 9–0 lead at the end of the first period.

The second quarter was filled with back-and-forth excitement. Packers guard Tiny Engebretsen intercepted an Ed Danowski pass, and Arnie Herber followed that with a 40-yard touchdown pass to Hutson's backup, Carl Mulleneaux. Danowski got that one back with a 21-yard touchdown pass to rookie Hap Barnard, but the Packers matched it on a Clarke Hinkle short run after a 66-yard pass play to Wayland Becker. At the half, New York led 16–14.

In the third quarter, the Packers drove down to the Giants' 5, but they were forced to settle for an Engebretsen field goal to take their first and only lead of the day, 17–16. The Giants drove from their 34 to the Packers' 44, where they converted a fourth-and-one on a Hank Soar line buck.

GAME DETAILS

New York Giants 23 • Green Bay Packers 17

Date: December 11, 1938

Location: Polo Grounds, New York

Attendance: 48,120

Significance: NFL title game

Box Score:

Packers	0	14	3	0	**17**
Giants	9	7	7	0	**23**

Scoring:
NYG Cuff 14-yard FG
NYG Leemans 6-yard run (Gildea kick failed)
GBP Mulleneaux 40-yard pass from Herber
   (Engebretsen PAT)

NYG Barnard 21-yard pass from Danowski (Cuff PAT)
GBP Hinkle 1-yard run (Engebretsen PAT)
GBP Engebretsen 15-yard FG
NYG Soar 23-yard pass from Danowski (Cuff PAT)

Team	FD	YDS	RUSH	PASS	RTN	A-C-I	PUNT	FUM	PEN
Packers	14	378	36-164	214	14	19-8-1	8-38	2-2	2-20
Giants	10	212	43-115	97	42	15-8-1	6-52	1-1	2-10

Packers: Herber 123P

Four plays later, from the 23, Danowski and Soar engineered the game-winning play. Danowski took a direct snap with New York aligned in a spread formation. Wingback Soar and end Poole were side by side as they ran straight downfield. Danowski was rushed hard by Packers end Milt Gantenbein, but a great cross block by guard Orville Tuttle obliterated him. Danowski fired into a crowd at the 7-yard line, and Hank Soar outfought teammate Poole and Packers Clarke Hinkle and Herm Schneidman for the ball. Soar then broke Hinkle's tackle at the 3 and plunged into the end zone for a 23–17 lead.

The Packers continued to move the ball, but the sturdy Giants defense refused to yield. The final quarter was scoreless, and the Giants were NFL champions for the third time. Under head coach Steve Owen, New York would return to the NFL Championship Game five more times— but lose each time. This game was the high point of Stout Steve's long career.

HANK SOAR

Hank Soar caught just two regular-season touchdown passes in his nine-year NFL career, so it was surprising that he was the recipient of the game-winner in this NFL title game. Soar was renowned as perhaps the top defensive back of his time. On offense, he was a versatile runner, receiver, and blocker, but not a big star.

Soar left Providence College after his junior year and signed with the Boston Shamrocks of the AFL. One year later, in 1937, he signed with the Giants and

> **I**t was just a jump ball, and I outjumped a bunch of guys from Green Bay.
>
> —HANK SOAR, QUOTED IN *THE NEW YORK TIMES*

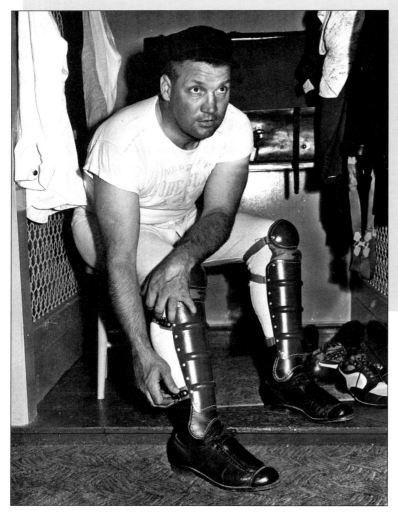

played for them through 1946. He was a tough player who sustained 17 fractures throughout his career, but missed no appreciable time due to his injuries. He was a brash individual who continually mouthed off to head coach Steve Owen, but Owen later called Soar his favorite player because of his spirit and his nose for the ball.

After his football career ended, Soar moved on to other sports. He coached the Providence Steamrollers in the NBA's predecessor, the Basketball Association of America, in 1947. He spent some time refereeing college basketball games in his native New England and then became a baseball umpire. Soar worked as a respected umpire in the major leagues from 1950 through 1975; he then held a supervisory position until 1989, when he retired at age 75. Soar worked first base during Don Larsen's perfect game in the 1956 World Series; he also worked four other World Series and three All-Star games.

Hank Soar scored the game-winning touchdown in the 1938 title game, and later became a distinguished Major League Baseball umpire.
(Photo courtesy of AP Images)

Ed Danowski

Ed Danowski is pretty well forgotten by time, but as his key role in two NFL championships demonstrates, he was one of the finest passers of his era. He did not have a particularly strong arm, but he had great touch and accuracy. He was a clever play caller, protected the ball well, and was a skilled punter and defensive back as well.

The Giants signed Danowski off the nearby Fordham campus, where Wellington Mara was a sophomore in 1934. When starting passer Harry Newman went down to a season-ending injury that year, rookie Danowski led the Giants to the title in the famous "Sneakers Game."

The following season, Danowski held on to the starting job and led the NFL in passing. New York returned to the title game, where they lost to the Lions. Danowski again led the league in passing in 1938, and he topped that with the title-winning touchdown pass to Hank Soar in this game against Green Bay. Ed led the Giants to another title game in 1939 and then retired to play semipro ball in 1940.

The three-time All-Pro returned to the Giants for the second half of 1941, but he then went into the navy for the bulk of World War II. Danowski was named varsity football coach at Fordham in 1946 and continued there until the Rams gave up the sport in 1955. He spent the remainder of his career as a local high school gym teacher and coach.

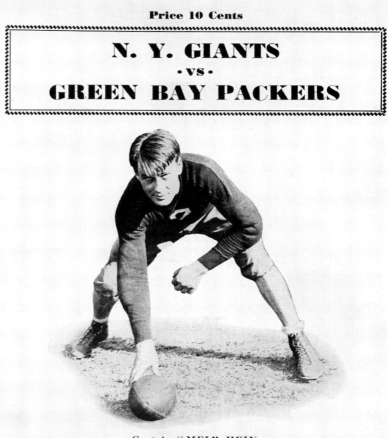

Price 10 Cents

N. Y. GIANTS
· vs ·
GREEN BAY PACKERS

Captain "MEL" HEIN
New York Giants Center
WINNER OF MOST VALUABLE PRO. FOOTBALL PLAYER AWARD

National League Championship Playoff
POLO GROUNDS
Sunday, December 11, 1938

Giants All-Pro Mel Hein sustained a concussion, but Hank Soar scored the game-winning touchdown for the Giants in the 1938 NFL Championship Game. *(Photo courtesy of WireImages)*

TRIUMPHANT TITTLE TOSSES SEVEN TOUCHDOWNS

Giants Bombard Redskins 49–34

The last bastion of the color line in the NFL fell in 1962 when Washington obtained their first black player, Hall of Fame receiver Bobby Mitchell. Just like that, a Redskins team that finished 1–12–1 in 1961 went into Yankee Stadium in Week 7 of the 1962 season undefeated and in first place at 4–0–2. The Giants trailed Washington with a 4–2 record and were expected to be slowed by two key injuries. First, Pro Bowl wide receiver Del Shofner had injured his shoulder in Week 5 against the Steelers, and he had played sparingly in Week 6 against the Lions. Second, ace quarterback Y. A. Tittle hurt his arm against Detroit and hadn't practiced all week. Knowing this, no one would have predicted what unfolded that day.

Tittle got off to a slow start, with six of his first seven passes falling incomplete. Things got worse after the Giants' Johnny Counts muffed a punt and Redskins quarterback Norm Snead hit Bobby Mitchell for a 44-yard score on the next play. After the ensuing kickoff, New York finally got a drive going despite two holding penalties, and Tittle hit Joe Morrison for a 22-yard touchdown to even the score.

The second quarter got underway with an interception of Snead by Erich Barnes. Tittle drove the Giants down the field on passes to Shofner, and then hit former Redskins tight end Joe Walton for a four-yard touchdown. Snead countered with another drive and touchdown pass, although Sam Huff blocked the extra point to retain a one-point New York lead. Another long pass to Shofner took the Giants to the Washington 4-yard line, and Tittle's two-yard pass to Joe Morrison right before the half was his third touchdown pass of the day.

On the first play of the second half, Snead got the Redskins back in the game with an 80-yard bomb to Mitchell, but the Giants took complete control of the game on the ensuing posession. Five straight

Y. A. Tittle tosses one of his seven touchdown passes against the Redskins on October 28, 1962.

GAME DETAILS

New York Giants 49 • Washington Redskins 34

Date: October 28, 1962

Location: Yankee Stadium, New York

Attendance: 62,844

Significance: Midseason showdown of the two teams atop the East

Box Score:

Redskins	7	6	7	14	**34**
Giants	7	14	21	7	**49**

Scoring:
WSH Mitchell 44-yard pass from Snead (Khayat PAT)
NYG Morrison 22-yard pass from Tittle (Chandler PAT)
NYG Walton 4-yard pass from Tittle (Chandler PAT)
WSH Dugan 24-yard pass from Snead
  (Khayat kick blocked)
NYG Morrison 2-yard pass from Tittle (Chandler PAT)
WSH Mitchell 80-yard pass from Snead (Khayat PAT)
NYG Shofner 32-yard pass from Tittle (Chandler PAT)
NYG Walton 26-yard pass from Tittle (Chandler PAT)
NYG Gifford 63-yard pass from Tittle (Chandler PAT)
NYG Walton 6-yard pass from Tittle (Chandler PAT)
WSH Snead 1-yard run (Khayat PAT)
WSH Junker 35-yard pass from Snead (Khayat PAT)

Team	FD	YDS	RUSH	PASS	A-C-I	PUNT	FUM	PEN
Redskins	19	374	19-59	316	40-17-3	6-31	1	35
Giants	25	602	28-97	505	39-27-0	4-47	0	127

Redskins: Snead 346P, Mitchell 158C
Giants: Tittle 505P, Shofner 269C, Gifford 127C

It would have been in bad taste.

—Y. A. TITTLE, IN RESPONSE TO CALLS FROM TEAMMATES AND FANS TO GO FOR EIGHT TOUCHDOWN PASSES

Y. A. Tittle

Y. A. Tittle was just the third quarterback in NFL history to throw for seven touchdowns in a game, and his 505 yards passing was a Giants record until 1985, when Phil Simms threw for 513 in a game. In fact, Tittle's three-year stretch of unparalleled quarterbacking in the early 1960s catapulted him into the Hall of Fame.

Tittle began his career in the All-America Football Conference with the original Baltimore Colts. He then spent a decade in San Francisco as part of the 49ers' "Million-Dollar Backfield" with Joe Perry, Hugh McElhenny, and John Henry Johnson. Tittle was a very precise passer with a sidearm throwing motion. He was one of the better quarterbacks in the league, but he never got to a championship game. In 1961, the 49ers shifted to the shotgun offense and felt they had no need for a 35-year-old quarterback, so they traded Tittle to New York for forgettable lineman Lou Cordileone.

Tittle came into a difficult situation in New York—supplanting the 40-year-old respected veteran Charley Conerly—but ultimately his leadership knit the whole team together into one unit. Tittle led the aging Giants to three straight NFL Championship Games from 1961 to 1963; he won Player of the Year recognition each year. In those three years, Tittle threw for 86 touchdowns, including a record 33 in 1962 and a record 36 the following season. In the two latter seasons, he threw for more than 3,000 yards and ran the best passing offense in the NFL. The Giants lost all three title games, however, and then time ran out on Tittle and the team in 1964. Despite his brief time in blue, the Giants retired Tittle's No. 14 jersey because of his unequalled passing.

Tittle completions culminated with a 32-yard touchdown to Shofner. Tittle's fifth touchdown pass went to Walton for 26 yards, and his sixth to Frank Gifford for 63 yards. The league record for touchdown passes in a game was seven, held by Sid Luckman and Adrian Burk, so that left Tittle just one shy. In the midst of this scoring explosion, Y. A. completed 12 passes in a row, just one short of another NFL record, as the Giants took a commanding 42–20 lead into the fourth quarter.

Midway through the final period, Tittle hit Shofner again for 50 yards to take the ball to the Washington 15. Three plays later came the record-tying seventh touchdown pass on a well-crafted play. With Walton and Gifford on the right side, the two ran crisscrossing patterns—Gifford in and Walton out—that confused Washington's secondary and left Walton all alone by the flag, where Tittle hit him for the last touchdown. The crowd began calling for touchdown pass number eight, but Tittle took the air out of the ball with the Giants up by 29 points. The Redskins managed two late touchdowns to make the score closer, but Tittle did not counter with any further air strikes.

For the day, Shofner caught 11 passes for 269 yards, and Tittle completed 27-of-39 for 505 yards and those seven touchdowns—not bad for a couple of banged-up veterans. The Giants were within a game of first place; they would not lose again until the championship game against the Packers. By contrast, the upstart Redskins would lose seven of their last eight games and finish in fourth place in the East.

DEL SHOFNER

Y. A. Tittle's roommate also came to the Giants in a 1961 trade, and he gave Tittle the best target he ever had. Del Shofner was a tall, wispy, injury-prone receiver who had great hands and blazing speed. He and Tittle teamed up to form the best long-ball threat in the game, as they showed on a 32-yard touchdown on this day of seven touchdown passes.

Shofner was originally drafted by the Rams with a number-one pick they had obtained from the Giants for Hall of Fame defensive end Andy Robustelli. Shofner first played defensive back but then was shifted to receiver, and he led the NFL in receiving yards in his second season.

After an injury-riddled 1960 season, Shofner was dealt to the Giants for a first-round draft pick. He led the Giants in receiving for the next three seasons, setting a club record in 1961 with 68 catches. He went over 1,000 yards each year from 1961 to 1963 and scored 32 touchdowns in that time, only missing one game to injury. Age and injuries caught up to him after 1963, though. In his last four seasons, he only played in 37 games and caught 54 passes for just three touchdowns. For his career, he averaged 18.5 yards per catch and was a five-time All-Pro.

Wide receiver Del Shofner teamed with Y.A. Tittle to form one of the game's most dangerous passing combinations. *(Photo courtesy of WireImages)*

THE SEVENTH SCORE

On the final touchdown pass, Joe Walton (80) and Frank Gifford (16) are on the right side. Both head straight down the field, and then Gifford breaks in and Walton breaks out as they crisscross. Both Washington's safety (41) and cornerback (20) stay with Gifford, although the corner should have switched his coverage to Walton after the crisscross. The result is an uncovered Walton at the flag, and he catches an easy toss from Tittle (14) for the score.

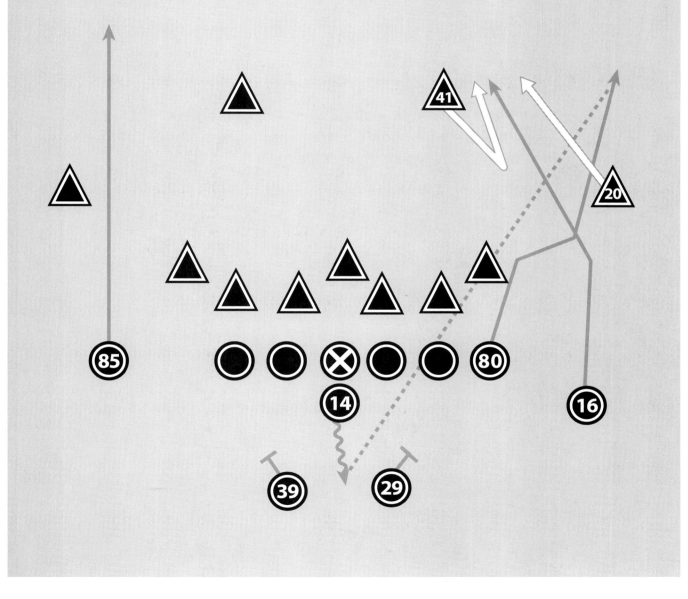

December 9, 1934

21 A STRONG RUN FOR THE TITLE

Giants Perform Soft-Shoe on Bears in Fourth Quarter

The defending champion Chicago Bears came into this NFL title game against the Giants with a 13–0 record. They had the best offense in the league and their defense was second only to the Lions. The Giants were a good team that finished 8–5, but they had lost to the Bears twice already in 1934, and six out of the last seven times the two teams had met. Furthermore, end Red Badgro was out with a broken leg and tailback Harry Newman was out with broken vertebrae, which he had suffered in a loss to the Bears three weeks before. In their places, end Ike Frankian and tailback Ed Danowski would perform heroically on this icy nine-degree day at the Polo Grounds.

New York scored first with a Ken Strong field goal in the first quarter, but they were nearly run out of the stadium in the second period. Behind a pounding running attack, the Bears marched down the field and scored early in the quarter on a Bronko Nagurski one-yard thrust. Nagurski led the Bears back into the Giants' red zone on their next possession, but the Giants held, and Jack Manders kicked a field goal to extend the Bears' lead to 10–3.

Nagurski next recovered a fumble by Ken Strong at the 6-yard line and then scored on the next play, but the play was erased by an offside penalty. Manders then missed a 24-yard field-goal attempt. Once more, however, Chicago marched deep into Giants territory. Once more, Nagurski plunged into the end zone only to have the play nullified by a penalty, and once more Manders missed a field goal. The Giants were fortunate to go to halftime only down 10–3.

> **I** think the sneakers gave them the edge in the second half. They were able to cut back when they were running with the ball, and we weren't able to cut with them.
>
> **—BRONKO NAGURSKI, IN *THE GIANTS OF NEW YORK* BY BARRY GOTTEHRER**

The Bears and Giants collided on the icy field at the Polo Grounds in the 1934 NFL Championship Game, forever known as the "Sneakers Game." *(Photo courtesy of WireImages)*

Lineman John Dell Isola and the Giants switched to basketball shoes for the second half of the "Sneakers Game," giving them a huge edge over the Bears.

GAME DETAILS

New York Giants 30 • Chicago Bears 13

Date: December 9, 1934

Location: Polo Grounds, New York

Attendance: 35,059

Significance: NFL title game

Box Score:

Bears	0	10	3	0	**13**
Giants	3	0	0	27	**30**

Scoring:
NYG Strong 38-yard FG
CHI Nagurski 1-yard run (Manders PAT)
CHI Manders 17-yard FG
CHI Manders 24-yard FG

NYG Frankian 28-yard pass from Danowski (Strong PAT)
NYG Strong 42-yard run (Strong PAT)
NYG Strong 11-yard run (Strong kick failed)
NYG Danowski 8-yard run (Molenda PAT)

Team	FD	YDS	RUSH	PASS	RTN	A-C-I	PUNT	FUM	PEN
Bears	10	165	46-89	76	83	13-6-3	9-41	5-0	4-30
Giants	12	276	37-173	103	76	13-7-2	6-46	5-2	0-0

Before the game, end Ray Flaherty told head coach Steve Owen that rubber-soled sneakers might provide better footing on the iced-over Polo Grounds surface. Locker-room attendant Abe Cohen was dispatched to Manhattan College to borrow some basketball shoes, since sporting-goods stores were closed on Sunday. At halftime, Cohen returned with several pairs of sneakers, and some of the Giants slipped them on. As the third quarter progressed, the rest of the team changed their footwear during breaks in the action.

The Bears upped their lead to 13–3 on another Manders field goal in the third period, but things began to turn around as the Giants moved the ball to the Bears' 12. But Chicago's Ed Kawal ended the threat by intercepting an Ed Danowski pass at the 4. Ken Strong returned the subsequent Bears punt to the Chicago 30, though, and the Giants were in business as the fourth quarter began.

Danowski dropped back to pass and appeared to underthrow Dale Burnett in the end zone. Chicago's Carl Brumbaugh got his hands on the ball at the 2, but end Ike Frankian wrestled it out of Brumbaugh's arms for a 28-yard touchdown pass, drawing the Giants within three points of the Bears.

Soon, New York had the ball in Chicago territory again at the 42, and it was Ken Strong's turn. This play offered convincing proof that the Giants were now in control. Strong took a direct snap as the entire Giants

Ken Strong

In addition to his 17 points, Ken Strong also ran for 94 yards on just nine carries in this title game. Strong was a triple-threat back who could pass, punt, and kick as well as block and catch. He was a slashing, battering runner who scored 484 points in the NFL, more than 300 of them in his stop-and-go career as a New York Giant.

Strong led the nation with 162 points as a senior at NYU in 1928. The Giants tried to sign him but were outbid by the Staten Island Stapletons. Ken led Staten Island in scoring all four years he played there, and topped them in rushing three times. He scored 47 percent of the team's points, but the Stapes could only win 43 percent of their games and went out of business in 1932. Strong was also a Detroit Tigers baseball prospect who hit 41 home runs in the minors in 1930, but a broken wrist and a subsequent botched surgery devoted him wholly to football.

Strong finally signed for his first tour with the Giants in 1933; he tied for the league lead in points that year with 64. In 1936, though, he got into a salary dispute with the team and signed with the fledgling American Football League. However, the AFL lasted only two seasons, and Strong found himself banned from the NFL for three years for jumping leagues. After a year with the Giants' Jersey City farm team, Strong rejoined the Giants as a 33-year-old kicker in 1939, but he retired at the end of the season owing to a bleeding ulcer. Then during World War II, the Giants brought Strong back for a third tour of duty, again just as a place-kicker. After four seasons, he retired for good at age 41 in 1947.

The Giants weren't done with Ken yet, though. In 1950, he wrote an instructional book on kicking called *Football Kicking Techniques*, and the Giants brought Strong back for a fourth time—as kicking coach, in 1962—when punter Don Chandler was being asked to place-kick. After four seasons as a kicking advisor, Strong was let go when the team signed soccer-style kicker Pete Gogolak in 1966. The following year, Strong was elected to the Hall of Fame, honoring a long and winding career spent entirely in New York. The Giants retired his No. 50 jersey.

---

line surged straight ahead (with Bo Molenda as the lead blocker from the backfield), shoving the entire Bears line onto its collective back. Strong slid to the left, pushed off the referee standing in his path at the 35, broke a tackle at the 32, and thundered untouched the remaining 30 yards for the go-ahead touchdown.

Another long drive by the Giants was capped by an 11-yard Strong cutback run to the right for his second touchdown. Although he missed the extra point, Strong had tallied 17 points, and the Giants led 23–13. A desperate Bears pass was then nabbed by Molenda, and the Giants took over on the Chicago 22. Four plays later,

Ed Danowski slithered in from the 9 to conclude the scoring in this huge upset, which has been known ever since as the "Sneakers Game."

The Giants were NFL champions for the second time, owing their victory to a four-touchdown detonation in the fourth quarter that was at least partly fueled by their change of footwear. However, another advantage for New York in that final period came when their water buckets froze and trainer Gus Mauch substituted swigs of whiskey from paper cups during timeouts. This frigid title game gave everyone a real warm feeling.

RAMBO RUMBLES THROUGH SAN FRANCISCO

Bavaro's 31-Yard Reception Keys Comeback Win over 49ers

Tied with the Redskins for first place in their division, the Giants rolled into San Francisco on a five-game winning streak for a *Monday Night Football* battle with the resurgent 49ers. This demanding and vital game would prove just how resilient and resourceful the 1986 Giants were on the road to the Super Bowl. However, it would take an extra-effort play by their sturdy tight end to spark them in the second half.

This Monday night showdown was Joe Montana's fourth game after returning from early-season back surgery that could have ended his career. But there was no rustiness evident in the first half. The 49ers dominated offensively and were up by 17–0 at the half on two touchdowns by Jerry Rice. Meanwhile, the ground attack of the ball-control Giants was being shut down by the stingy 49ers defense. For the game, the Giants would gain a paltry 13 yards rushing.

It was up to Phil Simms to shake things up with his arm. Ten minutes and 15 plays in the third quarter would prove crucial; the first play was the most decisive of all. The Giants first got the ball on the 49ers' 49-yard line, and Simms promptly hit tight end Mark Bavaro with a nine-yard pass over the middle. Two

49ers linebackers immediately tried to bring down Bavaro with arm tackles, but they slid right off him. Then Ronnie Lott jumped on Bavaro's back, but the tight end carried the fierce 49ers safety for a rough 17-yard ride as four other San Francisco defenders came in and hit Bavaro from the side, finally bringing him down at the 18.

Bavaro's astounding 31-yard reception got New York unstuck. Even though he later modestly attributed the gain to poor tackling, the dynamic catch-and-carry fired up the team. Three plays later, Simms slipped a short pass to Joe Morris, who went into the end zone from the 17 for the first Giants touchdown.

The next time the Giants got the ball, they started at their own 29. Four plays later, they faced a fourth-and-two at their own 49. Aggressively, New York went for it on fourth down; as Bill Parcells forcefully explained later, "I was trying to win the game." Simms handed the ball to Morris, who had thus far carried nine times for zero yards, and he ran around the weak-side end for a 17-yard pickup and a first down. On the next play, Simms hit Stacy Robinson for a 34-yard touchdown pass that Robinson let roll down to his legs before he secured the ball, and the

Game Details

New York Giants 21 • San Francisco 49ers 17

Date: December 1, 1986

Location: Candlestick Park, San Francisco

Attendance: 59,777

Significance: Two top teams trying to keep pace in their divisions on *Monday Night Football*

Box Score:

Giants	0	0	21	0	**21**
49ers	3	14	0	0	**17**

Scoring:
SF Wersching 30-yard FG
SF Rice 11-yard pass from Montana (Wersching PAT)
SF Rice 1-yard run (Wersching PAT)
NYG Morris 17-yard pass from Simms (Allegre PAT)
NYG Robinson 34-yard pass from Simms (Allegre PAT)
NYG Anderson 1-yard run (Allegre PAT)

Team	FD	YDS	RUSH	PASS	RTN	A-C-I	Sacked	PUNT	FUM	PEN
Giants	20	397	19-13	384	136	38-27-2	1-4	3-41	2-1	1-5
49ers	26	367	27-116	251	99	52-32-1	0-0	5-43	1-0	6-25

Giants: Simms 388P; 49ers: Montana 251P

Giants were within three points.

In short order, the Giants got the ball at their own 29 again. They moved the ball to midfield in three plays, and then Simms hit Robinson for a 49-yard bomb to the 1. From there, Ottis Anderson punched in the go-ahead touchdown with more than three minutes still left in the third quarter. Simms had completed eight of nine passes for 175 yards in the three rapid-fire Giants scoring drives.

When the Giants intercepted Montana's next pass and returned it to the San Francisco 39, it looked like New York was ready to put the game away for good. However, Bavaro fumbled the ball at the 6, and the last quarter was a hard-fought struggle between two great teams. In the final minutes, Montana began one of his patented comeback drives, leading the 49ers to the Giants' 17 with 1:16 left to play.

But on third-and-four, Wendell Tyler was stopped for a three-yard loss by Gary Reasons. He also fumbled the ball, but the play was allowed to stand. Then on fourth-and-seven from the 20, Montana was hit by linebacker Andy Headen as he tried to throw to Roger Craig over the middle, and the pass dropped harmlessly to the ground. The Giants had a great comeback win over a tough rival and were on track for a super season.

MARK BAVARO

Mark Bavaro did not like the handle "Rambo"—which his teammates gave him for his resemblance to the Sylvester Stallone movie character—because he found it disrespectful to the men who fought in the Vietnam War. Out of respect for this quiet, powerful tight end and popular teammate, his fellow Giants quickly dropped the nickname.

Bavaro was a tough football player who sank to the fourth round of the 1985 draft after suffering through knee and shoulder injuries and coaching problems at Notre Dame. In New York, he gamely played through foot and toe injuries, a broken jaw, neck sprains, and multiple knee surgeries during his six years as a Giant. While this famous reception against the 49ers may have been extreme, it was not unusual for Bavaro to drag tacklers with him as he gained extra yards after a catch. Perhaps even more impressive was

> **M**ark [Bavaro is] very intelligent. He's also very gentle, although I don't suppose that the 49ers would agree with that.
>
> —PHIL MCCONKEY, *SIMMS TO MCCONKEY*

his blocking; he regularly took on defensive ends all by himself. He took pride in being a complete tight end, excellent at both blocking and receiving.

Bavaro missed the 1991 season after having knee surgery, and then signed on for a year in Cleveland and two in Philadelphia before retiring. He set a Giants record for receptions in a game, catching 12 in a 1985 game against Cincinnati (later broken by Tiki Barber with 13), and was a two-time All-Pro.

Tight end Mark Bavaro's sure-handed heroics fueled the Giants' second-half comeback against the 49ers on *Monday Night Football*.

JOE MORRIS

Joe Morris's key 17-yard power burst on a fourth-and-two at midfield was typical of his reliability in the clutch. Bill Parcells liked to say of the undersized runner, "He's not small, he's short." Morris was 5'7" but was solidly built at 195 pounds. He had broken all the rushing records at Syracuse set by notable predecessors Jim Brown, Ernie Davis, Floyd Little, and Larry Csonka. The Giants picked him in the second round of the 1982 draft, but Morris found himself lodged behind first-round pick Butch Woolfolk. Morris finally began to earn playing time in 1984 as Woolfolk fell into disfavor, but then the Giants drafted George Adams with the 19th pick in 1985.

By then, though, Morris was ready to break out. He rushed for a team-record 1,336 yards and 21 touchdowns in 1985, and he exceeded 100 yards rushing in six different games as Adams faded from view. Both Parcells and offensive coordinator Ron Erhardt cited Morris's increased patience and improved ability to read his blocking as the factors that enabled Joe's great advance. Morris followed that season with 1,516 yards rushing and eight 100-yard games in the 1986 Super Bowl season. That record-setting season included back-to-back 181-yard games against the Redskins and the Cowboys in leading the Giants to the playoffs.

After those two great seasons, though, it was a quick downhill slide. Those two seasons were two of only three in his eight-year career in which he averaged more than four yards per carry. In 1985 and

> **P**hil Simms was great today. He proved you can shut down Joe Morris, but then you have to deal with Phil Simms.
>
> —JOE MORRIS

1986, Morris gained more than half his career rushing yards and scored 70 percent of his touchdowns. In that time, though, he was arguably the best runner in the league and a giant on the field who keyed New York's ground attack.

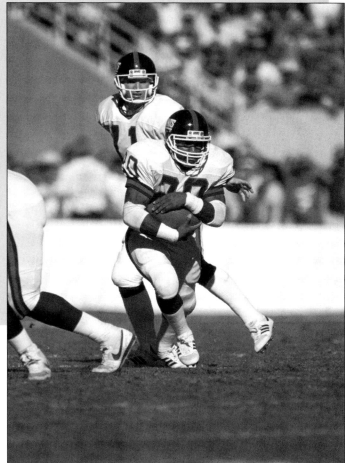

Running back Joe Morris led the Giants in rushing during the 1985–1986 seasons.

October 1, 1950

19 Owen Opens Umbrella on Browns

Giants Shut Out Cleveland 6–0

The Cleveland Browns laid waste to the rest of the All-America Football Conference in the late 1940s, winning four championships in four years and losing only four games total. In their first two games in the NFL after the two leagues merged in 1950, the Browns continued right on, outscoring the Eagles and the Colts 66–10 on the road. The Eagles, who lost 35–10, were the defending NFL champs and had the best defense in the league. For their first home game, however, the Browns would receive a surprising comeuppance from the Giants.

The Giants were coming off a mediocre 6–6 1949 season, but they had been bolstered by an influx of five talented players from the AAFC's disbanded New York Yankees. In particular, the Giants' defense had been remade, now featuring Hall of Fame defensive tackle Arnie Weinmeister and three terrific defensive backs—Otto Schnellbacher, Harmon Rowe, and Tom Landry. Those three defensive backs joined with holdover safety Emlen Tunnell to form

the key to the new defensive formation that Steve Owen unveiled for this first meeting with the Browns, the 6-1-4, or umbrella defense.

Most defenses at the time consisted of six- or seven-man lines with just three defensive backs. The onset of vibrant passing attacks like Cleveland's, though, called for a new scheme. Owen's approach was a six-man line with the two ends dropping back into coverage, backed by a middle linebacker and four defensive backs. It stymied the great Browns offense.

The Giants scored midway through the first quarter on a short run by Eddie Price to conclude a 51-yard drive. Meanwhile, Cleveland's great quarterback Otto Graham completed none of his 10 passes and threw three interceptions in the first half.

Cleveland improved a bit in the second half by relying on short passes, and Graham completed 12 of 21 for 123 yards. Twice in the fourth quarter, the Browns threatened to score. The first time, they reached the 10-yard line, but on first down Landry

Coach Steve Owen unleashed the umbrella defense on the Browns in 1950—the rest is football history. *(Photo courtesy of AP Images)*

STEVE OWEN

Owner Tim Mara called 250-pound tackle "Stout Steve" Owen to his office before the 1931 season and told him that he was tired of looking for uniforms that would fit him—so he was making Owen the new coach of the Giants. Steve would last for 23 years as coach and would establish the precepts of Giants football—tough defense, ball-control offense, and a reliable kicking game—that have guided the team throughout its history. The garrulous Owen was popular with the New York press; he stated in his autobiography, "Coaching is a matter of fundamentals, the hardest kind of work, and an understanding of human relations."

Even before the umbrella defense, Owen was quite an innovator. George Halas credited him with being the first to emphasize defense and to highly value field goals over touchdowns. During his time, the Giants were known for the special defenses Steve would devise to control opposing superstars like Don Hutson and Sammy Baugh.

Moreover, Owen was the first to keep his troops fresh by substituting virtually an entire unit each quarter. He was the first to regularly elect to kick off when his team won the opening coin toss, so that his defense could get on the field first. Owen also ran his own version of the single-wing—the A-formation—in which the line would be unbalanced to one side and the backfield shifted to the opposite side.

Owen was a disciplinarian who was described by his older players as being good-hearted and down-to-earth. However, by the 1950s, time was beginning to pass him by. He had to be pushed hard to move to the T-formation, and he was one of the last coaches to do so. In his autobiography, *The Whole Ten Yards*, Frank Gifford remembered Owen as "a fat snarly Oklahoman who dipped snuff—the juice would dribble onto his dirty rubber jacket—and stuck rigidly to his 'old ways' of doing things." Indeed, Owen's Giants were 110–60–14 from 1931 to 1946, but in his last seven years only 41–40–3.

Wellington Mara remembered the firing of Steve Owen, who never had a written contract with the Giants, as one of the worst days of his life. Owen never got over it, although he later coached the defense for the Eagles and even returned as a head coach in the 1960s in the Continental Football League. He was elected to the Hall of Fame posthumously.

Some call me a defensive coach and sneer when they say it. Well, I'll take that, if you allow that the object of the game is to win. I would rather win by 3–0 than lose by 38–36. Defense is still half the game, and I like defense. As a coach, I would have to like it, because it has to work if I want to win.

—STEVE OWEN, *MY KIND OF FOOTBALL*

GAME DETAILS

New York Giants 6 • Cleveland Browns 0

Date: October 1, 1950

Location: Municipal Stadium, Cleveland

Attendance: 37,647

Significance: A revolutionary defense shuts down the best team in football

Box Score:

Giants	6	0	0	0	**6**
Browns	0	0	0	0	**0**

Scoring:
NYG Price 2-yard run (Poole missed kick)

Team	FD	YDS	RUSH	PASS	RTN	A-C-I	PUNT	FUM	PEN
Giants	8	197	136	61	45	13-4-0	10-41	2-1	6-62
Browns	12	250	123	127	42	31-12-4	7-50	2-1	8-71

knocked a pass away from Dante Lavelli, and on second down Marion Motley fumbled the handoff and lost the ball to New York. Then, in the closing minutes of the game, Graham faced fourth-and-10 from the Giants' 11 and tried to hit Horace Gillom, but Schnellbacher batted the pass away to clinch the victory.

The 6–0 final score marked the first time that the Browns had ever been shut out; they would not be shut out again until the Giants repeated the trick in a 1958 playoff game. Owen said of his defense, "We have a smart, alert group of men whose defensive maneuvers kept the Browns off balance throughout the game."

The Giants would beat the Browns again three weeks later, 17–13, by altering their defensive strategy, having the ends rush the passer more than dropping into coverage, and at times going to a 5–1–5 nickel coverage defense. Both teams finished the season at 10–2. When they met in a playoff game, the Browns finally got the best of New York in another defensive slugfest, 8–3. The Giants' lone touchdown in that loss was nullified by a penalty.

THE UMBRELLA DEFENSE

The two keys to the Giants' umbrella defense were a defensive backfield of four men and a front line of six, including two ends who had the responsibility to drop into short pass coverage. In retrospect, it's easy to see how this basic concept would be developed further by Tom Landry into the 4-3-4 defense, which has been the base defense of professional football for more than 50 years. At the time, though, the umbrella—so named because the dropping ends combine with the defensive backs to resemble an opening umbrella, with the middle linebacker looking like the stem—was revolutionary; it offered a variety of blitz, shift, and zone coverage options for its practitioners.

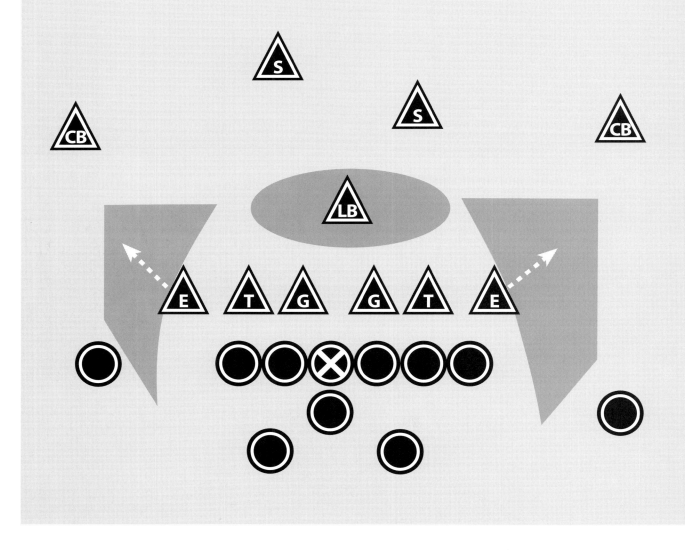

Tom Landry

All Steve Owen announced to his team as they were getting ready to face the Browns for the first time in 1950 was that the defense would play in a 6-1-4 arrangement. With that, he called 26-year-old defensive back and de facto defensive coach, Tom Landry, to the blackboard and handed him the chalk.

In Landry's phrase, Owen was "not a detail man"; Landry was very much a detail man, though. Remarkably, World War II veteran Landry was in his first year as a Giants player at the time, having spent his rookie season with the Yankees in the All-America Football Conference. Thus began a Hall of Fame coaching career that would last nearly 40 years.

While Landry is primarily remembered as the expressionless genius in the Homburg hat who prowled the Dallas Cowboys sideline, he first honed his skills in New York. In the mid-1950s, he combined the Giants' umbrella defense and the Eagles' 5-2 defense to come up with the 4-3 base defense that NFL teams have

used ever since. Landry's defense relied on maintaining discipline, reading formation and movement keys, and carrying out assignments precisely. He was never comfortable with freelancers, even if they were Hall of Fame players like Emlen Tunnell in New York or Herb Adderley in Dallas. He preferred system players like Andy Robustelli, Harland Svare, and Sam Huff.

A case could be made that Landry was the greatest coach in NFL history, in that he not only devised the base defense used by most teams in the past half-century but also introduced the multiple-set motion offense to the league in response to that defense. Let's not forget, either, that when he was in New York, he also was the kicking coach for Pat Summerall. With Landry coaching the defense and Vince Lombardi the offense, the Giants of the late 1950s had the two greatest assistant coaches in NFL history. It's ironic that neither was available to replace Jim Lee Howell when he stepped down in 1961.

Hall of Fame quarterback Otto Graham and his Cleveland teammates were befuddled by Steve Owens's defensive formation.

September 17, 2006

18 Eli's Coming Back
Manning Hits Burress in Overtime to Ground Eagles

One never knows what strange things to expect from an Eagles-Giants game, and this one was as unpredictable as could be. After the Giants took the opening kickoff and drove right down the field to score on a touchdown pass to Amani Toomer, the lights went out for New York. The Eagles scored the next 24 points over the first three quarters and led 24–7 going into the fourth. Philadelphia had outgained the Giants 406 yards to 108, and Donovan McNabb had outpassed Eli Manning 320 yards to 146. Manning had been sacked six times, and Eagles-killer Tiki Barber had just 14 yards on 10 carries.

It all changed in the most improbable fashion: the Giants started their magnificent road comeback by fumbling. As the fourth quarter started, the Giants had reached their own 45-yard line, having started the drive at their own 9 four minutes before. A run and a pass gave New York a first down on the Eagles' 39. Manning dropped back again and hit Plaxico Burress over the middle. As Burress was being tackled, Brian Dawkins stripped the ball at the 16. Eagles safety Michael Lewis tried to fall on the ball at the 5, but it bounced into the end zone,

where the Giants' Tim Carter recovered it for an incredible touchdown.

But even with this good fortune, time was running out. Neither the Eagles nor the Giants could move the ball the next two times they had it, and the Eagles started to run out the clock. However, Eagles star Brian Westbrook fumbled at his own 32, and the Giants recovered the ball with 4:11 to play. Four plays later, Manning hit Amani Toomer for a 22-yard touchdown, and New York trailed by only three with 3:28 to go.

Philadelphia managed just one first down and then punted back to the Giants, who took over on their own 20 with no timeouts and 58 seconds left. New York moved to midfield with 15 seconds to go. Manning then hit Jeremy Shockey at the Eagles' 32, and Eagles defensive end Trent Cole was flagged 15 more yards for trying to kick Giants guard Kareem McKenzie. That loss of composure by Philadelphia allowed Jay Feely to kick his game-tying field goal from 35 yards away instead of 50. The game was sent into overtime.

While both teams were physically drained on this 79-degree day, the Eagles were shell-shocked as well. Neither team could score on its first possession, but New

York began to move on its second chance. Twelve plays took the Giants from their own 15 to the Eagles' 31 and set the stage for the game-winning play. Facing a third-and-11, Manning realized an all-out blitz was coming and alerted Burress to look up fast.

Manning dropped back swiftly, but just as quickly blitzing safety Brian Dawkins was in his face. Eli tossed a high arcing pass to the 6'5" Burress over the head of Eagles cornerback Sheldon Brown; Burress caught it at the 5, carrying Brown into the end zone with him for the win. Burress jumped up and threw the ball into the stands while the normally stoic Manning leaped into the arms of guard Chris Snee to punctuate this thrilling Giants victory. Meanwhile, the thoroughly dehydrated Amani Toomer and Tim Carter had to be helped from the field and needed multiple IV bags in the locker room before they could truly savor this great win.

Plaxico Burress catches the 31-yard game-winning touchdown pass ahead of reaching Eagles cornerback Sheldon Brown. *(Photo courtesy of AP Images)*

We knew it would be an all-out blitz, so I told Plaxico I was going to drop back as fast as I could and throw it up as high as I could. At 6'6", either he's going to catch it or no one else is. On that play, I don't want to take a sack because that puts us out of field-goal range. It's a great play by Plax, making that catch.

—ELI MANNING

ELI MANNING

Every time Eli Manning gave a great performance, football pundits would speculate about whether it signaled a new level of his maturation or was merely an exceptional game that again indicated his immense potential. In his first four years, Manning exhibited a strong penchant for inconsistency not uncommon for young quarterbacks, but as his days of youthful inexperience dwindled, his tendency to mix great throws with awful misses or confounding interceptions began to look like the real Eli.

Eli Manning, of course, followed his famous father Archie (number two overall draft pick in 1971) and brother Peyton (number one overall draft pick in 1998) as the number one overall draft choice of San Diego in 2004. Except, à la John Elway in 1983, he announced before the draft that he would never play for the Chargers, and thus forced a trade to the Giants who coveted him. The Giants gave up their 2004 number one pick (quarterback Philip Rivers) as well as another number one pick, plus a third and a fifth, for Manning's rights. Before Super Bowl XLII, Giants fans wondered whether he was worth the high price.

From season to season, there was incremental improvement in Manning's completion percentage and passer rating, but the maddening inconsistency of both quarterback and team continued. While his arm and ability were unquestioned, his quiet demeanor and somewhat lethargic personality bred doubt as to his eventual success. Before he died, quarterback guru Bill Walsh said that it was time for Eli to stop being Peyton's little brother and become the Giants' quarterback. It was time in 2007. In his fifth year, Phil Simms made a quantum leap forward and spent the next decade as a top NFL quarterback; Giants fans saw Manning make that leap in winning the title as Super Bowl MVP. Ultimately, it's only in retrospect that we will know his historic rank among quarterbacks, but he has come of age. There will be times when he reverts to his skittish inaccuracy, but he scaled the NFL mountain in 2007.

Leading the late comeback against Philadelphia in 2006 was a major step in the maturation of quarterback Eli Manning.

GAME DETAILS

New York Giants 30 • Philadelphia Eagles 24

Date: September 18, 2006

Location: Lincoln Financial Field, Philadelphia

Attendance: 69,241

Significance: Division rivals at it again

Box Score:

Giants	7	0	0	17	6	**30**
Eagles	7	10	7	0	0	**24**

Scoring:
NYG Toomer 37-yard pass from Manning (Feely PAT)
PHL Stallworth 20-yard pass from McNabb (Akers PAT)
PHL Akers 37-yard FG
PHL Brown 23-yard pass from McNabb (Akers PAT)
NYG Carter fumble recovery in end zone (Feely PAT)
NYG Toomer 22-yard pass from Manning (Feely PAT)
NYG Feely 35-yard FG
NYG Burress 31-yard pass from Manning

Team	FD	YDS	RUSH	PASS	RTN	A-C-I	Sacked	PUNT	FUM	PEN
Giants	24	404	26-86	318	109	43-31-1	8-53	8-44	3-0	9-75
Eagles	23	451	30-107	344	134	45-27-0	1-6	5-44	1-1	10-66

Giants: Manning 371P, Toomer 137C, Burress 114C
Eagles: McNabb 350P, Smith 111C

EXTENDING THE PLAYBOOK

The beautiful thing about football is that things can turn around in a hurry at any time in the strangest ways. The Giants won this game because Plaxico Burress was stripped of the ball in Eagles territory, and the ball bounced just right for them. When Brian Dawkins pried the ball loose, the closest player to it was Eagles safety Michael Lewis. Lewis fell on the ball at the 5. However, tight end Visanthe Shiancoe knocked Lewis off the ball, and it rolled into the end zone, where a hustling Tim Carter beat the Eagles' Joselio Hanson to the ball.

Burress said, "I told Tim Carter I owe him a steak dinner, lobster, a glass of merlot—something. It's probably one of the best fumbles I've ever had."

PETE PREVITE SPECIAL BURNS BIRDS

Equipment Manager's Play Results in a Touchdown

The 6–2 Giants met the 7–1 Eagles midway through the 1961 season in a game for first place in the East; it was a game of spectacularly designed plays and lucky bounces. Both high-flying teams had new coaches and new starting quarterbacks this year. The defending champion Eagles were now coached by Nick Skorich and led by Sonny Jurgensen, while the Giants were coached by Allie Sherman and quarterbacked by veteran Y. A. Tittle. In a game of major importance and with Hall of Fame stars on both sides, however, it was a Yankee Stadium clubhouse attendant who made the most memorable contribution to New York's victory.

The Giants drove down the field the first time they got the ball, and fans got an early indication that this would be a game of surprises. From the Eagles' 30-yard line, Tittle went back to pass and scrambled to his right. Spotting Kyle Rote in the end zone, Tittle let go on the move but badly underthrew his target. Cornerback Jimmy Carr batted the ball in the air at the 5, and it bounced off safety Don Burroughs's hands at the goal line. Alertly, Del Shofner streaked in,

grabbed the sinking ball at the 3, and scampered into the end zone for a 7–0 lead.

Later in the first quarter, an 80-yard drive led to a Rote touchdown to put the Giants up 14–0. Another Giants drive was extended fortuitously on a botched reverse—Shofner fumbled and then tossed the ball back to a surprised Tittle, who completed an 18-yard pass to halfback Bob Gaiters. That drive led to a field goal which answered the first Eagles score, extending New York's lead to 17–7. The Giants weren't done, though. With just a minute left in the half, Allie Sherman ordered the Pete Previte Special.

Previte worked the locker room for the Giants and the Yankees. He thought of how teams in baseball often bring in their fastest runners to pinch-run in key situations, and imagined that might apply in football as well. Previte suggested this to Giants assistant coaches Don Heinrich and Harland Svare, and they brought the idea to Sherman, who worked up a play in which the two running backs are replaced by speedy defensive backs Erich Barnes and Jimmy Patton. With Barnes and Shofner going deep on one side

Physical cornerback Erich Barnes was the fastest player on the Giants and ideally suited for the Pete Previte Special in 1961.

THE PETE PREVITE SPECIAL

In a play named the Pete Previte Special in honor of the clubhouse attendant who had suggested it, the Giants lined up in a spread, shotgun formation with flanker Kyle Rote (44), tight end Joe Walton (80), and Jimmy Patton (20) all spread to the right and split end Del Shofner (85) and Erich Barnes (49) spread to the left. Tittle (14) took the deep snap as Rote, Walton, and Patton ran underneath routes and Shofner and Barnes headed deep. Shofner drew double coverage while Barnes drew single coverage on a post pattern. Tittle hit the wide-open Barnes in stride, and the speedy defensive back ran untouched to the end zone.

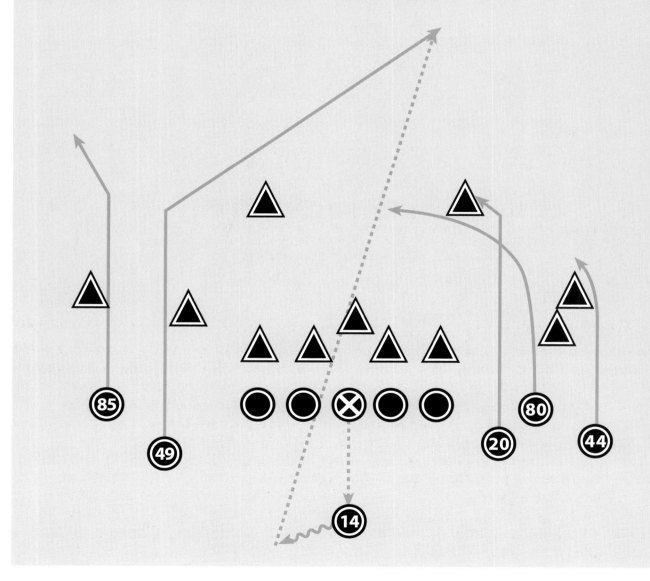

GAME DETAILS

New York Giants 38 • Philadelphia Eagles 21

Date: November 12, 1961

Location: Yankee Stadium, New York

Attendance: 62,800

Significance: Game with first-place divisional rival

Box Score:

Eagles	0	7	0	14	**21**
Giants	14	10	14	0	**38**

Scoring:

NYG Shofner 30-yard pass from Tittle (Summerall PAT)
NYG Rote 12-yard pass from Tittle (Summerall PAT)
PHL Lucas 2-yard pass from Jurgensen (Walston PAT)
NYG Summerall 11-yard FG
NYG Barnes 62-yard pass from Tittle (Summerall PAT)
NYG Gaiters 5-yard run and fumble recovery in the
 end zone (Summerall PAT)
NYG Scott 65-yard pass interception (Summerall PAT)
PHL Lucas 4-yard pass from Jurgensen (Walston PAT)
PHL Brown 17-yard pass from Hill (Walston PAT)

Team	FD	YDS	RUSH	PASS	RTN	A-C-I	PUNT	FUM	PEN
Eagles	23	372	27-132	240	40-19-4	3-41	1	4-0	20
Giants	22	440	37-164	270	24-18-0	6-38	1	3-1	60

Giants: Webster 100R, Tittle 307P, Shofner 137C

and Patton, Rote, and tight end Joe Walton running shorter patterns from the other, *someone* was bound to get open in a coverage mismatch.

When Philadelphia elected to double-cover Shofner, that left Barnes going against linebacker Maxie Baughan. Barnes streaked right past the linebacker, caught a strike from Tittle, and sprinted to the end zone in a 62-yard touchdown that sent the Giants to the locker room—where Previte was listening to the game on the radio—leading 24–7.

The Giants sealed the game on the first drive of the second half. They drove 76 yards and scored on a handoff to Bobby Gaiters, who fumbled into the end zone, recovered it, fumbled it again, and then recovered it for good. Linebacker Tom Scott closed out New York's scoring with a 65-yard interception return, and the Eagles got two garbage-time touchdowns to make the score more respectable.

The two teams were tied for the Eastern Conference lead and would still be tied four weeks later when they met in Philadelphia. The Giants prevailed 28–24 in that one, too, to win the conference title.

With Y. A. Tittle at the controls of his innovative offense, Allie Sherman was named Coach of the Year in 1961 and 1962.

ALLIE SHERMAN

The Brooklyn-born Allie Sherman was riding high at this early point in his career. He was succeeding dramatically in his dream job and was being lionized in the press and by the fans for his innovative passing game and exciting offensive approach. He successfully dealt with a potentially nasty quarterback controversy between holdover Charley Conerly and newly acquired veteran Y. A. Title, and he had revitalized a Giants team that was picked to finish in the middle of the pack in 1961.

Allie got his start as an undersized, left-handed backup quarterback for Greasy Neale's Eagles in the 1940s. Neale thought highly of Sherman, though, and frequently insisted he was the "smartest man in football." Neale recommended Sherman to his friend Steve Owen when Steve was installing the T-formation in 1949, and Sherman coached the Giants' backs for five years under Owen.

When Jim Lee Howell replaced Owen in 1954, Sherman took a head-coaching job in Canada while Vince Lombardi was hired as New York's offensive coach. Sherman returned to the Giants as a scout and replaced Lombardi as offensive coach when Vince left for Green Bay in 1959. Two years later, Howell stepped down and the Giants tried to get Lombardi out of his Packers contract,

just two years into his tenure there. Commissioner Pete Rozelle vetoed that possibility, however, and Sherman was hired, once more the second choice behind Lombardi.

Sherman's team won the Eastern Conference his first three years and he was named Coach of the Year in 1961 and 1962, although his Giants lost to Lombardi's Packers in both title games. Afraid that his aging team was on the verge of collapse, Sherman began trading away some veterans, while others retired. The problem was that he did not get much value back in his trades and did not have comparable talent on hand to replace the veteran stars.

The worst move he made was trading icon Sam Huff for nonentities Dick James and Andy Stynchula in 1964, which was the year everything turned sour for Sherman. After a 33–8–1 record in his first three seasons, Sherman's teams went 24–43–3 over the next five years. Amidst a host of "Good-bye Allie" chants and signs from fans, and after an embarrassing loss to the crosstown Jets in a 1969 preseason game, Sherman was fired with five years still remaining on his contract. He would never coach again, but he worked in broadcasting and even turned around a dysfunctional New York City off-track betting operation in the 1990s.

I thought, *Wouldn't it be a good idea to use speed late in a game as baseball uses pinch-runners for speed late in the game?* So I suggested to Heinrich and Svare that they use Barnes and Patton, two of our fastest men, for catching a pass maybe when we were behind late in the game or some such spot.

—PETE PREVITE, YANKEE STADIUM LOCKER-ROOM ATTENDANT

December 31, 2005

BARBER BURSTS 95 YARDS TO PLAYOFFS

Giants Pound Raiders 30–21

While the Giants had already clinched a spot in the 2005 play-offs as they entered the season finale, they needed a victory in Oakland to win the division title and possibly secure a first-round bye. To add to the challenge, the 4–11 Raiders were led by former Giants quarterback Kerry Collins, who had extra motivation against his old club. To make matters worse, New York's defense was banged-up, and it featured three linebackers who had just been signed in the past week. In the face of these adversities, Giants MVP Tiki Barber loaded the team on his back and hauled them into the postseason.

The key play in this lackluster game—played in a half-empty stadium—came halfway through the first quarter. The Giants faced a second-and-14 from their own 5-yard line. Barber took the handoff from Eli Manning and slid through a hole between center Shaun O'Hara and guard Chris Snee. A quick juke faked out Raiders safety Stuart Schweigert, who dove and missed Barber as Tiki made a sharp cut to the left and headed up the sideline, Amani Toomer and Plaxico

Burress in front of him for interference. Tiki went 95 yards untouched to the end zone for the first touchdown of the game. In the process, he broke a 75-year-old team record formerly held by Hap Moran, who had raced 91 yards against the Packers in 1930 (although Moran was tackled at the 1 and did not score).

Big plays kept the Giants ahead through-out the game. With the score 10–7 in the second quarter and New York at its own 22, Manning hit Burress at the 35 and Plaxico sprinted untouched for a 78-yard score. Early in the third quarter, Chad Morton returned a Raiders punt 57 yards to the Oakland 3, and Brandon Jacobs pounded the ball in from there to extend the lead to 27–14. While Randy Moss would catch a second touchdown pass after that, the outcome of the game was never seriously in doubt.

Barber ended up with 203 yards rushing for the game, making it the third time that year and the second consecutive game in which he surpassed 200 yards on the ground. He also broke Rodney Hampton's

Tiki Barber heads upfield for a 95-yard touchdown run, the longest run from scrimmage in Giants history, on the road against the Raiders in 2005.

team record of 49 rushing touchdowns and ended up with a Giants-best 1,860 yards rushing for the season.

The Giants won the NFC East and secured home-field advantage but it would do no good. One week later, the Carolina Panthers came into the Meadowlands, shut down Barber, and shut out the Giants 23–0 in Eli Manning's inauspicious playoff debut.

TIKI BARBER

Tiki Barber is the greatest Giants running back in the team's history. In his 10-year career, he scored 68 touchdowns, averaged 4.7 yards per carry, gained more than 10,000 yards rushing and more than 5,000 yards receiving, and retired as the team's all-time leading rusher *and* receiver. Drafted in the second round of Jim Fassel's first draft in 1997, the 5'10" Barber was projected as the new Dave Meggett, a third-down back to catch passes out of the backfield and return kicks. In the weight room, though, Barber built himself up to 200 pounds, and proved himself to be an every-down feature back for New York.

Barber's main flaw was that he started out as a fumbler. In seven years under Jim Fassel, Tiki averaged one fumble every 42 touches. Once new coach Tom Coughlin showed Barber a better way to carry the ball, that average dropped in his last three seasons to one fumble every 130 touches.

Barber also craved the spotlight and loved to talk to the media, but that did not always have a positive impact on his teammates or his coach. When he announced his pending retirement early in the 2006 season, it served as just one more distraction that the collapsing Giants did not need. Barber's seamless transition to *The Today Show* and NBC Sports immediately after the season came as no surprise.

At the end of his final game as a Giants player, a playoff loss to the Eagles in which Barber gained 137 yards rushing, Philadelphia safety Brian Dawkins paid his longtime rival the ultimate compliment by telling him, "You're a warrior."

Barber was a team leader throughout a 10-year period in which the Giants went to the playoffs five times and the Super Bowl once. That they never won it all during his career was no fault of the ever-elusive and surprisingly powerful Barber, and the team's Super Bowl victory the year after he retired was, to some, a cruel twist of fate.

Tiki Barber retired as both the leading rusher and leading receiver in Giants history.

GAME DETAILS

New York Giants 30 • Oakland Raiders 21

Date: December 31, 2005

Location: McAfee Coliseum, Oakland

Attendance: 44,594

Significance: The Giants were trying to clinch a playoff spot in the season finale

Box Score:

Giants	7	13	7	3	**30**
Raiders	7	7	7	0	**21**

Scoring:

NYG Barber 95-yard run (Feely PAT)
OAK Moss 15-yard pass from Collins (Janikowski PAT)
NYG Feely 25-yard FG
NYG Burress 78-yard pass from Manning (Feely PAT)
NYG Feely 38-yard FG
OAK Gabriel 8-yard pass from Collins (Janikowski PAT)
NYG Jacobs 1-yard run (Feely PAT)
OAK Moss 44-yard pass from Collins (Janikowski PAT)
NYG Feely 46-yard FG

Team	FD	YDS	RUSH	PASS	RTN	A-C-I	Sacked	PUNT	FUM	PEN
Giants	13	402	34-211	191	173	24-12-0	2-13	6-39	1-0	9-70
Raiders	21	325	17-25	300	163	48-26-0	3-31	9-47	1-0	8-54

Giants: Barber 203R, Manning 204P
Raiders: Collins 331P, Moss 116C, Gabriel 100C

> **H**e's been outstanding. He's played with great consistency. He's taken good care of the ball. He's an extremely durable guy.
>
> —TOM COUGHLIN ON TIKI BARBER

EXTENDING THE PLAYBOOK

Tiki Barber's 95-yard run wasn't the only record-setting play in this game. In the second quarter, Eli Manning and Plaxico Burress teamed up for the longest pass play of either player's career, 78 yards. On second-and-six from the 22, Manning dropped back to pass and spotted a wide-open Burress streaking across the middle of the field, but he badly underthrew the pass and it fell incomplete.

On the next play, Manning went back to Burress on a shorter crossing route. Burress caught the ball at the 35 between two defenders. Raiders safety Stuart Schweigert dove and missed Burress as Plaxico turned upfield and outraced the rest of the Raiders to the end zone for a 17–7 lead.

November 23, 1986

MARTIN ENTRAPS ELWAY
Lineman Scores Giants' Only Touchdown in Win over Denver

Just one week after the last-minute heroics against the Vikings (Play 8), the 1986 Giants were at it again against a tough Broncos squad on a late November day at the Meadowlands. New York was trying to win its fifth straight game for the second time this year, and they relied on the big play for this battle.

In this nail-biter, the Broncos kicked a field goal on their first possession. The Giants answered with their own three-pointer by Raul Allegre on the first play of the second quarter, capping a 16-play, 63-yard drive. Denver got a break late in the period when Stacy Robinson fumbled at the Broncos' 18-yard line. Denver turned that into another field goal, aided by a 39-yard interference call on Perry Williams. Quarterback John Elway had the Broncos on the move again in the closing seconds of the half—until defensive end George Martin altered the course of the game.

On first down from the New York 13, Elway tried to loft a swing pass to Gerald Willhite, but he didn't factor in the agility of Martin, who had played basketball at the University of Oregon. Martin had gotten by tackle Ken Lanier and jumped to bat the pass back to himself. Grabbing the

interception, he turned upfield at the 22. Elway had the angle on Martin at the 35, and George held the ball in his outstretched right hand, hoping to lateral it to Lawrence Taylor. Elway grabbed for Martin high to prevent the lateral, but Martin switched hands and shoved the quarterback down with his right arm at the 50. With Taylor and Harry Carson leading interference, Martin plodded on. At the 20, Mark Collins raced in to knock down the last Broncos player, Sammy Winder. Martin leapfrogged Winder at the 15 and trudged into the end zone as an elated L.T. leaped on his back and tackled him. The 78-yard play took a full 17 seconds, and it gave the Giants the lead.

In the third quarter, the teams exchanged field goals, and Allegre booted still another field goal five minutes into the final period, making the score 16–9. However, Elway brought the Broncos back with one of his patented fourth-quarter drives. Denver traveled 73 yards in nine plays and scored the tying touchdown on a Winder run with 1:55 to go.

Phil Simms had had a quiet day, so it was time for him to go to work. Quickly, though, he faced a third-and-21 from his own 18. With the dangerous Elway on the

GAME DETAILS

New York Giants 19 • Denver Broncos 16

Date: November 23, 1986

Location: The Meadowlands

Attendance: 75,116

Significance: Late-season contest between eventual Super Bowl participants

> **A** great play by a great athlete.
>
> —JOHN ELWAY

Box Score:

Broncos	3	3	3	7	**16**
Giants	0	10	3	6	**19**

Scoring:

DEN Karlis 40-yard FG

NYG Allegre 31-yard FG

DEN Karlis 32-yard FG

NYG Martin 78-yard interception return (Allegre PAT)

NYG Allegre 45-yard FG

DEN Karlis 42-yard FG

NYG Allegre 46-yard FG

DEN Winder 4-yard run (Karlis PAT)

NYG Allegre 34-yard FG

Team	FD	YDS	RUSH	PASS	RTN	A-C-I	Sacked	PUNT	FUM	PEN
Broncos	26	405	22-80	325	148	48-29-2	2-11	3-34	2-2	4-60
Giants	14	262	36-143	119	189	20-11-0	3-29	6-49	2-2	9-89

Broncos: Elway 336P

Giants: Morris 106R, Simms 148P

other sideline, the Giants needed a first down. They called a double-seam route, in which both wide receivers run straight up the seam of the zone coverage. Just like the previous week on fourth-and-17 against the Vikings, Simms found Bobby Johnson at the crucial time, and Johnson caught the ball for a 24-yard gain to the 42. Two plays later, from their 39, Simms tried the double-seam again and found Phil McConkey for a 46-yard gain to the Broncos' 15. With only six seconds left, Allegre came in and kicked the 34-yard game-winning field goal.

The Giants were in the midst of a 12-game winning streak and were starting to believe they were a team of destiny. They would meet the Broncos again in the Super Bowl and complete their mission by winning the franchise's first NFL title in 30 years.

GEORGE MARTIN

George Martin intercepted three passes in his career, and he returned each one for a touchdown. Martin also scored on two fumble recoveries, a lateral after a blocked field goal, and a pass reception as a tight end during his 14 years as a Giants defensive end. He also tackled John Elway for a safety in the Super Bowl. Only Jason Taylor scored more times as a defensive lineman.

The undersized Martin was a lowly 11th-round draft pick in 1975, but he became a starter at defensive end in his second season. When the Giants switched to the 3-4 defense in 1981 under new defensive coordinator Bill Parcells, the quick and nimble Martin became a situational pass-rushing specialist. He is credited with 46 career sacks from the time sacks began to be officially counted in 1982, but is thought to have accumulated more than 80 sacks unofficially. In the Super Bowl season of 1986, Martin returned to the starting lineup at age 33 and had an excellent year, capped by that Super Bowl safety. Having lived through some very bad years with the Giants, he and longtime teammate Harry Carson were respected team leaders who appreciated that first championship even more than most of their teammates.

Martin was an unselfish teammate who co-founded the team's Bible study group; he was the Giants' candidate for the league's community service Whizzer White Award for 10 consecutive years. (He finally won the award in 1987.) He and Carson both retired after the 1988 season, but Martin has stayed active with the Giants and in the local community. In 2007, he embarked on a 3,000-mile walk across the U.S. to raise money for 9/11 rescue and recovery workers.

It was one of the greatest plays I ever saw. People forget that Denver had gone the length of the field. The defense was exhausted, and for a lineman who had been chasing Elway for seven or eight plays in a row, to run the ball all the way back like that was something else.

—BILL PARCELLS

When I caught it, it was a bright sunny day. When I got to the end zone, it was cloudy. The weather had changed considerably.

—GEORGE MARTIN

George Martin picks off John Elway and lumbers toward the goal line late in the first half on November 23, 1986. It was the seventh career touchdown for Martin, and the only Giant touchdown of the game. *(Photo courtesy of AP Images)*

January 9, 1994

HAMPTON HIES AWAY HOME

Giants Vanquish Vikings 17–10 in Wild-Card Game

In Dan Reeves's first season as head coach, the Giants had the second-best record in the NFC on the strength of having the best defense in the NFL, allowing only 205 points. By losing the final game of 1993 to Dallas in overtime, however, New York found itself as a wild-card entry in the playoffs, playing host to a 9–7 Vikings team that gave up more points than it scored on the year. What seemed like a mismatch, though, turned out to be a dogfight on this windy 23-degree day with a minus-5-degree wind chill.

New York opened the scoring in the first quarter, on a 26-yard field goal with the wind. They lined up for a second field-goal try in the second quarter, but that kick into the wind was blown way off course. All the points in this game would be scored by the team that had the wind at their backs.

Late in the second quarter, Minnesota took advantage of the wind and scored on a 40-yard pass from veteran Jim McMahon to Cris Carter with 1:53 left in the period. The Vikings forced a punt before the half and received a gift when punter Mike Horan's kick was blown into the shoulder of teammate

Greg Jackson and traveled just 13 yards, to the Giants' 36-yard line. Two plays later, Fuad Reveiz kicked a 52-yard field goal on the final play of the first half, and the Giants went off the field trailing by a touchdown to a chorus of boos from the stands.

In the locker room, the players would get an earful from superstar Lawrence Taylor and other veterans, imploring the team to step it up. Meanwhile, Reeves was making some alterations to a base play in the playbook that would change the momentum of the game.

On the fourth play of the second half, Phil Simms took the snap at the 49 and handed off to Hampton, who was sweeping to the right. Defensive tackle John Randle got a hand on Hampton in the backfield, but Hampton cut back behind Doug Riesenberg's block on Roy Barker. Linebacker Fred Strickland got a piece of Hampton at the Vikings' 47 but was pushed away by tight end Howard Cross. Hampton took off, with Chris Doleman and Carlos Jenkins in pursuit. Hampton stiff-armed Jenkins to the ground at the 30 and picked up speed. Downfield, receiver Chris

> **W**hen you've got a back like Rodney running the ball, you want to do everything
> you can to get him in the secondary.
>
> —GUARD WILLIAM ROBERTS

Head coach Dan Reeves's halftime adjustments helped lead the Giants to playoff victory.
(Photo courtesy of WireImages)

THE RIGHT 38 H LEAD

H-back Aaron Pierce (84) comes in motion to the right and at the snap goes upfield and drives the cornerback to the outside. Tight end Howard Cross (87) chips the defensive end and then seals the linebacker by blocking down on him. Rodney Hampton (27) takes the quick pitch from Phil Simms (11) and drives through the alley created on the right side. Well downfield, Chris Calloway (80) cuts off the Minnesota safety and Hampton scores. This play was a halftime adjustment by head coach Dan Reeves; normally, Pierce would go in motion to the left.

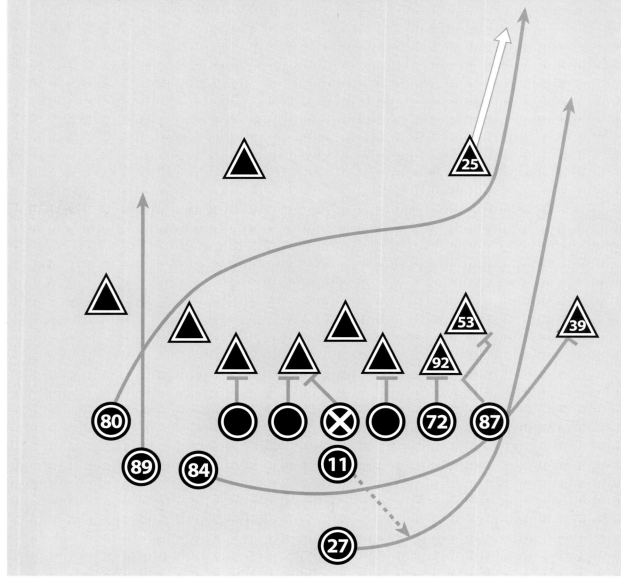

GAME DETAILS

New York Giants 17 • Minnesota Vikings 10

Date: January 9, 1994

Location: The Meadowlands

Attendance: 75,089

Significance: Wild-card playoff game

Box Score:

Vikings	0	10	0	0	**10**
Giants	3	0	14	0	**17**

Scoring:

NYG Treadwell 26-yard FG

MIN Carter 40-yard pass from McMahon (Reveiz PAT)

MIN Reveiz 52-yard FG

NYG Hampton 51-yard run (Treadwell PAT)

NYG Hampton 2-yard run (Treadwell PAT)

Team	FD	YDS	RUSH	PASS	RTN	A-C-I	Sacked	PUNT	FUM	PEN
Vikings	11	260	22-79	181	69	34-15-0	3-11	6-38	2-1	6-28
Giants	17	270	41-176	94	17	26-17-0	0-0	7-32	0-0	2-20

Vikings: McMahon 145P

Giants: Hampton 161R

Calloway was shielding safety Vencie Glenn, but Glenn slipped by Calloway at the 5—only to run face-first into another Hampton stiff-arm. Rodney went over him to complete a dominating 51-yard touchdown, which tied the game with 12:06 left in the third quarter.

A few minutes later a shanked Viking punt gave New York the ball on the Minnesota 26. Eight plays after that, Hampton powered in from the 2 to put the Giants up 17–10 with 5:37 left in the third period. The extra-point snap was high, but kicker David Treadwell hoofed it into the end zone, pulling a calf muscle in the process. With the way the Giants were playing on defense, though, they would need no more points.

Rodney Hampton carried 33 times for 161 yards on the day, while Phil Simms could only manage 94 yards passing on what he ranked as one of the three worst weather days he ever experienced. It was the last home game and last win for both Simms and Lawrence Taylor. By contrast, it was the first playoff win for rookie stars Michael Strahan and Jesse Armstead. The next week, Simms's and Taylor's careers would end with a loss in San Francisco, but New York was raising a new crop of leaders.

RODNEY HAMPTON

The 51-yard touchdown run by Rodney Hampton in this game showcased the power and speed of this remarkable Giants running back. It was the high point of a 161-yard rushing performance that carried the Giants past the Vikings in what would prove to be Hampton's last chance for a postseason win.

Hampton was a first-round draft pick in 1990, but unlike other first-round runners who flopped for New York such as Rocky Thompson, Butch Woolfolk, and George Adams, Hampton proved he was the real deal right from the start. As a rookie, he and Ottis Anderson were the team's lead ball carriers, but Hampton broke his leg in a playoff victory over the Bears and missed the Super Bowl run.

Under new coach Ray Handley, Hampton had his two best seasons, gaining more than 1,000 yards, averaging more than four yards per carry, and serving as a useful passing outlet. The next Giants coach, Dan Reeves, cast Hampton as a battering ram. He gained more than 1,000 yards three times but twice went over 300 carries, and averaged less than four yards a carry all four years.

Hampton was overworked under Reeves and began to break down physically with knee and back injuries. By the time Jim Fassel arrived in 1997, Hampton was a 28-year-old running back who had just 23 carries left in his career. His speed was gone and his power was diminished.

Hampton gained more than 1,000 yards in five consecutive seasons, and he played in two Pro Bowls. He retired as the all-time leading Giants rusher, having passed Joe Morris, although Tiki Barber was already on hand and would pass Hampton in the next decade.

> **I** got a good block and was able to find a seam. I put a stiff arm on one guy and got a good block downfield from Chris [Calloway].
>
> —RODNEY HAMPTON

Rodney Hampton stiff-armed his way to a 51-yard touchdown run against the Vikings in a playoff win on January 9, 1994.

January 14, 2001

COLLINS CONNECTS WITH COMELLA AND COLLARS VIKINGS

Giants Return to Super Bowl

With the 7–4 Giants having lost two games in a row, head coach Jim Fassel made his famous guarantee that New York was going to the playoffs, and the team caught fire, winning its last five games to clinch home-field advantage in the postseason with the best record in the NFC. By contrast, the deep passing attack of the Minnesota Vikings staked them to an 11–2 record before they came back to earth, losing the last three games of the season while giving up 104 points—35 per game. Still, the flawed Vikings were the heavy favorites when they came into Giants Stadium for the 2000 NFC Championship Game. The football world was in for a shock.

From his film study, Giants offensive coach Sean Payton was convinced that Minnesota's cornerbacks were a real weakness that could be exploited, so the Giants came out throwing. After returning the opening kickoff to the 26-yard line, New York took just four plays to score: a 16-yard pass to Amani Toomer, a 10-yard pass to Toomer, a two-yard run, and then a 46-yard bomb from Kerry Collins to a wide-open Ike Hilliard for a 7–0 lead two minutes into the game. When Moe Williams of the Vikings fumbled the ensuing kickoff and the Giants' Lyle West recovered at the Vikings' 18, the Giants went for the quick strike to an unlikely target. It was the play of the day.

Greg Comella was a free-agent fullback who was known for his blocking prowess and for having decent hands. On the next play, Comella flared to the right flat to draw in linebacker Dwayne Rudd before running for the end zone. As he turned at the goal line, Collins's pass was upon him quickly, and he grabbed it at face level in self-defense, falling awkwardly backward on his left foot, out of bounds. New York

Bulky, blocking fullback Greg Comella falls clumsily backward after making an awkward grab of a Kerry Collins pass for the Giants' second score against the Vikings on January 14, 2001. *(Photo courtesy of AP Images)*

GAME DETAILS

New York Giants 41 • Minnesota Vikings 0

Date: January 14, 2001

Location: The Meadowlands

Attendance: 79,310

Significance: NFC Championship Game

Box Score:

Vikings	0	0	0	0	**0**
Giants	14	20	7	0	**41**

Scoring:

NYG Hilliard 46-yard pass from Collins (Daluiso PAT)

NYG Comella 18-yard pass from Collins (Daluiso PAT)

NYG Daluiso 21-yard FG

NYG Jurevicius 8-yard pass from Collins (Daluiso PAT)

NYG Daluiso 22-yard FG

NYG Hilliard 7-yard pass from Collins (Daluiso PAT)

NYG Toomer 7-yard pass from Collins (Daluiso PAT)

Team	FD	YDS	RUSH	PASS	RTN	A-C-I	Sacked	PUNT	FUM	PEN
Vikings	9	114	9-54	60	133	28-13-3	4-18	6-35	2-2	5-61
Giants	31	518	41-138	380	31	40-29-2	1-5	1-30	1-0	4-36

Giants: Collins 381P, Hilliard 155C

had a two-touchdown lead 2:07 into the game, and they would not relent.

Minnesota's best scoring chance all day came midway through the first quarter, when Daunte Culpepper hit Cris Carter in the end zone, but cornerback Emmanuel McDaniel muscled the ball free for an interception and a touchback. A poor Vikings punt led to a Giants field goal on the first play of the second quarter, and New York would add three more scores in the period. After a 43-yard pass to Ron Dixon, Collins hit Joe Jurevicius for an eight-yard touchdown pass four minutes later. A 10-play, 62-yard drive five minutes after that culminated in another field goal. Finally, just 12 seconds before the half, Collins capped another long drive with a seven-yard touchdown pass to Hilliard for a 34–0 lead.

Minnesota's ever-so-slim hopes were erased on the very first play of the second half, when Giants safety

KERRY COLLINS

Kerry Collins chose a great platform to have a career day and reward the confidence shown him by general manager Ernie Accorsi and coach Jim Fassel two years before. Unfortunately, two weeks later he chose the international stage of Super Bowl XXXV to reverse that career day with a 15-for-39, four-interception performance. So it was for his career.

Collins led Penn State to a Rose Bowl win in 1995 and a claim to the national championship. He was the first-ever draft choice of the expansion Carolina Panthers, and he led them to the NFC Championship Game in his second season. The wheels came off after that. Alcohol-fueled, racially tinged remarks to teammates got him a black eye from guard Norberto Garrido and the mistrust of the rest of the Panthers. When he went to Carolina coach Dom Capers and asked to be benched while he cleared his head, Capers saw him as a quitter and cut him midseason in 1998. Mike Ditka gave him a two-month trial in New Orleans, but released him at the end of the season.

The Giants then shocked everyone by signing the unwanted Collins to a $16-million contract in 1999. Accorsi and Fassel had thoroughly checked out Collins and were convinced he had confronted his alcoholism and turned his life around. They were proven correct, and Fassel and quarterbacks coach Sean Payton were able to accentuate Collins's positives to produce his best work in New York.

Collins was big and durable with a strong arm. He also had limitations that kept him from being a great quarterback: he was immobile, inconsistent, a record-setting fumbler, and he threw costly interceptions.

The Giants got Collins's five best seasons—four years with more than 3,000 yards and one with more than 4,000—but he left with some bitterness when New York traded for Eli Manning in 2004. After two more mediocre seasons as a starter in Oakland, Collins found his ideal role as Vince Young's backup in Tennessee.

Shaun Williams blitzed in and stripped Culpepper of the ball while he was sacking him. Cornelius Griffin recovered for New York at the 29, and five plays later Collins hit Amani Toomer for a seven-yard touchdown and the 41-0 final score.

It was a game of total domination on both sides of the ball for New York. Kerry Collins threw for 381 yards and five touchdowns; meanwhile, the sturdy Giants defense held the spectacular Vikings to 114 yards of total offense. The difference of 404 yards between Minnesota's total and the Giants' 518 was the largest disparity in the history of the NFL playoffs. For Minnesota, Cris Carter did not catch a pass until the fourth quarter, while Randy Moss caught just two passes for 18 yards. The Giants were going to the Super Bowl.

Jim Fassel

With a simple statement the day before Thanksgiving 2000, Jim Fassel defined the season for the Giants: "This is a poker game. I'm shoving my chips to the center of the table. I'm raising the ante. This team is going to the playoffs." That statement of assurance and purpose seemed to have a visceral effect on the team; the players became more focused and determined. This NFC Championship Game would punctuate those words and prove to be the high point of Fassel's tenure in New York.

Fassel had a 25-year coaching apprenticeship before being named head coach of the Giants in 1997. He served as an assistant coach in college, the World Football League, and the USFL before earning a stint as head coach of the University of Utah in the 1980s. Then it was on to the NFL as an assistant with the Giants, the Broncos, the Raiders, and the Cardinals. Along the way, he worked with such names as John Elway, Phil Simms, and Jeff Hostetler, and won their trust and confidence.

Fassel's years as the Giants' coach were inconsistent and up-and-down; the team went 58–53–1. New York surprisingly made the playoffs in his first season, but they stumbled to mediocrity the next two seasons and Giants defensive players were openly dubious of Fassel's decisions. With his job in jeopardy, Fassel changed his own destiny by rescuing the career of troubled quarterback Kerry Collins. Fassel got the best out of Collins and the team made the Super Bowl in 2000, but then stumbled again in 2001. The 2002 season seemed to be a new start, but the awful playoff collapse to the 49ers that year (see Play 50) carried over to 2003, when Fassel lost control of a team that finished 4–12—and lost his job as well.

While waiting for another head coaching position in 2004, Fassel signed on as offensive coordinator for his old friend Brian Billick in Baltimore, but he suffered the humiliation of having Billick take over the offense halfway through the season in 2006. He was passed over for the Washington Redskins head coaching position in early 2008 and is currently working in broadcasting.

This is the Giants team that was referred to as the worst ever to win home-field advantage in the National Football League. And today, on this field of painted mud, we proved that we're the worst team to ever win the National Football Conference Championship.

—WELLINGTON MARA

Jim Fassel's bold playoff prediction paid off with a trip to Super Bowl XXXV, the highpoint of his tenure with the Giants. *(Photo courtesy of AP Images)*

December 21, 1958

HOT-POTATO TRICK PLAY BEATS BROWNS

First Quarter Touchdown and Giants Defense Tops Cleveland

One week after beating Cleveland 13–10—on an improbable 49-yard field goal through the wind and snow—to tie for the Eastern Conference lead (Play 3), the Giants and the Browns returned to Yankee Stadium for a playoff to determine the Eastern crown on an overcast 25-degree day. With a stalwart defense and a bit of surprising trickery on offense, New York took on a Browns team demoralized by the previous week's loss.

Cleveland coach Paul Brown tried to mix up his attack for this rematch. The previous week, he had called 37 runs, mostly by Jim Brown, and just 12 passes. In this game, he reversed that by calling 13 runs and 27 passes. Jim Brown was held to the lowest rushing total of his career, gaining a mere eight yards on just seven carries.

The Giants controlled the ball and the tempo from the start, getting off 71 plays to the Browns' 40. Both teams had trouble holding on to the ball; each had four turnovers. But the Giants kept their grip tight at just the right time.

In the first quarter, New York reached the Cleveland 19-yard line when Charley Conerly called a brand-new play the team had practiced all week. Conerly handed off to right halfback Alex Webster, who was heading left while guard Al Barry pulled to the right. Left halfback Frank Gifford slipped behind fullback Mel Triplett heading to the right and took a

> **B**ut all week in practice when [Gifford] got through the line, the linebacker would grab him—you know how you do in practice, around the shoulders. And Conerly was just loping along out there behind the line, so Gifford would toss him the ball. We all laughed about it.
>
> —KYLE ROTE, IN *THE GOLDEN AGE OF PRO FOOTBALL* BY MICKEY HERSKOWITZ

The Giants' Charley Conerly, Alex Webster, and Frank Gifford completed a double hand-off and lateral to beat the Browns for the 1958 Eastern Division championship. *(Photo courtesy of AP Images)*

CHARLEY CONERLY

The last thing that 37-year-old Charley Conerly wanted to do in his 11th NFL season was to run with the ball, but once Frank Gifford lateraled to him in this playoff game, Charley had no choice. Conerly scored his first touchdown in more than a year on the play.

Conerly came through for the Giants countless times during the 14 seasons the taciturn Mississippian spent in New York. He was originally drafted by Washington in 1945, but Charley was serving his country as a Marine involved in several island assaults in the Pacific at the time. After he finished his college eligibility, Conerly was traded to the Giants for Howie Livingston in 1948.

The Giants bested the AAFC's Brooklyn Dodgers to sign Chuckin' Charley, and in his rookie season, he set a personal best for touchdowns and passing yards. However, for the next five years, he struggled. He had to learn the T-formation when coach Steve Owen was forced to switch to that, and Owen kept bringing back his own outdated A-formation to confuse matters. Conerly and the Giants were plagued by a poor line, slow receivers, and an unimaginative attack, and Conerly felt the brunt of it. He was sacked repeatedly and booed unmercifully, and the stands were festooned with signs reading "Back to the Farm," "Charley Must Go," and worse.

> **W**ell, I was supposed to be there. The lateral was an option. Vinnie [Lombardi] set it up that way. I was supposed to be there if Gifford needed me. I don't know how long it'd been since I scored a touchdown, but it was great for an old guy like me to run it in.
>
> —CHARLEY CONERLY, IN *GIANTS IN THEIR OWN WORDS* BY RICHARD WHITTINGHAM

In 1954, Vince Lombardi was hired to handle the offense, and Conerly's career turned around at age 33. For the next eight seasons, under Lombardi and then Allie Sherman, Conerly enjoyed a golden era in which the team won and the fans were on his side at last. His teammates had always been behind this quiet, calm, forceful, respected leader who was named league MVP in 1959, when he led the league in passing at age 38. When he retired at age 40 in 1961, only Otto Graham had won more quarterback starts than Charley's 77.

Conerly also led 20 fourth-quarter game-winning comebacks and finished as the Giants' all-time leader with more than 19,000 yards passing and 173 touchdowns. His No. 42 jersey was retired by the team.

> **T**he double reverse didn't surprise me, but the lateral to Conerly? They couldn't have planned it. What the hell was he doing there?
>
> —PAUL BROWN

GAME DETAILS

New York Giants 10 • Cleveland Browns 0

Date: December 21, 1958

Location: Yankee Stadium, New York

Attendance: 61,254

Significance: Eastern Conference playoff

Box Score:

Browns	0	0	0	0	**0**
Giants	7	3	0	0	**10**

Scoring:

NYG Conerly 10-yard lateral from Gifford after 8-yard run (Summerall PAT)

NYG Summerall 26-yard FG

Team	FD	YDS	RUSH	PASS	RTN	A-C-I	Sacked	PUNT	FUM	PEN
Browns	7	86	13-24	62	35	27-10-3	6-52	8-38	1-1	2-20
Giants	17	317	53-211	106	23	18-8-2	0-0	7-47	6-2	4-35

> **N**ext time I give you the f*cking ball, you keep it.
>
> —CHARLEY CONERLY TO FRANK GIFFORD, IN *THE WHOLE TEN YARDS*

handoff from Webster on a reverse. Gifford cut upfield, between Al Barry blocking Bob Gain on the outside and Dick Yelvington closing off Willie McClung on the inside. Gifford faked a lateral to get Gain to rise up and lean the wrong way as Gifford slid by. With linebacker Galen Fiss closing from the sideline and safety Ken Konz coming from the goal line, Gifford then lateraled the ball out to the sideline, where Conerly caught the ball at the 10. Gain and Konz were out of position, but safety Junior Wren hustled over to drill the 37-year-old Conerly as he dove into the end zone with what proved to be the only touchdown of the game.

Those are the only points the Giants would need on this inspired day, although Pat Summerall added a field goal in the second quarter for insurance. The closest Cleveland came to scoring was when they reached the Giants' 6 in the fourth quarter, but a Sam Huff interception ended that threat. The Browns would have the ball for only one out of the last 11 minutes of the game.

New York outgained Cleveland 211 to 24 on the ground and 317 to 86 in total yards, soundly beating their chief rival of the past decade. It was the first time Paul Brown's team had been shut out in 106 games; the last time had been when Giants coach Steve Owen opened his umbrella defense on Cleveland in October 1950. The Giants had earned their slot in the NFL title game against the Colts the next week in Yankee Stadium.

SAM HUFF

Above all, Sam Huff had a sense of timing and drama. He came along at the right time in the right system, and he knew how to make the most of the opportunity. Tom Landry's 4-3 defense was designed to funnel plays to the middle linebacker, and Huff filled that role to the hilt. His furious battles with great runners like Jim Brown and Green Bay's Jim Taylor were rugged grudge matches that made all three deservedly famous.

Huff was a third-round draft pick in 1956 as a guard; he was shifted to linebacker in training camp. He won the starting job in his rookie year. Over his eight seasons in New York, Huff became a legend as the leader of the first defense to get the acclaim and cheers normally reserved for the offense. In 1959, he became the first NFL player ever to appear on the cover of *Time* magazine, and one year later he was

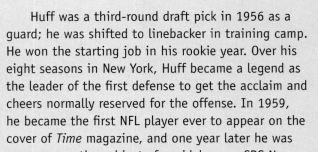

the subject of a widely-seen CBS News documentary called "The Violent World of Sam Huff." The documentary was narrated by Walter Cronkite; it was the first time a player had been wired with a microphone for a game. Huff was a hard and sometimes late tackler who also had the speed to cover passes. He set a record for linebackers with 30 interceptions for his career.

Huff, along with many Giants fans, cried when he learned that Allie Sherman had traded him to Washington in 1964 as part of a youth movement. Huff got his revenge on Sherman in 1966, when he sent the Redskins' field-goal unit onto the field—without Washington coach Otto Graham's approval—to kick an insulting three-pointer in the closing seconds of a 72–41 pounding of the Giants. The five-time Pro Bowl player was elected to the Hall of Fame in 1982; he has broadcast Redskin games for more than 30 years.

Legendary linebacker Sam Huff was the foundation of Tom Landry's 4-3 defense.

LOMBARDI'S TRICK PLAY

On this double-handoff special designed by Vince Lombardi, Charley Conerly (42) hands off to Alex Webster (29) heading left. Webster then hands the ball to Frank Gifford (16) in the backfield as Gifford heads through a gap created by right tackle Frank Youso (72) and pulling left guard Al Barry (68), while Conerly trails the play near the sideline. When Gifford nears Browns linebacker Galen Fiss (56) at the 10, he pitches back to Conerly, who scurries the rest of the way for the touchdown.

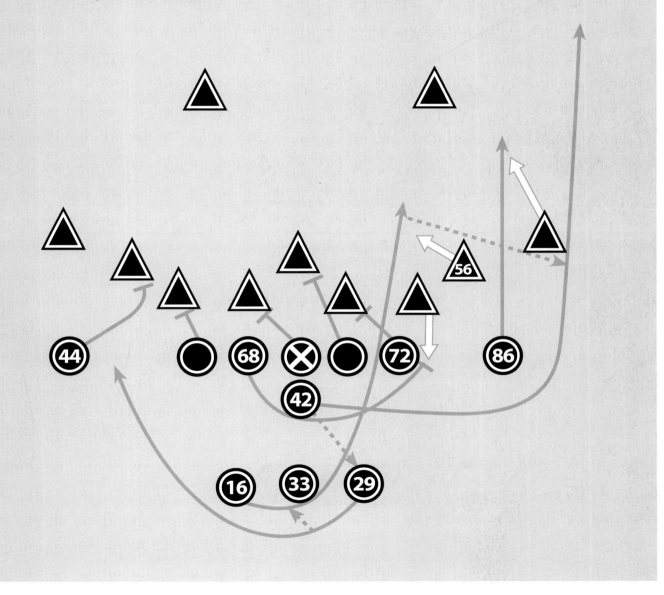

11 JASON FLEECES THE EAGLES

Sehorn's Pick Plucks Philadelphia

In a surprising season in which coach Jim Fassel guaranteed the Giants were going to the playoffs, New York stepped up and not only did that, but secured home-field advantage as well by achieving the best record in the NFC in 2000. For their first postseason opponent, the Giants drew their division rivals, the Philadelphia Eagles, under second-year coach Andy Reid and second-year quarterback Donovan McNabb. The Eagles came into this game fresh off a playoff victory over Tampa Bay, but Philadelphia had lost eight straight games to the Giants over the last four years.

Although the game turned out to be a sloppy defensive battle in which both teams turned the ball over three times, New York was in control and in the lead from the first play of the game. Philadelphia kicked off, and underachieving speedster Ron Dixon caught the kick at the 3-yard line. He traveled straight up the middle of the field, broke right at the 40 to avoid kicker David Akers, and then sailed untouched to the end zone for a 97-yard touchdown and a 7–0 New York lead 17 seconds into the game.

The Giants would not need much more. Although New York's offense was stalled, the Eagles were completely ineffectual. The Giants defense assigned defensive tackle Cornelius Griffin as a "spy" to follow the mobile McNabb's every move, and the Eagles would only keep the ball for 23 minutes during the contest.

A second score came early in the second quarter when a fumble by Eagles receiver Torrance Small led to a Brad Daluiso field goal. Then in the closing minutes of the period, Michael Strahan, who had two sacks on the day, forced another fumble in Eagles territory, but Tiki Barber fumbled the ball right back to Philadelphia on the 15. The Eagles managed a rare first down to set up the play of the day.

Donovan McNabb dropped back to pass, looking right the entire time. He fired a low sideline pass to Torrance Small on his knees. Jason Sehorn literally jumped the pattern by diving in front of Small to grab the ball at the 32, but it popped loose as Sehorn

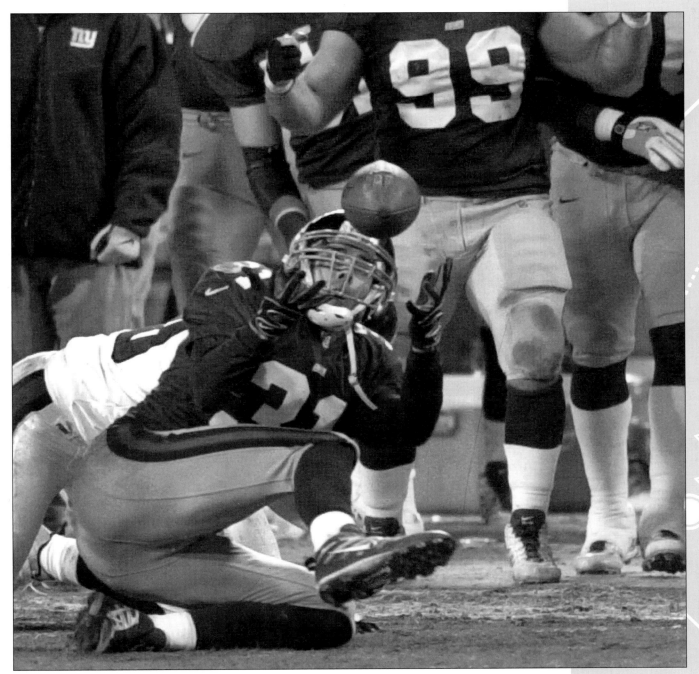

After having batted the ball into the air while rolling on the ground, cornerback Jason Sehorn manages to get to his feet and race to the end zone for a 32-yard game-changing touchdown against the Eagles. *(Photo courtesy of AP Images)*

JASON SEHORN

With this brilliant, juggling interception, Jason Sehorn displayed the unique, raw athletic ability that caused teammates to call the only white cornerback in the NFL "Species." Sehorn was 6'2" and 215 pounds, with 4.3 speed in the 40 and the stylish good looks to attract media overexposure.

Sehorn was not much of a student in high school, and he first tried minor league baseball in the Cubs organization. After finding curveballs too tough to hit, he went to junior college, where his football skills won him a transfer to USC. The Giants drafted him in the second round in 1994 on the strength of two years starring in the Trojans' defensive backfield. Sehorn became a Giants starter in his third year, and the following season, 1997, he was twice named the NFL's Defensive Player of the Week.

Injuries would prove to be his downfall, however. Over the years, his leg, ankle, rib, and knee problems caused him to miss 28 of 101 games after becoming a starter. Of most significance, he tore his ACL and MCL in the 1998 preseason trying out as a return man, a slot for which he had long lobbied coach Jim Fassel. It cost him the entire season.

He was slow to come back from the knee injury in 1999 and was never quite the same player again. He also became increasingly difficult to coach, and his teammates started referring to him as "Rodman" in reference to NBA star Dennis's spoiled, belligerent attitude. Released in a contract move by New York in 2003, he signed on for one last disappointing season with the Rams. Ultimately, aside from this signature play, he is most remembered for proposing to actress Angie Harmon on *The Tonight Show*. Despite his vast talent and potential, he never made a Pro Bowl roster and belongs in the category of What Might Have Been.

> As I popped it, it just hung there for a second, and I thought to myself, *Just go.* It was a slow-motion thing where everything seemed to work.
>
> —JASON SEHORN

> I thought only Torrance could get it, but [Sehorn] went down and got it and kept it alive. He made a great play.
>
> —DONOVAN MCNABB

> I saw him tapping it around and trying to gain control of it. I was trying to get up myself.
>
> —TORRANCE SMALL

GAME DETAILS

New York Giants 28 • Philadelphia Eagles 10

Date: January 7, 2001

Location: The Meadowlands

Attendance: 78,765

Significance: Divisional playoff game

Box Score:

Eagles	0	3	0	7	**10**
Giants	7	10	0	3	**20**

Scoring:

NYG Dixon 97-yard KO return (Daluiso PAT)
NYG Daluiso 37-yard FG
NYG Sehorn 32-yard interception return (Daluiso PAT)

PHL Akers 28-yard FG
NYG Daluiso 25-yard FG
PHL Small 10-yard pass from McNabb (Akers PAT)

Team	FD	YDS	RUSH	PASS	RTN	A-C-I	Sacked	PUNT	FUM	PEN
Eagles	11	186	14-46	140	127	41-20-1	6-41	8-42	3-2	6-50
Giants	15	237	43-112	125	187	19-12-0	1-0	7-32	3-3	4-18

Eagles: McNabb 181P
Giants: Collins 125P

hit the ground. Sehorn rolled over and batted the ball forward as he rose to one knee and caught it. As Sehorn stood up at the 26, teammate Emmanuel McDaniel crashed into him and was knocked down, but Jason took off, cutting inside Eagles tackle Jon Runyan at the 17 and beating McNabb to the corner of the end zone. Sehorn's amazing interception and touchdown return put New York up by a commanding 17–0 score.

While the Eagles managed a field goal to close the first half and even scored a touchdown late in the fourth quarter after blocking a punt, they were never in the game. Two big plays and a suffocating Giants defense ended the Eagles' playoff hopes. For the Giants, their relatively unimpressive win contributed to their being dangerously underestimated for the NFC Championship Game against Minnesota one week later. See Play 13 for how that turned out.

January 20, 2008

10 SUPER COOL

Webster's Overtime Interception Brings Redemption and Victory Over the Packers

The story of the 2007 NFL season was the explosive New England Patriots' attempt at an undefeated season. In the final week of the season, the 15–0 Patriots came to the Meadowlands, with both the Pats and Giants having already clinched their playoff seeding. Other teams in similar situations around the league were resting starters. However, the Patriots had committed to playing 60 minutes each game all year, so there was no doubt they would be going all out. To his credit, Tom Coughlin played his starters and went for the win as well. Despite losing 35–31 to New England in one of the best games of the year, the Giants gained league-wide respect and launched themselves on a stunning road playoff run.

New York had a losing record at home, but its steadily improving defense helped pave a 7–1 road record. In the wild-card round, the Giants took apart a well-rested but weak Tampa Bay team 24–14. In the divisional round, the Giants outlasted a well-rested but disorganized top-seeded Cowboys team 21–17. For the conference championship, the Giants would have to travel to frigid Green Bay where the second-seeded Packers,

who had taken a middle route by resting some starters in the finale, waited.

At kickoff, the temperature at Lambeau Field was minus-2 degrees with a minus-23 wind chill; it was the third-coldest game in recorded NFL history. The first time New York had the ball, the team drove 71 yards in 14 plays and bled nearly eight minutes off the clock in taking a 3–0 lead. This drive set the tone for the Giants, with its sure-handed mix of runs and passes, especially passes from Eli Manning to the uncoverable Plaxico Burress, who would catch 11 balls on the day to set a team playoff record.

A short drive to open the second quarter led to a second Lawrence Tynes field goal. However, the 6–0 lead was short-lived as Green Bay scored on the most spectacular play of the day immediately following the kickoff. From the Green Bay 10, Brett Favre dropped back to pass. Receiver Donald Driver pushed past an attempted chuck by cornerback Corey Webster and broke free as Webster slid to the ground. Favre hit a wide-open Driver around the 30, and he outraced Webster for the goal line on a 90-yard touchdown. The momentum seemed to be turning as Green Bay forced New York to punt on its next two possessions, and then drove to the Giants' 19 where Favre threw a screen pass to Brandon Jackson with two blockers in front of him. In a key stop, middle linebacker Antonio Pierce outflanked guard Jason Spitz and made the tackle for a one-yard gain. Green Bay settled for a field goal and a 10–6 halftime lead.

New York received the second half kickoff and took more than seven minutes to drive 69 yards for the go-ahead touchdown on a short run by Brandon Jacobs. Favre answered with a second touchdown pass to retake the lead, but Manning marched the Giants right back down the field for a 20–17 lead. Green Bay knotted the game at 20 early in the fourth quarter on a drive that was aided by Packers tackle Mark Tauscher's fumble recovery after Giants cornerback R.W. McQuarters picked off Favre, but lost the handle on the ball. Manning, who looked quite comfortable throwing the ball in the frosty conditions, again took the Giants deep into Packers territory, but Tynes missed a 43-yard field goal with less than seven minutes to play. Favre, who looked older and older as the game went on, was unable to move the Packers, and Manning gave Tynes a second chance from 36 yards with four seconds to play. After a bad snap by Jay Alford, though, Tynes missed a second time. Overtime.

Green Bay won the coin toss and started at their own 26. On the second

Much-maligned cornerback Corey Webster picks off Brett Favre on the second play of overtime, setting up Lawrence Tyne's game-winning field goal that sent the Giants to Super Bowl XLII.

TOM COUGHLIN

The extreme chill of the weather was clear on this evening in Green Bay from the deepening red on Tom Coughlin's cheeks, but he probably didn't even notice the cold as he watched his Giants playing the game the way he had wanted them to all along. Just one year before, it was widely suspected that Coughlin would be fired for the underachieving performance of his noisy, out-of-control players.

Coughlin was hired to be a disciplinarian, but before the close of this season, the Giants had been criticized for their streaky, inconsistent play and for a marked lack of discipline on the field. Coughlin spent three seasons as the receivers coach under Bill Parcells before moving on to the head coaching job at Boston College in 1991. In 1993, he was the Giants' first choice to replace Ray Handley, but turned them down

to remain at B.C. A year later, he took the dual head coach/general manager position for the expansion Jacksonville Jaguars and did an impressive job in getting them to two AFC Championship Games in his eight years before he was fired in 2003.

The Giants hired him to run a tighter ship than his predecessor Jim Fassel did. Coughlin instituted an intense, autocratic atmosphere where "on time" meant 5-10 minutes early, but it took the retirement of Tiki Barber and an injury to Jeremy Shockey to be fully accepted by the players. His teams have featured a lot of high-priced talents and have gotten off to good starts each year, but then faded down the stretch just as badly. In 2007, Coughlin softened his approach a bit and hired dynamic new defensive coordinator Steve Spagnuolo to turn things around. In the playoffs, the Giants at last played as a team, with few turnovers and penalties, all units contributing equally and without finger-pointing and selfish emotional displays. With the team's recent history, no one expected that to last for a four-game playoff run, but Coughlin took this underrated team all the way to the Super Bowl. What will he do for an encore in 2008?

> **W**e like it on the road. Our guys have heart. They're something. They never say die and find a way to win.
>
> —TOM COUGHLIN

The 2007 season was sweet redemption for embattled head coach Tom Coughlin.

GAME DETAILS

New York Giants 23 • Green Bay Packers 20

Location: Lambeau Field, Green Bay

Attendance: 72,740

Significance: NFC Championship Game

Box Score:

As a DB, we have to have a short-term memory, but I wanted to come back and make a play so bad. I just wanted to make a play and the coaches said, 'You will get an opportunity.'

—COREY WEBSTER

Giants	3	3	14	0	3	**23**
Packers	0	10	7	3	0	**20**

Scoring:
NYG Tynes 29-yard FG
NYG Tynes 37-yard FG
GBP Driver 90-yard pass from Favre (Crosby PAT)
GBP Crosby 36-yard FG

NYG Jacobs 1-yard run (Tynes PAT)
GBP Lee 12-yard pass from Favre (Crosby PAT)
NYG Bradshaw 4-yard run (Tynes PAT)
GBP Crosby 37-yard FG
NYG Tynes 47-yard FG

Team	FD	YDS	RUSH	PASS	RTN	A-C-I	Sacked	PUNT	FUM	PEN
Giants	24	380	39-134	246	165	40-21-0	2-8	4-33	5-1	6-50
Packers	13	264	14-28	236	104	35-19-2	0-0	6-32	1-0	7-37

Giants: Manning 254P, Burress 154C
Packers: Favre 236P, Driver 141C

When you're out on the field, it's hot. But once you got back to the sideline, your fingers started to ache, and you really felt it. It was miserable.

—CHRIS SNEE

play from scrimmage, the Packers ran a play they had run three times earlier in the game. Tight end Donald Lee shifts back into the backfield before the snap while Donald Driver moves up to the line. While it appears that Lee will act as a lead-blocking fullback on a run, instead Favre drops back and throws an out pattern. The play had worked twice before—but not this time. Cornerback Corey Webster stayed right with Driver and was in perfect position to jump the pattern and intercept Favre's underthrown pass at the 43. A skittering nine-yard return gave the Giants the ball at the Green Bay 34. Two runs by Ahmad Bradshaw placed the ball at the 29, and Tynes nailed the 47-yard field goal. Tynes and Corey Webster had their atonement, and New York had a rematch with the undefeated 18–0 Patriots.

January 20, 1991

9 TAKING THE HEART FROM SAN FRANCISCO

Giants Win NFC on Final Play

The Giants and the 49ers stormed through the 1990 season on a collision course for a *Monday Night Football* showdown in San Francisco in Week 12. Both teams won their first 10 games and then lost in Week 11 before the most anticipated game of the year.

In the prime-time, hard-fought defensive battle, the two-time defending champion 49ers survived, 7–3, despite the Giants twice having a first-and-goal—New York could only manage a field goal in those eight plays. Both teams would lose just one more game before the playoffs, but New York suffered an even bigger loss against the Buffalo Bills: starting quarterback Phil Simms went down to a season-ending foot injury. The team's fortunes fell into the hands of career backup Jeff Hostetler and the rugged Giants defense.

The first half set the fierce tone for the NFC Championship Game. The 49ers took the opening kickoff and drove far enough for a field goal. The Giants answered with a 15-play drive for their own field goal. These were the two best defenses in the league, and the hitting was ferocious right from the start. Defenders on both sides were delivering shots that left bodies strewn on the field. The second quarter saw two more field goals and a 6–6 tie at the half.

Early in the third quarter, Joe Montana hit John Taylor for a 61-yard scoring pass (which Everson Walls just missed intercepting) for the only touchdown in the game. The Giants continued with their game plan, though—a slow and steady ground game that would result in time-of-possession dominance of 39 to 21 minutes.

However, in the fourth quarter, New York still trailed 13–9. They needed some big plays, and soon. With less than 10 minutes to play, the 49ers faced third down at their own 23-yard line when Joe Montana rolled right to pass. Giants end Leonard Marshall was blocked and knocked down, but he scrambled to his feet and chased after Montana. Marshall nearly ran right through the 49ers quarterback, sending the ball flying and knocking Montana out of the game.

San Francisco punted, but New York's ensuing drive stalled at its own 46. As the Giants lined up to punt on fourth-and-two,

Let's say that Roger fumbles two plays later. That could have been the difference, not giving them enough time. When you lose a game like this one, you can put your finger on a thousand little things. And even if Joe is in there in that situation, he would have been handing off, too, trying to run out the clock. I'll just give the Giants the credit they deserve and leave it at that.

—BOBB MCKITTRICK, 49ERS LINE COACH

Lawrence Taylor recovers a San Francisco fumble to help set up Matt Bahr's game-winning field goal. *(Photo courtesy of AP Images)*

LEONARD MARSHALL

The remarkable sequence of big plays in the last eight minutes of this championship game was started by Giants defensive end Leonard Marshall, who got up off his knees to run down Joe Montana and send both the quarterback and the ball flying. Marshall made a habit of making big plays during his 10-year career with the Giants. He was a complete player, strong against both the pass and the run.

A second-round draft pick out of LSU in 1983, Marshall was called "the steal of the draft" by the Raiders' Al Davis. It did not look that way at first. Marshall reported to training camp 20 pounds overweight and out of shape, with little pass-rushing technique. The Giants even assigned an assistant trainer to trail Marshall in the evenings and prevent him from making any late-night fast-food runs. Marshall worked hard, however, and

> **We left our heart here last time. But we knew we'd be back here to recapture it.**
>
> **—LEONARD MARSHALL**

within two years, Bill Parcells referred to him as one of the best "weight-room guys" on the team and cited that as the reason for his improvement as a player.

Marshall often teamed up with Lawrence Taylor on the right side, and the two formed a knockout punch for the Big Blue Wrecking Crew for several seasons. There were three seasons in which Marshall would record double-digit sacks, and he was twice named All-Pro. With the Giants, Marshall would sometimes play inside as a tackle on passing downs, and when he signed with the Jets as a free agent in 1993, he was moved to defensive tackle. After one injury-plagued year there, he was cut; he then played one final season with the Redskins before retiring. But he will always be remembered as a big-time player in two Giants Super Bowl runs.

Leonard Marshall separates Joe Montana from the football and ends the quarterback's day to start the Giants' fourth-quarter comeback in the 1990 NFC Championship Game.

GAME DETAILS

New York Giants 15 • San Francisco 49ers 13

Date: January 20, 1991

Location: Candlestick Park, San Francisco

Attendance: 65,750

Significance: NFC Championship Game on the road against two-time Super Bowl champs

Box Score:

Giants	3	3	3	6	**15**
49ers	3	3	7	0	**13**

Scoring:
SF Cofer 47-yard FG
NYG Bahr 28-yard FG
NYG Bahr 42-yard FG
SF Cofer 35-yard FG

SF Taylor 61-yard pass from Montana (Cofer PAT)
NYG Bahr 46-yard FG
NYG Bahr 38-yard FG
NYG Bahr 42-yard FG

Team	FD	YDS	RUSH	PASS	RTN	A-C-I	Sacked	PUNT	FUM	PEN
Giants	20	311	36-152	159	81	29-15-0	3-17	5-42	0-0	5-45
49ers	13	240	11-39	201	125	27-19-0	3-14	5-40	3-1	9-63

Giants: Hostetler 176P
49ers: Montana 190P

Bill Parcells gave blocking back Gary Reasons a green light for a fake if he saw a hole. Reasons saw daylight, took the snap, and rumbled 30 yards to the 49ers' 16. Four plays later, Matt Bahr kicked his fourth field goal, and the Giants trailed by just a point with under six minutes to go.

With Steve Young now at quarterback, San Francisco tried to run out the clock. Roger Craig fumbled on the first play, but the 49ers recovered. Young then hit Brent Jones for 25 yards. After a couple more runs, the 49ers had a first down on the Giants' 30. On the next play, Roger Craig took the handoff as Giants tackle Eric Howard dropped to one knee to knife past guard Guy McIntyre and blast the ball out of Craig's grasp. Craig immediately swung around to grab it, but in that instant Lawrence Taylor popped up and snatched the ball out of the air.

The Giants had the ball at their own 43 with 2:36 left. Hostetler hit Mark Bavaro for 19 yards and Stephen Baker for 13 in a seven-play drive to the 49ers' 24, where Matt Bahr hit his fifth field goal as time expired. Giants 15, 49ers 13. There would be no three-peat; New York was headed for the Super Bowl to face the Buffalo Bills.

November 16, 1986

Simms Saves Game with Sensational Strike on Fourth-and-17

Giants Edge Vikings 22–20

In a tense, tight struggle between two teams with playoff aspirations, the Giants prevailed because of the efforts of their much-maligned quarterback, a disrespected receiving corps, and their fifth option at place-kicker in 1986. Neither the Vikings nor the Giants could run the ball very effectively during the game, but both passers were on target.

The two teams traded field goals throughout the first half, with Raul Allegre hitting three for New York. Trailing 9–6, Minnesota finally crossed the goal line in the third quarter, on an eight-yard pass from Tommy Kramer to Allen Rice. Another Allegre field goal late in the third period brought New York to within a point, and a few minutes later, Phil Simms hit Bobby Johnson for a 25-yard touchdown to go up by six with 10 minutes to play. An injured Kramer was replaced at quarterback by Wade Wilson, but the Vikings roared down the field in seven plays behind their backup quarterback, taking a 20–19 lead on a 33-yard pass to Anthony Carter with just seven minutes to play.

The teams' defenses stiffened and they exchanged punts, with New York getting the ball at its own 41-yard line with 2:14 left in the game. After making a first down at the Vikings' 45, though, two incompletions and a sack left the Giants facing a seemingly impossible fourth-and-17 with 1:12 to play. Minnesota was in a three-deep zone with four down linemen, one linebacker, and six defensive backs.

After consulting with Bill Parcells, Simms called "half right 74," in which the Giants lined up with three receivers spread wide. Phil McConkey went in motion to the right before the snap and broke downfield untouched. To his right, Bobby Johnson ran for the right sideline, while Stacy Robinson ran a crossing pattern on the left. Simms first looked for Robinson and then turned right and floated one for Johnson, as defensive tackle Mike Stensrud crashed into Simms. The pass to Johnson was perfectly

GAME DETAILS

New York Giants 22 • Minnesota Vikings 20

Date: November 16, 1986

Location: Hubert H. Humphrey Metrodome, Minneapolis

Attendance: 62,003

Significance: A game with playoff implications

Box Score:

Giants	3	6	3	10	**22**
Vikings	3	3	7	7	**20**

Scoring:
NYG Allegre 41-yard FG
MIN Nelson 39-yard FG
NYG Allegre 37-yard FG
MIN Nelson 44-yard FG
NYG Allegre 24-yard FG

MIN Rice 8-yard pass from Kramer (Nelson PAT)
NYG Allegre 37-yard FG
NYG Johnson 25-yard pass from Simms (Allegre PAT)
MIN Carter 33-yard pass from Wilson (Nelson PAT)
NYG Allegre 33-yard FG

> **I** just ran to the first-down marker and stopped. And when I turned, the ball was there.
>
> —BOBBY JOHNSON

Team	FD	YDS	RUSH	PASS	RTN	A-C-I	Sacked	PUNT	FUM	PEN
Giants	23	383	25-90	293	90	38-25-2	2-17	2-56	1-0	5-25
Vikings	21	353	25-109	244	118	31-20-0	3-11	4-48	1-1	8-108

Giants: Simms 310P
Vikings: Kramer 187P

placed over the cornerback's head, and Johnson cradled it at the 30 and stepped out of bounds to stop the clock. The play kept the Giants' hopes alive.

The Giants moved the ball to the 15 and ran the clock down to 12 seconds before Raul Allegre came in to kick his fifth field goal of the game for the 22–20 win. Allegre, who wasn't signed by the team until the fourth week of the season, earned a game ball, but the cool leadership of Simms won the game. Simms later told reporter Dick Schaap that during the week Parcells had said to him, "You're a great quarterback, and you got that way by being daring and fearless, so let's go." Simms lived up to that billing on this day.

HALF RIGHT 74

On fourth-and-17, the Giants went with "half right 74." Phil McConkey (80) went in motion to the right before the snap and broke toward the end zone on a go-route inside Bobby Johnson's (88) out pattern. Bavaro sensed a blitz and stayed in to block, while runner Joe Morris (20) headed for the middle of the field. Simms (11) dropped back and hit Johnson on the sideline, just beyond the first-down marker.

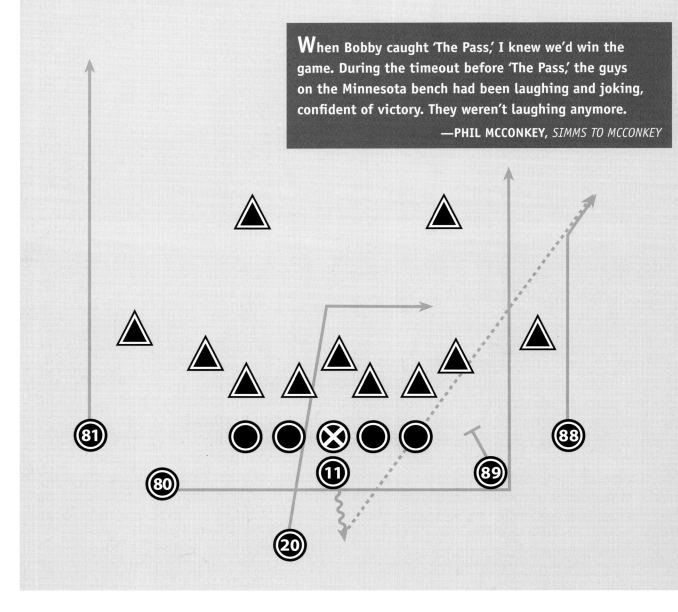

When Bobby caught 'The Pass,' I knew we'd win the game. During the timeout before 'The Pass,' the guys on the Minnesota bench had been laughing and joking, confident of victory. They weren't laughing anymore.

—**PHIL MCCONKEY**, *SIMMS TO MCCONKEY*

Phil Simms

In retrospect, many Giants players pointed to this comeback win over the Vikings as their biggest win—the win that showed them they could go all the way. It also established Phil Simms as a big-time quarterback. Bill Parcells told the media, "Anybody who doesn't think Phil Simms is a great quarterback should be covering another sport."

It wasn't always that way. When Simms was drafted number seven overall out of unknown Morehead State in 1979, Giants fans at the NFL Draft booed. Because the television cameras missed the Simms draft announcement, NBC asked Pete Rozelle to make the announcement again, and Simms was booed a second time as Rozelle snickered.

Following that omen, Phil was beset by shoulder separations, a knee injury, and a fractured thumb in his first five years. With Simms's propensity for interceptions, Parcells did not trust him, and he gave the starting job to Scott Brunner in 1983. Simms demanded a trade, but in 1984, he won the starting job back and threw for more than 4,000 yards, gaining Parcells's confidence and respect.

Even in 1986, though, there were doubters. Famous Giants fan and author Frederick Exley wrote a piece for *The New York Times* two weeks *after* this game in which he bemoaned that the Giants would ultimately fail because of Simms. Simms, however, proved to be a tough field general who wouldn't quit. He led the team to its first Super Bowl championship that year, forever silencing all critics.

Despite earning the respect of fans, teammates, and the media, the end of Simms's career was somewhat ignominious. After Phil's foot injury allowed the younger Jeff Hostetler to step forward and lead the Giants to a second title in 1990, a quarterback controversy was created, and new coach Ray Handley gave the starting nod to Hostetler in 1991. Simms didn't get his starting job back till 1993—when, at age 37,

> **P**arcells kissed me as I came into the locker room. 'You can play on my team anytime,' he said.
>
> —**PHIL SIMMS**, *SIMMS TO MCCONKEY*

he had one of the finest seasons of his 14-year career and led New York to the playoffs one last time.

Simms wanted to continue playing, but the Giants cut him in the off-season as a casualty of the new salary cap. He still dominates the Giants' passing record book, with more than 33,000 passing yards, 199 touchdowns, 21 games of more than 300 yards, 17 fourth-quarter comebacks, and 95 wins. The Giants retired his No. 11 jersey, and Phil has gone on to a very successful second career as a broadcaster.

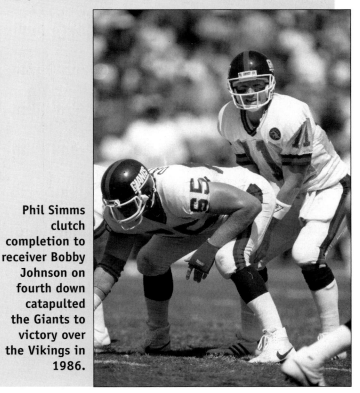

Phil Simms clutch completion to receiver Bobby Johnson on fourth down catapulted the Giants to victory over the Vikings in 1986.

January 4, 1987

Burt Delivers Knockout Blow

Giants Crumple 49ers 49–3

Whenever the Giants met the 49ers in the 1980s, it was like a heavyweight championship boxing match between a puncher and a boxer. The Giants excelled at a smash-mouth, run-oriented game, while the 49ers relied on their pass-oriented West Coast offense. The two teams played several competitive games throughout the decade, so this mauling by the Giants in the 1986 postseason is notable for its one-sidedness. The game had begun to slip away from the 49ers by the end of the first half, but it was nose tackle Jim Burt's brutal takedown of quarterback Joe Montana that fully decided the outcome.

Montana would best Giants quarterback Phil Simms in six of their nine head-to-head matchups over the years, but the Giants had roughed up Montana the previous year in the playoffs, and they had also come back from a 17–0 first-half deficit to beat the Niners in the 1986 regular season. Despite the fact that the Giants pulled out that game 21–17, Bill Parcells found just the needle to jab his offensive line as they prepared for the playoffs. One reason the Giants fell so far behind is that the team gained only 13 yards rushing all game. In the run-up to this divisional playoff game against those same 49ers, Parcells spent the week calling his offensive line "Club 13," just his way of telling them that they needed to do a lot better.

The game began as a competitive affair. On the 49ers' first series, Jerry Rice caught a slant from Montana at midfield with no blue shirts in front of him, and he headed for the goal line. At the 26-yard line, though, Rice inexplicably lost his grip on the football and was unable to pick up the bouncing ball. Trailing Giants safety Kenny Hill was able to fall on the ball in the end zone for a touchback. From the 20, Simms then led the Giants on an 80-yard drive, culminating in a 24-yard touchdown pass to Mark Bavaro. Before the first period ended, San Francisco answered with a field goal, but those three points would prove to be their only points of the game.

Midway through the second quarter, Herb Welch intercepted Montana, and on the next play, Joe Morris ran 45 yards for

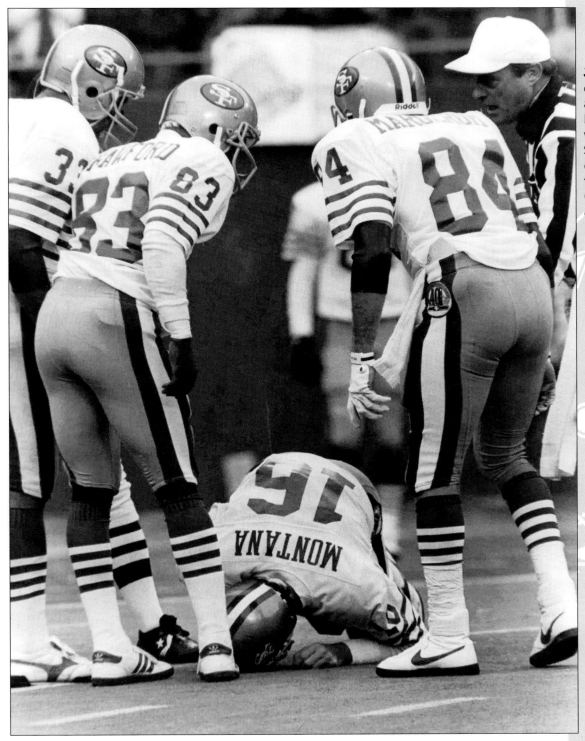

Joe Montana's day was over after being hit by Jim Burt, and with him went San Francisco's chance against the mighty Giants. *(Photo courtesy of WireImages)*

A FAKE FIELD GOAL

A second key play was the fake field goal in the second quarter. Leading 14–3 with two minutes left, the Giants faced fourth-and-six at the 49ers' 28. The field-goal unit that came onto the field included tight end Mark Bavaro (89) and fullbacks Maurice Carthon (44) and Tony Galbreath (30), who don't usually perform on that squad. When holder Jeff Rutledge (17) called "Shift," he rose up, Carthon shifted back, and the kicker, Raul Allegre (2), went out as a flanker. Allegre drew a defensive back in coverage even though he had never caught a pass in his life at any level. Bavaro easily shed the linebacker who covered him and caught a 23-yard pass for a first-and-goal at the 5.

> They played a perfect game. We were shattered by a great team. I believe they will go all the way.
>
> —BILL WALSH

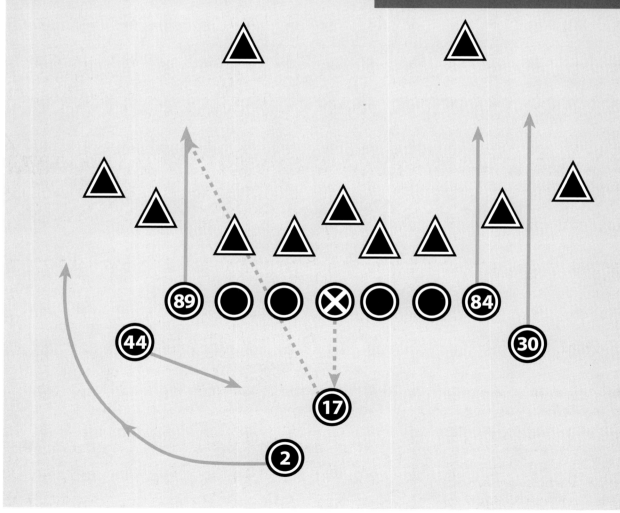

GAME DETAILS

New York Giants 49 • San Francisco 49ers 3

Date: January 4, 1987

Location: The Meadowlands

Attendance: 75,691

Significance: Divisional playoff game

Box Score:

49ers	3	0	0	0	**3**
Giants	7	21	21	0	**49**

Scoring:
NYG Bavaro 24-yard pass from Simms (Allegre PAT)
SF Wersching 26-yard FG
NYG Morris 45-yard run (Allegre PAT)
NYG Johnson 15-yard pass from Simms (Allegre PAT)
NYG Taylor 34-yard interception return (Allegre PAT)
NYG McConkey 28-yard pass from Simms (Allegre PAT)
NYG Mowatt 29-yard pass from Simms (Allegre PAT)
NYG Morris 2-yard run (Allegre PAT)

Team	FD	YDS	RUSH	PASS	RTN	A-C-I	Sacked	PUNT	FUM	PEN
49ers	9	184	20-29	155	130	37-15-3	1-7	10-40	2-1	11-62
Giants	21	366	44-216	150	166	20-10-0	1-9	7-44	0-0	3-23

Giants: Joe Morris 159R

a score to go up 14–3. Behind an inspired front line, Morris had more than 100 yards rushing in the first half; he ended the day with 159.

At the end of the second quarter, the Giants put the game away in a series of superlative plays from the offense, defense, and special teams. The Giants had driven to the 49ers' 28, where they faced a fourth-and-six. Parcells aggressively called for a fake field goal, and holder Jeff Rutledge hit Mark Bavaro for a 23-yard gain to the 5. After a holding call, Simms went back to pass from the 15. Just as Simms unloaded a 15-yard touchdown strike to Bobby Johnson, though, Dwaine Board drove Phil into the ground headfirst so that he never saw the play and left the field a bit woozy. The Giants led 21–3 with 50 seconds left in the half.

After the kickoff came the knockout blow from the defense. Montana went back to pass, looking for Rice. As he released the ball, nose tackle Jim Burt sent Montana flying backward; the quarterback landed on his head and was knocked unconscious. The pass was intercepted by Lawrence Taylor at the 34 and returned for a clinching touchdown. Montana, who had courageously come

Jim Burt

Because he was just 6'1" and injury-prone, Jim Burt was completely bypassed in the 1981 draft and signed with the Giants as a free agent, where he came under the influence of new defensive coordinator Bill Parcells. During a game in his rookie season, Burt was so upset at not getting in the defensive-line rotation that he gave Parcells a forearm to the back, knocking the coach onto the field. The two would have a love-hate relationship that extended beyond the eight years they spent together in New York. Burt's teammates saw the two as so similar in temperament that they referred to Burt as "Parcells Jr."

Burt was an emotional player who put forth maximum effort at all times and loved practical jokes and tall tales. Parcells said of Burt that he "runs two quarts low," and the coach used him as a whipping boy for severe criticism aimed indirectly at the overall team. In an attempt to even the score with the acerbic Parcells in 1984, Burt dumped a Gatorade container over his coach's head after a victory. That practice became a signature of the 1986 Giants during their Super Bowl run; it has since become part of football victory celebrations everywhere.

During his career, Burt developed back problems that led to his departure from New York. Although they re-signed him in the spring of 1989, the Giants got nervous about Burt's back and forced him to announce his retirement before training camp that year. Parcells said at the time: "He's one of the very, very best players I've been fortunate enough to coach. We have a very special relationship, not only as a player-coach, but personally. This is a very sad time for me. A little of my heart and soul is going. I love the guy." General manager George Young added that he "didn't want to see Jim Burt in a wheelchair."

In October of 1989, though, Burt signed with the 49ers, just three years after he drilled Joe Montana out of the playoffs. Before the two teams met that season, Burt referred to his ex-coach when he said he would be looking for "a fat guy with headphones on" to barrel over. He spent two years with San Francisco as a backup and won his second Super Bowl ring a year before his former Giants teammates won theirs. Preparing for that Super Bowl as a 49er, Burt told Frank Litsky of *The New York Times*, "The Giants? That was my life. My heart was broken. They made a business decision. I didn't look at it that way. I should have."

back in midseason from back surgery, had a concussion and was done for the day—and so were the 49ers. After the game, Burt said of the devastating hit, "It was clean, but I don't feel good about it."

In the third quarter, Simms threw two more touchdown passes and Joe Morris ran for a second score, while backup quarterback Jeff Kemp was able to do nothing for the Niners. By the end of the game, the Giants had accumulated 216 yards rushing and had controlled the clock for over 34 minutes. The defense picked off three passes, gobbled up a fumble, and limited San Francisco to just 29 yards rushing.

The worst thing about the game for Parcells was finding flaws to fire up his troops for the following week's conference championship game against the Redskins. Ever the motivator, Parcells greeted his linemen the day after the game with: "My quarterback took too many shots to the mouth." The Giants would thrash the Redskins 17–0 to advance to the Super Bowl.

Defensive tackle Jim Burt's hit on Joe Montana led to a Lawrence Taylor interception and a concussion for the 49ers quarterback in the Giants 49–3 playoff victory. *(Photo courtesy of WireImages)*

January 27, 1991

6 NEW YORK CLOCKS BUFFALO

Giants Control Ball and Bills in Super Bowl Upset

Super Bowl XXV was a classic matchup of two very different 13–3 teams. The AFC's Buffalo Bills led the league with 428 points in 1990—an average of 27 per game—and were noted as a pioneer of the fast-paced, attack-mode, no-huddle offense. The New York Giants, by contrast, led the NFL by allowing just 211 points during the season, an average of 13 per game. But they had finished just 15th in scoring and were further hampered by having lost their starting quarterback, Phil Simms, to a foot injury in a loss to these same Bills in Week 15. Since then, the Giants had relied on backup Jeff Hostetler and their defense to keep winning games. It was no surprise that the Bills were seven-point favorites in this clash of opposites.

The Giants' plan was simple: keep the ball out of the hands of Bills quarterback Jim Kelly by running the ball and avoiding turnovers. On defense, the Giants often employed just two down linemen, allowing Kelly time to throw but blanketing and roughing up his receivers.

The first quarter ran according to form. The Bills went three-and-out on their opening drive, while the Giants drove 58 yards in 10 plays and took 6:15 off the clock before kicking a field goal. Buffalo answered with a 61-yard bomb to James Lofton that set up an equalizing field goal.

Buffalo opened the second quarter with a 12-play, 80-yard drive, capped by a Don Smith touchdown run, to take a 10–3 lead. The Bills extended that lead midway through the second period when they pinned the Giants on their own 7-yard line. On second down, Hostetler tripped over Ottis Anderson's foot and was sacked in the end zone by Bruce Smith for a safety and a 12–3 Buffalo lead. However, New York's defense stiffened, and the Giants got the ball on their own 13 with 3:49 to play in the period. Hostetler mixed rollout passes and straight drops with an 18-yard Anderson run and a 17-yard Dave Meggett scamper to move 87 yards in 10 plays. The vital score came on third-and-10 from the Buffalo 14, when Hostetler hit Stephen Baker in the

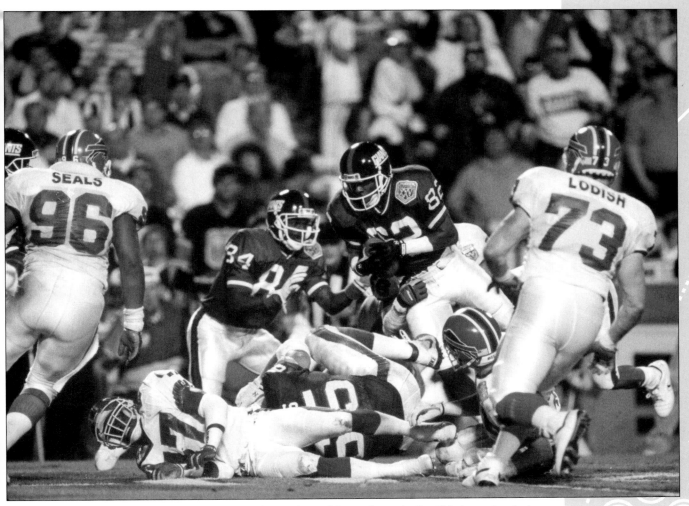

Mark Ingram's conversion of a crucial third-down play midway through the third quarter led to the Giants' second touchdown and eventual victory over the Bills in Super Bowl XXV.

corner of the end zone to narrow the gap to 12–10 at the half.

Hostetler was at his best during the opening drive of the second half. Again mixing rollouts, dropbacks, and runs by Anderson and Meggett, Hostetler slowly marched the Giants 75 yards in 14 plays that took 9:29 off the clock, the most time-consuming drive in Super Bowl history. Along the way, Hostetler converted four third downs. The most exciting conversion came on a third-and-13 from the Buffalo 32. Hostetler hit receiver Mark Ingram at the 26, where Ingram spun around converging tackler Kirby Jackson. At the 24, Ingram pivoted and spun in reverse as linebacker

Jeff Hostetler

In the locker room after this great Super Bowl victory, star backup quarterback Jeff Hostetler was surrounded by teammates joyfully mocking him with chants of "You can't win! You can't do it! You're just a backup!" At last, to the surprise of everyone outside the Giants' locker room, Hostetler had shown what he could do. However, Bill Parcells was not surprised at his success, saying, "We didn't put a rookie in the game."

Hostetler never had a smooth road. Once Todd Blackledge beat him out for the starting job at Penn State, he transferred to West Virginia, where he was an academic All-American and eventually married the daughter of coach Don Nehlen. The Giants drafted him in the third round of the 1984 draft, but he would not throw his first pass until 1988. During his time as the third-string quarterback, Jeff also served as emergency tight end and even blocked a punt. When he took over for the injured Simms in 1990, he had thrown just 58 passes as the Giants' frustrated backup quarterback.

His postseason success led to an immediate quarterback controversy. Head coach Ray Handley chose the younger and more mobile Hostetler, but Simms still got playing time during the next two unsuccessful seasons. Both quarterbacks found this to be an intolerable situation, so new coach Dan Reeves chose Simms as his starter in 1993 and allowed Hostetler to leave as a free agent.

Hostetler spent four seasons as the starter with the Raiders, throwing for more than 3,000 yards in two of those seasons, but his time there is most remembered for his coach Art Shell sneeringly dismissing him as a "white" quarterback. Hostetler moved on to the Redskins for a season and then retired. As a Giant, he only had 632 pass attempts for 20 touchdowns and 12 interceptions, but he will always be remembered as a Super Bowl hero.

Darryl Talley grabbed him by the neck, but Ingram shook loose. Ingram then juked Mark Kelso at the 23, ran right, stopped again at the 21, and spun once more as defender James Williams grabbed his foot. Talley reemerged and dove for Ingram's back as the receiver lunged fully forward to the 18, with Mike Lodish and Chris Hale piled on. Ingram had gotten past six Bills players for the first down in this key play that demonstrated the Giants' determination. The touchdown that followed on a short Anderson run gave the Giants a 17–12 lead that held into the fourth quarter.

The Bills took the lead back on the first play of the final period, in which brilliant runner Thurman Thomas broke two tackles on a shotgun draw play and scored from 31 yards out. Again, Hostetler bled the clock and moved the ball, this time for 74 yards in 13 plays over seven minutes and 32 seconds. A 21-yard Matt Bahr field goal gave New York a slim one-point lead, 20–19, with 7:20 to play.

Buffalo was unable to move the ball and punted to New York. The Giants could only make one first down, but they used up three minutes of clock and two Buffalo timeouts before giving the ball back to the Bills at their own 10-yard line with 2:16 to play. As the clock ticked away, New York's suffocating pass defense forced Buffalo to move the ball on the ground. Kelly could only complete two short passes for 10 yards, but three scrambles gained 18 yards, and two Thomas bursts gained 33 more. Kelly spiked the ball at the New York 29 with eight seconds left.

Scott Norwood's wide right 47-yard missed field goal gave the Giants the championship. It was a remarkable team accomplishment by an outgunned underdog. The Giants achieved an astounding time-of-possession

GAME DETAILS

New York Giants 20 • Buffalo Bills 19

Date: January 27, 1991

Location: Tampa Stadium, Tampa

Attendance: 73,813

Significance: Super Bowl XXV

Box Score:

Bills	3	9	0	7	**19**
Giants	3	7	7	3	**20**

Scoring:
NYG Bahr 28-yard FG
BUF Norwood 23-yard FG
BUF Smith 1-yard run (Norwood PAT)
BUF Smith tackled Hostetler for safety
NYG Baker 14-yard pass from Hostetler (Bahr PAT)
NYG Anderson 1-yard run (Bahr PAT)
BUF Thomas 31-yard run (Norwood PAT)
NYG Bahr 21-yard FG

Team	FD	YDS	RUSH	PASS	RTN	A-C-I	Sacked	PUNT	FUM	PEN
Bills	18	371	25-166	205	114	30-18-0	1-7	6-39	0-0	6-35
Giants	24	386	39-172	214	85	32-20-0	2-8	4-44	0-0	5-31

Bills: Thomas 135R, Kelly 212P
Giants: Anderson 102R, Hostetler 222P

> **I** was just trying to get to the first-down markers.
>
> —MARK INGRAM

> **H**e made two open-field, stop-and-start moves, pure change of direction moves that just stopped the tackler.
>
> —SAM WYCHE ON MARK INGRAM, QUOTED IN *THE NEW YORK TIMES*

supremacy of 40:33 to 19:27 as they choked off the most explosive offense in the league and outgained Buffalo—both on the ground and in the air. New York won behind the labors of its relentless, aging defense; a resourceful, mistake-free exhibit by their backup quarterback, who took a fearful physical beating in the game; and a punishing MVP performance by Ottis Anderson, the oldest running back in the NFL. No player exuded the Giants' fighting spirit more than receiver Mark Ingram, though, whose battling first-down catch in the third quarter exemplified this total team effort.

BILL PARCELLS

Bill Parcells's basic philosophy, "Power wins football games," prevailed in Super Bowl XXV. The Giants weren't going to outrun the Bills, but they proved they could overpower them. Unfortunately, it was the last game that Parcells would coach for the Giants. In May, he stepped down somewhat mysteriously, although it later became clear that he was having health problems that necessitated his taking a break from coaching.

The New Jersey native was a perfect fit in the Meadowlands. He began as the linebackers coach and defensive coordinator under Ray Perkins, and he impressed general manager George Young so much that he was quickly named head coach when Perkins left to succeed Bear Bryant at the University of Alabama.

It took a year for Parcells to assert himself and feel comfortable in the position, but once he did, few have done it better. Parcells was a players' coach that established real relationships with each player,

> The whole plan was to shorten the game.
>
> —BILL PARCELLS

treating each one differently as he tried to get the best out of them through various psychological prods and manipulations. It helped that Lawrence Taylor bought into his program, and in return Parcells showed great concern for the off-the-field problems of Taylor and others. Certain tough and gritty players even became known as Parcells's "guys," following the gruff coach from one coaching stop to another.

Parcells returned to coaching in New England in 1993 and took the Patriots to the Super Bowl in his fourth year, but then conflicts with owner Robert Kraft caused him to leave. Subsequent tours with the Jets and the Cowboys brought similar results: he took each team to the playoffs, but was never able to repeat the ultimate success he experienced twice as the coach of the New York Giants. In late 2007, Parcells agreed to become the head of football operations for the Miami Dolphins.

Super Bowl XXV was the final game in the Giants coaching career of Bill Parcells. *(Photo courtesy of AP Images)*

Jeff Hostetler went from backup quarterback to Super Bowl hero in 1991.
(Photo courtesy of AP Images)

Coach's Blunder, Quarterback's Bobble

Giants Fumble Away Season to Eagles

In Philadelphia, the play is still called the "Miracle of the Meadowlands" 30 years later, but in New York it will forever be "the Fumble." In 1978, neither the Giants nor the Eagles had been in a playoff game for at least 15 years. In fact, the Giants' record from 1964 through 1977 was 68–124–4, while the Eagles achieved a nearly identical mark of 68–122–6. In 1978, New York and Philadelphia were stumbling around on the outskirts of playoff contention and came into this Week 12 match with 5–6 and 6–5 records, respectively. It came as a surprise that this clumsily played game would be a turning point for each ill-managed franchise.

New York got off to an early lead as bargain-basement quarterback "Parkway Joe" Pisarcik led the Giants on a nine-play, 72-yard drive, capped by a touchdown pass to Bobby Hammond halfway through the first quarter. Less than two minutes later, Brad Van Pelt intercepted a Ron Jaworski pass, and Pisarcik cashed in on a 30-yard strike to Johnny Perkins for a 14–0 lead.

The Eagles got back into the game with 1:26 left in the half when Wilbert Montgomery ran for an eight-yard touchdown. A bad snap on the extra point proved costly to Philadelphia; their kicker Nick Mike-Mayer was injured trying to throw a pass on the botched play. The Giants then moved into scoring position quickly, but Pisarcik was picked off in the end zone at the end of the first half.

Joe Danelo extended the Giants' lead to 17–6 in the third quarter, but the Eagles closed the gap with less than four minutes remaining in the lackluster game when Mike Hogan bulled in from the 1-yard line. The touchdown came after the Birds had driven 91 yards in 13 plays, aided by three Giants penalties. Punter Mike Michel missed the extra point, and Philadelphia trailed 17–12.

Giants running back Doug Kotar fumbled the ball away at his 33 with 3:22 to play, but two minutes later cornerback Odis McKinney intercepted a Jaworski pass at the New York 10, seemingly preserving a victory that would leave both teams with 6–6 records. The Giants called three running plays and used up the Eagles' timeouts. With 31 seconds left in the game, New York faced a third-and-two at their own 28. All

That's the most horrifying ending to a ball game I've ever seen.

—GIANTS COACH JOHN MCVAY

After a botched exchange between Giants quarterback Joe Pisarcik and Larry Csonka, Eagles cornerback Herman Edwards pounces on the ill-timed fumble and returns it for the game-winning touchdown on November 19, 1978. *(Photo courtesy of AP Images)*

GEORGE YOUNG

Two years after Peter Finch won an Oscar for his role in the film *Network*, Giants fans empathized with his crazed character's catchphrase, "I'm mad as hell and I'm not going to take it anymore!" The day after "the Fumble," offensive coach Bob Gibson was fired. Two weeks later, 100 fans burned their tickets and mailed the ashes to owner Wellington Mara. The week after that, some fans rented a plane to fly a banner that read "15 Years of Lousy Football—We've Had Enough" over the stadium during the last home game of 1978.

The deleterious effect of this happening to one of the league's flagship franchises was not lost on NFL commissioner Pete Rozelle, who worked diligently behind the scenes to get Wellington Mara and his nephew Tim to put aside their feud and agree on a new general manager to restore the New York Giants to prominence. Finally, on Valentine's Day 1979, the Giants hired George Young to run their football operation.

Young had begun as a successful high school coach in Baltimore; he caught the eye of Don Shula, who hired him to work in scouting. Over the years, Young worked his way up in first the Colts and then the Dolphins organizations, mentored by Shula. The Dolphins' personnel director was ideally suited not only to rebuild the New York franchise through

astute drafts and coaching hires, but also to serve as a resilient buffer between the two incompatible Maras. Young hired disciplinarian Ray Perkins as coach, and New York made the playoffs three years later. When Perkins decided to leave to replace the legendary Bear Bryant at his Alabama alma mater, Young replaced him with defensive coach Bill Parcells, and Parcells would complete the restoration by leading the Giants to two Super Bowl wins in eight seasons.

When Young decided to step down in 1998, he left a legacy of accomplishment, organization, honor, dignity, and integrity. He also left an in-house successor in Ernie Accorsi, who carried on in the Young style and maintained the overall success of the franchise.

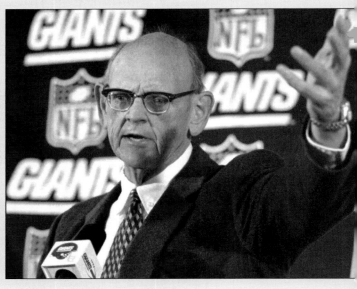

George Young ran the Giants' football operations from 1979 through 1998.
(Photo courtesy of AP Images)

they had to do was snap the ball and have Pisarcik take a knee and the clock would run out.

None of the Giants' offensive players could believe that offensive coordinator Bob Gibson sent in a play that called for a handoff to fullback Larry Csonka, and several of them vociferously protested against it in the huddle. Pisarcik chose to follow orders, though. He took the handoff gripping the back end of the ball, and turned to the right before swinging all the way around to find Csonka, who was headed to Joe's left. The aborted handoff bounced off Csonka's hip as he plowed into the line. Pisarcik dove for the bouncing ball, and Csonka

GAME DETAILS

New York Giants 17 • Philadelphia Eagles 19

Date: November 19, 1978

Location: The Meadowlands

Attendance: 70,318

Significance: Two struggling teams trying to make a run for the playoffs

Box Score:

Eagles	0	6	0	13	**19**
Giants	14	0	3	0	**17**

Scoring:

NYG Hammond 19-yard pass from Pisarcik (Danelo PAT)
NYG Perkins 30-yard pass from Pisarcik (Danelo PAT)
PHL Montgomery 8-yard run (Mike-Mayer kick failed)

NYG Danelo 37-yard FG
PHL Hogan 1-yard run (Michel kick failed)
PHL Edwards 26-yard fumble recovery (Michel PAT)

Team	FD	YDS	RUSH	PASS	A-C-I	PUNT	FUM	PEN
Eagles	23	314	45-150	164	31-15-3	3-25	2-0	5
Giants	14	281	31-100	181	23-13-1	5-43	2-2	70

Eagles: Jaworski 164P, Carmichael 105C
Giants: Pisarcik 181P

turned around too late: Eagles cornerback Herman Edwards pushed through a weak block by Kotar and scooped up the ball as it bounced right into his hands. Edwards carried the ball triumphantly in his left hand as he sprinted the 26 yards to the end zone with tight end Gary Shirk in fruitless pursuit. Edwards's monster spike signaled an impossible Giants loss and the low point for the franchise.

New York would lose three of their last four games to finish 6–10, while the Eagles would split their last four and improbably make the playoffs. The victory validated coach Dick Vermeil's turnaround of the franchise and enabled them to make the postseason, but it also contained a poison pill in the loss of their kicker. Vermeil tried to make it work by using his punter to place-kick, but Michel missed an extra point and two chip-shot field goals in a one-point playoff loss to Atlanta.

New York had at last bottomed out, and a new general manager in 1979 would begin restoring the team's greatness.

4 TRIPLETT TRAMPLES BEARS TO START ONSLAUGHT

New York Ices Chicago for Title

One month before the 1956 NFL Championship Game, the Bears and the Giants met in an odd game in which the Giants were in firm control throughout and led 17–3 with just five minutes to play. However, two bombs to tall, skinny speedster Harlon Hill—the Randy Moss of his day—enabled the Bears to pull out a tie in the closing seconds.

Chicago had the best offense in the league, and they came into the title game favored by three points. A storm hit New York the day before the game, though. The temperature at game time was a frosty 18 degrees and the field was a sheet of ice. Coach Jim Lee Howell's advice to offensive coach Vince Lombardi was to "keep it simple" on this slippery day.

Both teams came out wearing rubber soles, unlike the celebrated "Sneakers Game" between these same two teams for the 1934 NFL title. However, the Giants were shod in new sneakers supplied by Andy Robustelli's sporting goods store, while the Bears were wearing worn-out pairs of practice sneakers that some claimed dated from the 1930s. The difference was apparent right from the start. Giants halfback Gene Filipski caught George Blanda's opening kickoff at his own 7-yard line and smoothly negotiated New York's excellent open-field blocking to return the ball 53 yards to the Chicago 39. Three plays later, on third-and-10, nominal starting quarterback Don Heinrich hit Frank Gifford for 22 yards and a first down at the 17.

The next play demonstrated the Giants' dominance on this day. The Bears showed blitz and Heinrich audibled to a draw play. Burly fullback Mel Triplett took the handoff from Heinrich and burst off guard untouched, as the umpire in the middle of the field turned too late to flee in fear as Mel ran up his back. At the 5, Triplett shoved the umpire forward as defensive backs McNeil Moore and Stan Wallace converged on him from both sides. Triplett dragged the two Bears defenders into the end zone with him, and all three crashed on top of the flattened

New sneakers courtesy of Andy Robustelli's sporting goods store helped Frank Gifford and the Giants blow past the Bears 47–7 in the 1956 NFL Championship Game.

official. The Giants took a 7–0 lead; they would never trail.

On the second play following the kickoff, Andy Robustelli recovered a fumble by Bears fullback Rick Casares at the Chicago 15. On fourth down, toeless Ben Agajanian converted a field goal to make the score 10–0. Still in the first quarter, safety Jimmy Patton picked off quarterback Ed Brown at the New York 36 and returned

the ball 28 yards to the Chicago 36. Again, Agajanian converted the Bears' miscue into three points, and New York led 13–0.

The Bears were getting desperate. After Emlen Tunnell tackled J. C. Caroline for a loss on a fourth-down play, the Giants took over behind the real starting quarterback, Charley Conerly. Four runs and a 22-yard flare pass to Alex Webster brought them to the 3, and Webster powered in from there to

Jim Lee Howell

Kyle Rote told the story of walking down the hall in training camp and seeing defensive coach Tom Landry studying film in one room and offensive coach Vince Lombardi running the projector in another, while head coach Jim Lee Howell sat in a third room reading the newspaper. The self-deprecating Howell often joked, "I just blow up the footballs and keep order." It is true that Howell was a delegator, not a master strategist, but it is also true that he was very successful in that style, as the Giants' 1956 championship proves.

Howell was the epitome of the "company man." He signed with the Giants in 1937, as a 6'5" former basketball star from the University of Arkansas, and spent the rest of his working life commuting between his Arkansas farm and New York. Howell was a starting end under Steve Owen from 1937 through 1947, with three years as a Marine in World War II. He became the Giants' first end coach in 1948 and then succeeded the legendary Owen as head coach in 1954.

Howell ran the team for seven years, achieving a 55–29–4 record and appearing in three NFL title games. When the pressure got too great, he quit coaching and moved into the front office. Howell was the Giants' director of personnel from 1961 through 1979. He then served as a roving scout until 1986, when at last he retired, having spent 50 years with the Maras.

Howell was a disciplinarian with a booming voice who performed his own

bedchecks, but he gave a lot of freedom to his celebrated assistant coaches. He liked to say that fourth-down decisions were his responsibility. He had no tough choices in 1956, but in 1958 it was Howell who sent Pat Summerall in to try a 49-yard field goal in the snow, and it was Howell who sent Don Chandler in to punt the ball back to Johnny Unitas with two minutes left. One decision worked out and one didn't. The day after the last-minute heroics of Unitas, Howell was photographed in his office shrugging his shoulders, a sheepish grin on his face. He would never again experience the pure elation of December 30, 1956.

Though never a master strategist, coach Jim Lee Howell did lead his Giants to three NFL title games.

GAME DETAILS

New York Giants 47 • Chicago Bears 7

Date: December 30, 1956

Location: Yankee Stadium, New York

Attendance: 56,836

Significance: NFL Championship Game

Box Score:

Bears	0	7	0	0	**7**	
Giants	13	21	6	7	**47**	

Scoring:
NYG Triplett 17-yard run (Agajanian PAT)
NYG Agajanian 17-yard FG
NYG Agajanian 43-yard FG
NYG Webster 3-yard run (Agajanian PAT)
CHI Casares 9-yard run (Blanda PAT)
NYG Webster 1-yard run (Agajanian PAT)
NYG Moore recovered blocked punt in end zone
 (Agajanian PAT)
NYG Rote 9-yard pass from Conerly (Agajanian kick failed)
NYG Gifford 14-yard pass from Conerly (Agajanian PAT)

Team	FD	YDS	RUSH	PASS	A-C-I	PUNT	FUM	PEN
Bears	19	314	32-67	247	47-20-2	8-34	2-1	50
Giants	16	354	34-126	228	20-11-0	3-37	3-1	40

Bears: Blanda 140P
Giants: Conerly 195P, Gifford 131C

start the second quarter. A muffed punt by Tunnell led to the only Bears touchdown, but the Giants answered with a five-play, 71-yard drive that was highlighted by a 50-yard pass to Webster and capped by a one-yard Webster touchdown. To conclude the first half, Ray Beck blocked a Chicago punt and little-used rookie Henry Moore recovered the ball in the end zone for a 34–7 halftime lead.

The second half was a formality. George Blanda took over at quarterback for Chicago but engineered no points, while Charley Conerly threw touchdown passes to Kyle Rote in the third quarter and Frank Gifford in the fourth to make the final score 47–7. With the victory secure, Conerly gave way to third-stringer Bobby Clatterbuck. Chuckin' Charley threw just 10 passes on the day, but completed seven of them for an astounding 195 yards. Oddly, the touchdown caught by Rote was the only pass caught by a Giants end all day, but halfbacks Gifford and Webster were free throughout the game. In their first season in Yankee Stadium, the Giants had won their first NFL title in 18 years.

December 14, 1958

3 SUMMERALL LEGS OUT A GIANTS WIN

49-Yard Field Goal in the Snow Forces Playoff

The Giants trailed the Browns by a game in the East for most of the 1958 season. When the teams met in the season finale, New York had won three straight and were 8–3 on the year; Cleveland had won four straight and were 9–2. A tie or Cleveland victory would clinch the crown for the Browns. On a cold, windy, snowy day at Yankee Stadium, the Giants had to win.

On the Browns' first play from scrimmage, the Giants' vaunted defensive line and linebackers were completely wiped out, and the great Jim Brown burst up the middle for a 65-yard touchdown run. Brown was not touched until corner Dick Lynch tapped him with one hand at the 30-yard line. The Giants defense solidified after that initial lapse, though, and held Brown to 83 yards on 25 carries during the rest of the game.

The Giants got on the scoreboard themselves in the second quarter with a 46-yard field goal by Pat Summerall, following a fumble by Cleveland quarterback Milt Plum. The Browns' Lou Groza answered with a 22-yard field goal later in the quarter.

Cleveland had the fewest fumbles in the NFL in 1958, but fumbles were what did

in the Browns this day. Early in the fourth quarter, Milt Plum lost the ball a second time, and Andy Robustelli recovered it at the Browns' 45. Frank Gifford followed with a halfback option pass diagonally across the field to Kyle Rote at the 10, and Don Paul tackled Rote at the 6. After a failed run by Gifford, the Giants went back to the halfback option play, and Gifford hit Bob Schnelker for the tying touchdown with 10:10 to play.

The Browns would make only one more first down in the game, and they punted back to New York at the 30. The Giants drove inside the Browns' 30, where Summerall lined up for a 36-yard field goal with just under five minutes to play. Summerall missed the kick and felt like the goat. Again, however, the Browns could not move the ball, and Dick Deschaine shanked a 22-yard punt to the Cleveland 42.

As the clock wound down, Charley Conerly threw three incompletions. On one, he hit Alex Webster in the hands in the end zone, but the normally reliable Webster couldn't hang on to the wet ball. On fourth down, offensive coach Vince Lombardi wanted to try another pass. However, Jim Lee

You know you can't kick it that far.
—VINCE LOMBARDI TO SUMMERALL, AFTER THE KICK

After missing just minutes earlier, Giants kicker Pat Summerall connects on a 49-yard field goal to force a playoff for the 1958 division crown. *(Photo courtesy of AP Images)*

PAT SUMMERALL

Alex Webster would kid Pat Summerall that if Alex had held onto that third-down touchdown pass, Pat never would have had the chance to be a hero and no one would have ever heard of him. As it turned out, though, Summerall's kick is one of the greatest moments in team history, and it capped his first season in New York.

Summerall was a fourth-round draft pick of the Lions in 1952. He was on the roster of the NFL champions that year but only got into two games as an end. Traded to the Cardinals the following season, Summerall began the kicking career for which he is remembered. In five seasons with the hapless Cardinals, Pat never made 50 percent of his field goals. His fortunes changed in 1958, when the Giants traded Dick Nolan and a number-one pick to the Cardinals to obtain Summerall and Lindon Crow.

Summerall found a whole different atmosphere in New York. Center Ray Wietecha's snaps were sharp and accurate, while holder Charley Conerly's soft hands provided Summerall with a dependable spot throughout his four years as a Giants player. Coached by Tom Landry, Summerall became one of the best kickers in football.

> **I** couldn't believe Jim Lee was asking me to do that. That was the longest attempt I'd ever made for the Giants. It was a bad field and so unrealistic. Most of the fellows on the bench couldn't believe it either. They wanted another pass play.
>
> —PAT SUMMERALL, IN *THERE WERE GIANTS IN THOSE DAYS* BY GERALD ESKENAZI

After three title games in four seasons, Summerall retired at age 31 to go into radio and television. His smooth, vocal delivery afforded Pat a 45-year career in the booth. He not only broadcast football, but also annual major events in golf and tennis. He was known for his intelligent, minimalist, low-key style, which highlighted the game itself and gave his colorful analyst partners, Tom Brookshier and John Madden, room to shine. Late in life, Summerall achieved perhaps his most heroic act of all by confronting his alcoholism and changing his life.

EXTENDING THE PLAYBOOK

The option play was the bread and butter of the Giants offense (see Play 44), but the team executed it particularly well in an urgent situation in this game. Trailing 10–3 with 10 minutes left, the Giants had gotten into the red zone on a halfback option pass from Gifford to Rote. Now they were about to try it again from the 8.

On this play, Gifford took a pitchout to the right and was aided by two good blocks. First, quarterback Charley Conerly went low to take out linebacker Galen Fiss. Then fullback Mel Triplett dropped defensive tackle Bob Gain. Still, defensive end Willie McClung was unblocked and bearing down on Gifford as he scanned the end zone. Kyle Rote was open behind the left goal post, and Bob Schnelker was free behind the right one. Gifford leaped to get his pass over the outstretched hands of the charging McClung; he hit Schnelker for the touchdown as Junior Wren and Ken Konz converged too late on the big end.

GAME DETAILS

New York Giants 10 • Cleveland Browns 10

Date: December 14, 1958

Location: Yankee Stadium, New York

Attendance: 63,192

Significance: The Giants needed to beat the Browns to tie them for division crown

Box Score:

Browns	7	3	0	0	**10**
Giants	0	3	0	10	**13**

Scoring:

CLE Brown 65-yard run (Groza PAT)
NYG Summerall 46-yard FG
CLE Groza 22-yard FG
NYG Schnelker 8-yard pass from Gifford (Summerall PAT)
NYG Summerall 49-yard FG

Team	FD	YDS	RUSH	PASS	A-C-I	PUNT	FUM	PEN
Browns	9	257	37-150	107	12-6-0	6-33	2	55
Giants	12	226	22-64	162	37-15-0	7-43	0	63

Browns: Brown 148R

Howell shockingly sent Summerall, who had not practiced all week owing to a knee problem, onto the field to try a 49-yard field goal through the swirling snow.

With 2:07 remaining, Conerly took the snap and smoothly spotted the ball on the white field. Summerall made his straight-ahead approach and got full extension from his leg; the ball sailed through the dark, damp night and through the uprights for a 13–10 lead.

Teammates and coaches mobbed Summerall as he left the field, but the game wasn't over yet. Jim Brown returned the kickoff to the Browns' 45-yard line. A pass completion to Ray Renfro took them to the Giants' 41, but a 19-yard sack dropped Cleveland back to its own 40. One last completion took them back to Giants territory, and Groza came on to try a 55-yard field goal with 25 seconds left. It fell well short. Because of Summerall's unlikely clutch kick, the teams were tied for first and would meet in a playoff one week later to determine the Eastern champion.

GIANTS BREAK BRONCOS

Simms-McConkey Connection Puts New York on Top

It had been 30 years since the New York Giants had won the NFL championship, but 1986 seemed different. New York went 14–2 during the regular season and swept through the playoffs, outscoring the 49ers and the Redskins 66–3 to win a trip to Pasadena to play the Broncos in the Super Bowl. Coach Bill Parcells had been at Yankee Stadium in 1956 when the Giants had vanquished the Bears from start to finish to win the title. Now, with his Giants poised to repeat the feat, he would be fearless and gutsy in trying to win the game.

The Giants had beaten Denver at the Meadowlands in November on a last-minute field goal. There would be much less suspense in Super Bowl XXI. On offense, New York was led by little Joe Morris's 1,516 rushing yards and the underappreciated Phil Simms's 3,487 passing yards. But the core of the team, exemplified by Lawrence Taylor's 20.5 sacks, was its aggressive defense, which gave up the second-fewest points in the NFL.

Sparkplug Phil McConkey led the team onto the field, waving a white towel to get the crowd behind the Giants, but it was the Broncos who came out fastest. John Elway's first play in the Super Bowl was a 10-yard scramble, and he led Denver on a 45-yard opening drive to take a quick 3–0 lead.

For the run-oriented Giants, Phil Simms surprised the Broncos by coming out throwing on first down; in the first half, Simms threw on nine of 12 first-down plays. Simms was on target, too, hitting his first six passes in the first drive of 78 yards, which ended with a six-yard touchdown pass to tight end Zeke Mowatt. Elway, however, was just as hot. He completed all four passes on the next Broncos drive and scored on a four-yard quarterback draw to take a 10–7 lead, still in the first period.

When the Giants were forced to punt at the outset of the second quarter, though, the game started to turn sour for Denver. Elway drove them to a first-and-goal from the New York 1-yard line, but the ferocious Giants defense dug in and made a memorable stand. On first down, Taylor ran Elway down for a one-yard loss on a sweep. Harry Carson stoned Gerald Willhite up the middle on second down, and Carl Banks nailed Sammy Winder for a four-yard loss

As I caught the ball and turned up, I saw a wide-open field. I thought I was going to get in. I saw the goal line and thought, *My god, I'm going to get a touchdown in the Super Bowl.*

—PHIL MCCONKEY

Phil McConkey got his Super Bowl touchdown in the fourth quarter, snatching a pass that bounced off the hands of teammate Mark Bavaro.

PHIL McCONKEY

Championship teams are made up of many parts: superstars, stars, solid starters, and leaders. However, there is also a need for spirited guys who go all-out and take care of the little things. Phil McConkey led his teammates onto the field at the Super Bowl furiously waving a white towel to get the fans behind the team. He set up one touchdown with a 44-yard reception on a flea flicker, and then he caught a touchdown on a deflected pass that bounced off the hands of tight end Mark Bavaro. In fact, Bill Parcells had lauded McConkey as the field-position star of the 17–0 NFC championship win over the Redskins in gusty Giants Stadium two weeks before, for catching every punt and not letting them bounce the way his Washington counterpart had.

The smallish McConkey set receiving records at the Naval Academy in the 1970s but went undrafted by the NFL. Before his five-year navy commitment ran out, he wrote to his hometown Buffalo Bills and the Giants requesting a tryout. New York took a chance on the 5'10" 27-year-old helicopter pilot, and he made the team in 1984 as a return man and reserve receiver. He never caught more than 25 passes in a season and scored only twice in his career, but he was a reliable punt returner who three times led the NFL in fair catches.

In 1986, he fell too far on the receiver depth chart and was cut. When Lionel Manuel injured his knee early in the season, however, Parcells traded a late-round draft choice to Green Bay to bring back the lively McConkey in Week 5. Feisty Phil's inspirational "The grass is greener, my ass" message stayed on the Giants' bulletin board for the entire Super Bowl run of 1986.

McConkey was truly one of Parcells's guys, but he was still cut in 1989 at age 32. He spent the season in Arizona and San Diego and then retired. His appeal to coaches, teammates, and fans was summed up in a comment he once made to Dave Anderson of *The New York Times*: "Pressure is trying to land a helicopter on an aircraft carrier in the middle of the Mediterranean at night. Hey, that's pressure. Playing football isn't pressure. Football is fun."

Phil McConkey was upended by Broncos cornerback Mark Haynes, but held onto the ball to set up the game-changing touchdown in Super Bowl XXI.

GAME DETAILS

New York Giants 39 • Denver Broncos 20

Date: January 25, 1987

Location: The Rose Bowl, Pasadena, California

Attendance: 101,063

Significance: Super Bowl XXI

Box Score:

Broncos	10	0	0	10	**20**
Giants	7	2	17	13	**39**

Scoring:

DEN Karlis 48-yard FG
NYG Mowatt 6-yard pass from Simms (Allegre PAT)
DEN Elway 4-yard run (Karlis PAT)
NYG Martin tackles Elway for safety
NYG Bavaro 13-yard pass from Simms (Allegre PAT)

NYG Allegre 21-yard FG
NYG Morris 1-yard run (Allegre PAT)
NYG McConkey 6-yard pass from Simms (Allegre PAT)
DEN Karlis 28-yard FG
NYG Anderson 2-yard run (Allegre kick failed)
DEN Johnson 47-yard pass from Elway (Karlis PAT)

Team	FD	YDS	RUSH	PASS	RTN	A-C-I	Sacked	PUNT	FUM	PEN
Broncos	23	372	19-52	320	93	41-26-1	4-32	2-41	2-0	4-28
Giants	24	399	38-136	263	71	25-22-0	1-5	3-46	0-0	6-48

Broncos: Elway 304P, Johnson 121C
Giants: Simms 268P

> **B**obby Johnson was wide open for the touchdown, but McConkey took us to the 1-foot line, so I guess that's OK.
>
> —BILL PARCELLS

on a failed sweep on third down. To top it off, kicker Rich Karlis then missed a 23-yard field goal.

The next time Denver had the ball, Elway retreated all the way to his end zone on a third-and-12 from the Denver 13, and defensive end George Martin corralled him for a safety. Martin was Elway's nemesis—he'd had a 78-yard interception return in the regular-season meeting between these teams (see Play 15). Denver was still able to move the ball, though. Karlis had one more chance at three points with 13 seconds left in the period,

but he missed a 34-yard field goal to leave the score at 10–9 at the half.

The third quarter was a Giants onslaught, in which they outgained Denver by 161 yards. Simms, who had thus far thrown just three incompletions, would not miss another pass in the game. The opening Giants drive stalled at their own 46, but Parcells sent an unusual group on for the punt. Backs Lee Rouson and Maurice Carthon lined up as gunners on the outside, while quarterback Jeff Rutledge lined up as the blocking back. The three then

THE FLEA-FLICKER

Both wideouts lined up on the left, but Phil McConkey (80) went in motion to the right. Joe Morris (20) took the handoff from Phil Simms (11) and then stopped at the line and flipped the ball back to Simms. As the defense converged on the fake run, both wideouts went deep and Simms surveyed the field. Although Bobby Johnson (88) was wide open, Simms spotted McConkey first and hit him at the 20. McConkey was tackled at the 1, but the Giants scored on the next play.

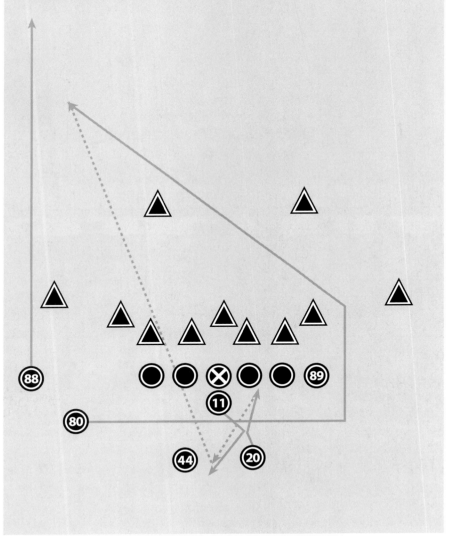

shifted to their normal positions while punter Sean Landeta went in motion as a flanker. Rutledge made sure that the Broncos linebackers were off the line, and then took the snap and made the first down on a quarterback sneak.

Five plays later, Simms hit Bavaro from 13 yards out, and New York took the lead for good, 16–10. Denver went three-and-out, and Phil McConkey returned the kick 25 yards to the Broncos' 36. Eight plays after that, Raul Allegre kicked a 21-yard field goal to extend the lead to 19–10.

Again, Denver went three-and-out. New York moved to the Broncos' 45, and Parcells sent McConkey in with the play of the game. Receivers McConkey and Bobby Johnson started out lined up on the same side, but McConkey went in motion to the right behind Mark Bavaro. Simms handed off to Morris. McConkey paused at the line to see if the safety was blitzing and then took off on a 45-degree angle across the field. Morris took two steps with the ball and then turned and tossed it back to Simms. Simms did not see Johnson open by the goal line, but he spotted McConkey and hit him at the 20. McConkey raced for the end zone, but was cut off at the 5 by cornerback Mark Haynes, who went low and sent McConkey spinning head over heels to the 1. Joe Morris powered in for the score on the next play, and with 24 seconds

ARAPAHOE

This punt fake was called ARAPAHOE: A Run A Pass A Hit On the Enemy. Lee Rouson (22) and Maurice Carthon (44) lined up as gunners on the outside, while Jeff Rutledge (17) lined up as the blocking back. None were normally on the punt team. Rouson and Carthon shifted to their running back positions, and quarterback Rutledge moved behind center. Sean Landeta (5), the punter, went in motion to the right. Rutledge first tried to draw Denver offside, but then took the snap and made the first down on a quarterback sneak.

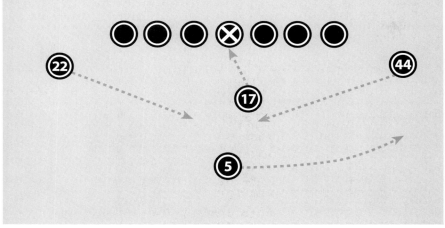

> **W**e've run the flea flicker in practice for I don't know how long, and we've never hit on the damn thing. When I hit McConkey down on the 1, I thought, *That's it. We've won it.*
>
> —PHIL SIMMS

left in the third quarter, the game was essentially over.

The Giants led 26–10 going into the fourth quarter, and Simms would throw just two more passes in the game. His last pass bounced off the hands of Mark Bavaro as the tight end was hit by two defenders. The ball bounded backward—where Phil McConkey was waiting. As he grabbed the ball just a foot from the ground, McConkey likened it to catching snowflakes as a kid in his native Buffalo. But this was a touchdown in the Super Bowl, and his friend Bavaro lofted him in the air exultantly.

In the closing minutes, Jim Burt, who had initiated the practice of dousing Parcells with the Gatorade bucket to celebrate a victory, was celebrating with the fans. In his stead, Harry Carson camouflaged himself in the overcoat of a security guard and drenched his coach with the quenching liquid. Simms, who had completed 22 of 25 passes for 268 yards and three touchdowns in a superlative performance, became the first Super Bowl quarterback to cash in by uttering the line "I'm going to Disney World!" as he left the field. Indeed, he had transformed Big Blue Nation to Fantasyland at long last.

February 3, 2008

1 SMACKED, WHACKED, AND SACKED

Undefeated Patriots Are Upset By Road Warrior Giants in Super Bowl

Just five weeks earlier, the 15–0 New England Patriots and the 10–5 Giants had met in a memorable regular season finale between two teams seemingly headed in opposite directions: the undefeated Patriots toward immortality and the inconsistent Giants toward a third straight quick playoff exit. Even after winning three playoff games on the road to advance to the Super Bowl, the Giants were still 12-point underdogs to the "invincible" Patriots in their quest for the Vince Lombardi Trophy. However, the battle-tested Giants were confident; wide receiver Plaxico Burress even predicted a 23–17 victory. In the other locker room, quarterback Tom Brady scoffed at the notion that New England would score just 17 points; by the end of the game, Brady would be hoping for that many.

As the game got underway, it was clear that the Giants had lost no momentum during the two-week break after the conference championship. New York took the opening kickoff and marched 63 yards in 16 plays to take a 3–0 lead on a Lawrence Tynes field goal. This masterful mix of runs and passes consumed the first 9:59 of the game and set a Super Bowl record for the lengthiest drive in history. Of most importance, it kept New England's offense, the highest scoring in NFL history, off the field. The Patriots used up the rest of the first quarter with their own 56-yard touchdown drive, scoring on the first play of the second quarter to go up 7–3.

The furious pass rush the Giants generated from their front four and occasional blitzers roughed up Brady and kept him out of rhythm by knocking him down 23 times. The Patriots' three second-quarter drives went three plays for seven yards, three plays for minus 14 yards with two sacks, and nine plays for 38 yards. The last drive took New England close to field goal position, but Giants lineman Justin Tuck stripped the ball from Tom Brady as he sacked him and the half ended.

The Patriots started to get a little rhythm by shortening their pass routes to start the third quarter. They took 8:17 off the clock and drove to the Giants' 25, but a Michael Strahan sack left New England facing a fourth-and-13

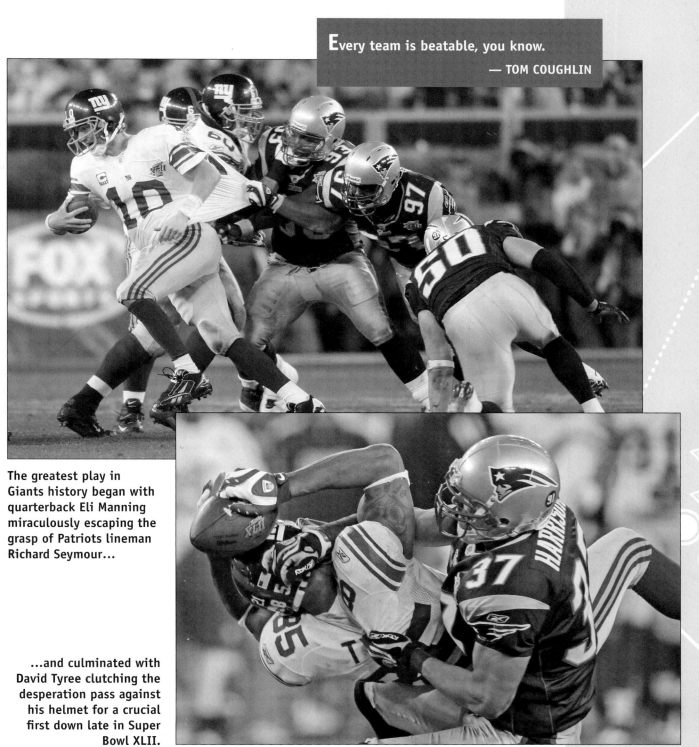

The greatest play in Giants history began with quarterback Eli Manning miraculously escaping the grasp of Patriots lineman Richard Seymour...

...and culminated with David Tyree clutching the desperation pass against his helmet for a crucial first down late in Super Bowl XLII.

EXTENDING THE PLAYBOOK

While David Tyree's spectacular catch of Eli Manning's scrambling lob pass was the play of the game, the Giants still needed to score a touchdown to take the lead. They turned to a familiar face for that. Plaxico Burress had been held to just one catch for 14 yards by the Patriots, who were continually rolling a safety to double-cover him. On first-and-10 from the Patriots' 13 with just 39 seconds left, Burress finally got single coverage and made New England pay. The Giants came out in a shotgun formation with three receivers to the right, Ahmad Bradshaw in the backfield, and Burress alone to the left. The Patriots came with an all-out seven-man blitz, leaving just four to defend the pass—single coverage all around. Manning spotted this as he took the snap and looked immediately for Burress. Burress ran a slant-and-go, or "sluggo" route, in which he fakes the slant and heads straight up the field. Cornerback Ellis Hobbs bit on the inside fake as Manning launched a fade pass that forced Burress to turn around for the easy game-winning grab.

at the 31. Inexplicably, coach Bill Belichick eschewed the 49-yard field goal attempt, and Brady threw incomplete on fourth down. The Patriots left a good chance at three points on the field and would later regret it.

After an exchange of punts, the Giants took over on their own 20 to start the fourth quarter with the score still improbably 7–3. Eli Manning dropped back and hit tight end Kevin Boss at the 40 and Boss rumbled another 25 yards before safety Rodney Harrison tripped him up at the Patriots' 35. Three Ahmad Bradshaw runs and a key third-down catch by Steve Smith took the ball to the 5. Manning's play-action slant pass to fourth receiver David Tyree darted past cornerback Asante Samuel, and the Giants had the lead back with 11 minutes to play. It would not be the last the Patriots would see of special teams ace Tyree.

After another exchange of punts, New England took over on their own 20 with 7:54 to play. Despite having struggled against a ferocious, but now tiring, Giants defense, Brady was not done. Just as he had done in his previous three Super Bowls, Brady directed the Patriots on a fourth-quarter drive to take the lead. Three completions to Wes Welker—who tied a Super Bowl record for catches with 11—two to Kevin Faulk, and three to Randy Moss culminated with a six-yard touchdown

to Moss with 2:45 to play. The Patriots led 14–10, and time was running out for New York. The unflappable Manning later said, "You kind of like being down four. You have to score a touchdown."

Starting at their own 17, the Giants faced fourth-and-one at their 37 with a minute and a half left, but Brandon Jacobs bulled for two yards to keep the drive alive. Manning scrambled for five on the next play, and then came a forgotten play that could have ruined Manning's reputation for good. On second-and-five, a hurried Manning threw an inaccurate deep out that hit cornerback Asante Samuel right in the hands. Fortunately for New York, the ball bounced harmlessly to the ground, and the stage was set for the play of the day, of the year, of the ages.

On third-and-five from the Giants' 44, Manning took the snap in shotgun formation. The Patriots only rushed four down linemen, but Adalius Thomas came hard from the edge and got a hand on Manning. As Eli stepped up to avoid Thomas, he stepped right into the big push up the middle from Richard Seymour and Jarvis Green, both of whom grabbed hold of Manning's jersey. Somehow Manning broke free and sprinted back five more yards, spotting David Tyree breaking off a deep post in the middle of the field. Manning launched a high floater

GAME DETAILS

New York Giants 17 • New England Patriots 14

Date: February 3, 2008

Location: University of Phoenix Stadium, Glendale, Arizona

Attendance: 71,101

Significance: Super Bowl XLII against an undefeated team

Box Score:

Giants	3	0	0	14	**17**
Patriots	0	7	0	7	**14**

Scoring:

NYG Tynes 32-yard FG

NEP Maroney 1-yard run (Gostkowski PAT)

NYG Tyree 5-yard pass from Manning (Tynes PAT)

NEP Moss 6-yard pass from Brady (Gostkowski PAT)

NYG Burress 13-yard pass from Manning (Tynes PAT)

Team	FD	YDS	RUSH	PASS	RTN	A-C-I	Sacked	PUNT	FUM	PEN
Giants	17	338	26-91	247	64	34-19-1	3-8	4-39	2-0	4-36
Patriots	22	274	16-45	229	132	48-29-0	5-37	4-44	1-1	5-35

Giants: Manning 255P

Patriots: Brady 266P, Welker 103C

that Tyree snagged over his head at the 24 while Rodney Harrison swatted at the ball and hooked Tyree's right arm, using his body as a fulcrum to bend Tyree backwards in the air. Tyree's left hand came off the ball, but his right hand pinned the ball to his helmet. As the ball started to slip during his descent, Tyree again secured it with his left hand. The brawny Harrison flipped Tyree backward on the ground, still trying to free the ball, but Tyree held onto the ball with a death grip even as he rolled over. It was a 32-yard broken play that left Harrison shaking his head in shock. "There were two or three guys who had [Manning], and he breaks free and throws up a Hail Mary that the guy comes down with," he said.

The Giants still needed a touchdown, though. Manning was sacked on the next play by Thomas and then threw incomplete, forcing another third down. Reliable slot receiver Steve Smith was open once more to convert the third down and stepped out of bounds at the 13. On the next play, Manning hit a wide-open Plaxico Burress for the game-winning score. New England still had 35 seconds, but one more sack, the fifth of the day, and three incompletions ended their last chance. The Giants were champions—they had beaten the unbeaten Patriots in perhaps the greatest upset in Super Bowl history.

That play will go down as one of the biggest ever.

—TOM COUGHLIN

Wide receiver Plaxico Burress hauls in the game-winning touchdown pass to complete one of the greatest upsets in Super Bowl history.

I felt like I was being grabbed a little bit, but got out of it. Saw Tyree in the middle of the field. I tried to get the ball to him and it just floated. He made an unbelievable catch, jumping up, holding onto that ball.

— ELI MANNING

JUSTIN TUCK AND OSI UMENYIORA

While Eli Manning played a fine game and was named the Super Bowl MVP for leading the Giants on the game-winning drive, the real MVPs of the game were Justin Tuck and the Giants defensive front four, who pressured Tom Brady all day, knocking him to the ground 23 times, including five sacks. Tuck had two of those sacks and also forced a Brady fumble that was recovered by linemate Osi Umenyiora. The Giants led the NFL in sacks in 2007, and Tuck and Umenyiora were the leading sackers on the team, both mentored by veteran Michael Strahan. Although both went to high school in Alabama, Tuck and Umenyiora took widely divergent paths to the NFL.

Umenyiora is a most unlikely NFL success story. He was born in London to Nigerian parents, but his family returned to Nigeria when Osi was seven. At 14, he was sent to Auburn, Alabama, to live with his sister and get an education. He was quite a soccer player and did not play American football until high school. Osi even gave up the game as a senior because his grades were slipping, but he still earned a football scholarship to Troy State, where he earned a degree in business and attracted the attention of the Giants, who selected him in the second round of the NFL Draft in 2003.

With so little football experience, Umenyiora had a difficult rookie season. He did have a breakout game in the season finale, though, with his first sack and two blocked punts. The Chargers noticed his potential and tried desperately to include him in the draft rights deal of Eli Manning for Philip Rivers, but Giants general manager Ernie Accorsi insisted it was a deal-breaker because he valued Osi's pass rushing talents. Umenyiora rewarded that faith with seven sacks in 2004 and 14.5 in 2005. Hip problems sidelined him in 2006, but he was back at full speed in 2007.

Tuck, meanwhile, went to Notre Dame and set school records for most sacks and tackles for loss. Justin himself was at a loss when he wasn't selected in the 2005 NFL Draft until the 10th pick of the third round. He had a promising rookie season backing up Strahan, but missed most of 2006 to a foot injury. New defensive coach Steve Spagnuolo knew just how to take advantage of Tuck's skills in 2007, though. Despite starting only two games, Tuck was used frequently as a defensive tackle on passing downs and helped create the most fearsome pass rush in the league. Tuck's 10 sacks bested Strahan's nine and trailed only Osi's 13, and led to Justin signing a five-year, $30-million contract extension during the playoffs.

Both Tuck and Umenyiora rely on speed, agility, and moves to get to the quarterback in a hurry. Likewise, both are strong and stout against the run as well, and neither ever quits on a play. Their dominant performance in Super Bowl XLII gave them a national profile. The two should anchor the Giants' front four for years to come.

APPENDIX

Fifty plays are a paltry sum for a team with as rich a legacy as the Giants. Here are the next 50, in chronological order: let the arguments begin.

Date	Play	Final Score
December 6, 1925	Bears player Red Grange scores on an interception in his New York debut	Giants 7, Bears 19
November 23, 1930	Hap Moran's record-setting 91-yard run	Giants 13, Packers 6
October 8, 1933	Harry Newman rushes for 108 yards, including an 80-yard run	Giants 20, Redskins 21
December 2, 1945	Arnie Herber brings the Giants back from a 21-point deficit with four touchdown passes	Giants 28, Eagles 21
October 20, 1946	Frankie Filchock throws a 55-yard pass to Frank Liebel, who laterals to Howie Livingston at the 5	Giants 28, Cardinals 24
December 15, 1946	Frankie Filchock, under a gambling cloud, throws six interceptions in the title game	Giants 14, Bears 24
November 21, 1948	Emlen Tunnell picks off three passes and returns one for a 43-yard touchdown	Giants 49, Packers 3
December 5, 1948	Charley Conerly throws for 363 yards and completes a touchdown from flat on his back	Giants 28, Steelers 38
November 13, 1949	Choo Choo Roberts grabs 212 receiving yards with three touchdowns	Giants 30, Packers 10
December 9, 1951	Eddie Price scores on an 80-yard run	Giants 23, Eagles 7
October 30, 1955	Jimmy Patton returns both a kickoff and a punt for scores	Giants 35, Redskins 7
October 21, 1956	Charley Conerly throws three touchdowns in his first Giants game in Yankee Stadium	Giants 38, Steelers 10

Date	Play	Final Score
December 2, 1956	Frank Gifford runs for two touchdowns, catches a touchdown pass, and throws one	Giants 28, Redskins 14
October 25, 1959	Frank Gifford catches a 77-yard touchdown	Giants 21, Steelers 16
November 29, 1959	Frank Gifford scores on a 79-yard run	Giants 45, Eagles 14
September 24, 1961	Y. A. Tittle relieves Conerly and completes 10 of 12 passes to lead to the winning score	Giants 17, Steelers 14
October 15, 1961	Erich Barnes returns an interception 102 yards for a touchdown	Giants 31, Cowboys 10
October 22, 1961	Charley Conerly throws two touchdown passes in the last four minutes	Giants 24, Rams 14
December 10, 1961	Conerly bails out Tittle with three touchdown passes in relief	Giants 28, Eagles 24
December 30, 1962	Sam Huff and Jim Taylor match up in the title game	Giants 7, Packers 16
December 29, 1963	Larry Morris ruins Tittle's knee on a blitz in the title game	Giants 10, Bears 14
December 6, 1964	Clarence Childs returns kickoff 100 yards	Giants 21, Vikings 30
December 12, 1965	Homer Jones catches touchdowns of 74 and 72 yards	Giants 27, Redskins 10
September 11, 1966	Homer Jones catches touchdowns for 98 and 75 yards	Giants 34, Steelers 34
September 22, 1968	Spider Lockhart returns an interception 68 yards for a touchdown	Giants 34, Eagles 25
November 15, 1970	Fran Tarkenton brings the Giants back from a 19-point deficit with three fourth-quarter scores	Giants 35, Redskins 33
September 7, 1980	Earnest Gray catches four touchdowns	Giants 41, Cardinals 35

Date	Play	Final Score
December 27, 1981	Giants recover two Wally Henry fumbles to win their first playoff game in 25 years	Giants 27, Eagles 21
September 9, 1984	Andy Headen scores on an 81-yard fumble return	Giants 28, Cowboys 7
October 13, 1985	Phil Simms throws for 513 yards and Mark Bavaro catches 13 passes	Giants 30, Bengals 35
December 21, 1985	Joe Morris scores three times, including a 65-yard run	Giants 28, Steelers 10
December 29, 1985	Mark Bavaro makes key one-handed catch in playoff win	Giants 17, 49ers 3
January 5, 1986	Sean Landeta whiffs on a punt in playoff game	Giants 0, Bears 21
October 27, 1986	Joe Morris's first 181-yard game	Giants 27, Redskins 20
November 2, 1986	Joe Morris's second straight 181-yard game	Giants 17, Cowboys 14
November 27, 1988	Lawrence Taylor has a monster game despite a torn deltoid	Giants 13, Saints 12
September 11, 1989	Dave Meggett catches a 62-yard touchdown	Giants 27, Redskins 24
December 24, 1989	Dave Meggett returns a punt 76 yards	Giants 34, Raiders 17
January 7, 1990	Flipper Anderson ends the Giants' season with a touchdown catch in overtime	Giants 13, Rams 19
January 13, 1991	Jeff Hostetler scrambles for touchdown in his first playoff game	Giants 31, Bears 3
November 24, 1991	Pepper Johnson has 4.5 sacks	Giants 21, Buccaneers 14
September 24, 1995	Rodney Hampton scores four touchdowns	Giants 45, Saints 29
October 8, 1995	Jesse Armstead returns an interception 58 yards for winning score in overtime	Giants 27, Cardinals 21

Date	Play	Final Score
December 6, 1998	Tiki Barber catches an 87-yard touchdown	Giants 23, Cardinals 19
January 6, 2002	Michael Strahan sets sack record with 22.5	Giants 25, Packers 34
December 28, 2002	Jeremy Shockey muscles tying touchdown from the hands of Brian Dawkins	Giants 10, Eagles 7
January 2, 2005	Tiki Barber wins game on the Giants' last play	Giants 28, Cowboys 24
December 17, 2005	Tiki Barber rushes for 220 yards	Giants 27, Chiefs 17
December 30, 2006	Tiki Barber carries Giants to playoffs with 234 yards rushing	Giants 34, Redskins 28
September 30, 2007	Osi Umenyiora sacks Donovan McNabb six times	Giants 16, Eagles 3

BIBLIOGRAPHY

BOOKS

Allen, George, with Ben Olan. *Pro Football's 100 Greatest Players: Rating the Stars of Past and Present.* Indianapolis: Bobbs-Merrill, 1982.

Asinof, Eliot. *Seven Days to Sunday: Crisis Week with the New York Giants.* New York: Simon and Schuster, 1968.

Barber, Tiki, and Gil Reavill. *Tiki: My Life in the Game and Beyond.* New York: Simon Spotlight, 2007.

Burt, Jim, and Hank Gola. *Hard Nose: The Story of the 1986 Giants.* San Diego: Harcourt Brace Jovanovich, 1987.

Callahan, Tom. *The GM: The Inside Story of a Dream Job and the Nightmares That Go with It.* New York: Crown, 2007.

Campbell, Jim. *Golden Years of Pro Football.* Avenel, New Jersey: Crescent Books, 1993.

Carroll, Bob, Michael Gershman, David Neft, and John Thorn. *Total Football: The Official Encyclopedia of the National Football League.* New York: Harper Collins, 1999.

Carroll, Bob. *When the Grass Was Real: Unitas, Brown, Lombardi, Sayers, Butkus, Namath and All the Rest: The Ten Best Years of Pro Football.* New York: Simon and Schuster, 1993.

Carson, Harry, and Jim Smith. *Point of Attack: The Defense Strikes Back.* New York: McGraw-Hill, 1987.

Claassen, Harold (Spike). *The History of Professional Football.* Englewood Cliffs, New Jersey: Prentice-Hall, 1963.

Cohen, Richard M., Jordan A. Deutsch, Roland T. Johnson, and David S. Neft. *The Scrapbook History of Pro Football.* Indianapolis: Bobbs-Merrill, 1976.

Conerly, Perian. *Backseat Quarterback.* Jackson, Mississippi: University of Mississippi Press, 2003, 1963.

Cope, Myron. *The Game That Was: An Illustrated Account of the Tumultuous Early Days of Pro Football.* New York: Crowell, 1974.

Curran, Bob. *Pro Football's Rag Days.* Englewood Cliffs, New Jersey: Prentice-Hall, 1969.

Daley, Arthur. *Pro Football's Hall of Fame.* New York: Grosset and Dunlap, 1968, 1963.

Daly, Dan, and Bob O'Donnell. *The Pro Football Chronicle: The Complete (Well Almost) Record of the Best Players, the Greatest Photos, the Hardest Hits, the Biggest Scandals, and the Funniest Stories in Pro Football.* New York: Collier Books, 1990.

De Laet, Dianne Tittle. *Giants and Heroes: A Daughter's Memories of Y. A. Tittle.* South Royalton, Vermont: Steerfoth Press, 1995.

DeRogatis, Al, and Dan Rubin. *The New York Giants: The Story of a Football Team.* New York: Duell, Sloan and Pearce, 1964.

DeVito, Carlo. *Wellington: The Maras, the Giants, and the City of New York.* Chicago: Triumph Books, 2006.

Didinger, Ray. *The Super Bowl: Celebrating a Quarter Century of America's Greatest Game.* New York: Simon and Schuster, 1990.

Eisen, Michael. *Stadium Stories: New York Giants.* Guilford, Connecticut: Insider's Guide, 2005.

Eskenazi, Gerald. *There Were Giants in Those Days*. New York: Grosset and Dunlap, 1976.

Exley, Frederick. *A Fan's Notes: A Fictional Memoir*. New York: Random House, 1968.

Flynn, George, ed. *Vince Lombardi on Football*. New York: New York Graphic Society Limited and Wally▮ Inc., 1973.

—. *The Vince Lombardi Scrapbook*. New York: Grosset and Dunlap, 1976.

Gifford, Frank, and Harry Waters. *The Whole Ten Yards*. New York: Random House, 1993.

Gillette, Gary, et al. *ESPN Pro Football Encyclopedia*. New York: Sterling, 2007.

Gottehrer, Barry. *The Giants of New York: The History of Professional Football's Most Fabulous Dynasty*. New York: Putnam, 1963.

Grier, Roosevelt, and Dennis Baker. *Rosey, an Autobiography: The Gentle Giant*. Tulsa, Oklahoma: Honor Books, 1986.

Gutman, Bill. *Parcells: A Biography*. New York: Carroll & Graf, 2000.

Harrington, Denis. *The Pro Football Hall of Fame: Players, Coaches, Team Owners and League Officials, 1963–1991*. Jefferson, North Carolina: McFarland, 1991.

Harris, David. *The League: The Rise and Decline of the NFL*. New York: Bantam Books, 1986.

Hersch, Hank. *The Greatest Football Games of All Time*. New York: Sports Illustrated [Time-Life], 1998.

Herskowitz, Mickey. *The Golden Age of Pro Football: NFL Football in the 1950s*. Dallas, Texas: Taylor Publishing, 1990.

Hubbard, Mary Bell. *Strike Three! And You're Out: The Cal Hubbard Story*. Marceline, Missouri: Walsworth, 1986.

Huff, Sam, and Leonard Shapiro. *Tough Stuff: The Man in the Middle*. New York: St. Martin's, 1988.

Izenberg, Jerry. *Championship: The Complete NFL Title Story*. New York: Four Winds Press, 1966.

—. *The New York Giants: Seventy-Five Years*. Alexandria, Virginia: Time-Life Books, 1999.

—. *No Medals for Trying: A Week in the Life of a Pro Football Team*. New York: Macmillan, 1990.

King, Joe. *Inside Pro Football*. Englewood Cliffs, New Jersey: Prentice-Hall, 1958.

King, Peter. *Football: A History of the Professional Game*. New York: Bishop Books [Time Inc. Home Entertainment], 1997.

King, Peter, et al. *75 Seasons: The Complete Story of the National Football League, 1920–1995*. Atlanta, Georgia: Turner Publishing Inc., 1994.

Klein, Dave. *The Game of Their Lives*. New York: Random House, 1976.

—. *The New York Giants: Yesterday, Today and Tomorrow*. Chicago: Regnery, 1973.

Lamb, Kevin. *Giants: The Unforgettable Season*. New York: Macmillan, 1987.

Landry, Tom, with Gregg Lewis. *Tom Landry: An Autobiography*. Grand Rapids, Michigan: Zondervan Publishing and New York: Harper Collins, 1990.

Leuthner, Stuart. *Iron Men: Bucko, Crazy Legs, and the Boys Recall the Golden Days of Professional Football*. New York: Doubleday, 1988.

Lichtenstein, Michael. *The New York Giants Trivia Book*. New York: St. Martin's Griffin, 2001.

Maraniss, David. *When Pride Still Mattered: A Life of Vince Lombardi*. New York: Simon and Schuster, 1999.

March, Harry. *Pro Football, Its "Ups" and "Downs:" A Lighthearted History of the Post-Graduate Game*. Albany, New York: J. B. Lyon, 1934.

Maule, Tex. *The Game: The Official Picture History of the NFL and AFL*. New York: Random House, 1967.

McCallum, Jack, with Chuck Bednarik. *Bednarik: Last of the Sixty-Minute Men*. Englewood Cliffs, New Jersey: Prentice-Hall, 1977.

MacCambridge, Michael. *America's Game: The Epic Story of How Pro Football Captured a Nation*. New York: Random House, 2004.

McConkey, Phil, Phil Simms, and Dick Schaap. *Simms to McConkey: Blood, Sweat and Gatorade*. New York: Crown, 1987.

Murphy, Austin. *The Super Bowl: Sport's Greatest Championship*. New York: Sports Illustrated [Time-Life], 1998.

Neft, David S., Richard M. Cohen, and Richard Korch. *The Football Encyclopedia: The Complete History of Professional Football from 1892 to the Present*. New York: St. Martin's, 1994.

O'Brien, Michael. *Vince: A Personal Biography*. New York: William Morrow, 1987.

Owen, Steve, and Joe King. *My Kind of Football*. New York: D. McKay, 1952.

Peterson, Robert. *Pigskin: The Early Years of Pro Football*. New York: Oxford University Press, 1997.

Porter, David L., ed. *Biographical Dictionary of American Sports: Football*. New York: Greenwood Press, 1987.

Rathet, Mike, and Don R. Smith. *Their Deeds and Dogged Faith*. New York: Rutledge Books, 1984.

Robustelli, Andy, and Jack Clary. *Once a Giant: My Two Lives with the New York Giants*. Boston: Quinlan Press, 1987.

Riger, Robert. *Best Plays of the Year 1962: A Documentary of Pro Football in the National Football League*. Englewood Cliffs, New Jersey: Prentice-Hall, 1963.

—. *Best Plays of the Year 1963: A Documentary of Pro Football in the National Football League*. Englewood Cliffs, New Jersey: Prentice-Hall, 1964.

Schwartz, Paul. *Tales from the New York Giants Sideline*. Champaign, Illinois: Sports Pub., 2004.

Smith, Myron J. *Pro Football: The Official Pro Football Hall of Fame Bibliography*. Westport, Connecticut: Greenwood Press, 1993.

Steinbreder, John. *70 Years of Championship Football*. Dallas, Texas: Taylor, 1994.

Strahan, Michael, and Jay Glazer. *Inside the Helmet: My Life as a Sunday Afternoon Warrior*. New York: Gotham, 2007.

Strother, Shelby. *NFL Top 40: The Greatest Football Games of All Time*. New York: Viking, 1988.

Taylor, Lawrence, and Steve Serby. *LT Over the Edge: Tackling Quarterbacks, Drugs and a World Beyond Football*. New York: HarperCollins, 2003.

Terzian, James. *New York Giants*. New York: Macmillan, 1973.

Tittle, Y. A., and Don Smith. *I Pass*. New York: Franklin Watts, 1964.

Tunnell, Emlen, with Bill Gleason. *Footsteps of a Giant*. Garden City, New York: Doubleday, 1966.

Whittingham, Richard. *The Giants: An Illustrated History*. New York: Harper & Row, 1986.

—. *Giants: In Their Own Words*. Chicago: Contemporary Books, 1992.

—. *The Illustrated History of the New York Giants*. Chicago: Triumph Books, 2005.

—. *What a Game They Played*. New York: Harper and Row, 1974.

—. *What Giants They Were: New York Greats Talk About Their Teams, Their Coaches, and the Times of Their Lives*. Chicago: Triumph Books, 2000.

Wiebusch, John, ed. *Lombardi*. Chicago: Follett Publishing, 1971.

BT
3/30/09

NEWSPAPERS

The Philadelphia Inquirer
Philadelphia Daily News
New York Daily News
New York Post
The New York Times
Newsday
The Washington Post

PERIODICALS

Colliers
Football Digest
Life
Newsweek
Saturday Evening Post
Sports Illustrated
Time

DVDS

The New York Giants: The Complete History. NFL Films/Warner Home Video, 2004.

WEBSITES

Current Team Histories (http://www.jt-sw.com/football/pro/teams.nsf)
DatabaseFootball.com (http://www.databasefootball.com/index.htm)
NFL History Network (http://nflhistory.net)
NFL.com (http://www.nfl.com)
New York Giants (http://www.giants.com)
Pro Football Hall of Fame (http://www.profootballhof.com)
Professional Football Researchers Association (http://www.footballresearch.com)